Fade to Gray

Fade to Gray

AGING IN AMERICAN CINEMA

Timothy Shary and Nancy McVittie

University of Texas Press *Austin*

Printed in the United States of America
First edition, 2016

Requests for permission to reproduce material from this work should be sent to:

Permissions
University of Texas Press
P.O. Box 7819
Austin, TX 78713-7819
http://utpress.utexas.edu/index.php/rp-form

♾ The paper used in this book meets the minimum requirements of ANSI/NISO Z39.48-1992 (R1997) (Permanence of Paper).

LIBRARY OF CONGRESS CATALOGING-IN-PUBLICATION DATA
Names: Shary, Timothy, 1967–, author.
McVittie, Nancy, 1980–, author.
Title: Fade to gray : aging in American cinema / Timothy Shary and Nancy McVittie.
Description: First edition. Austin : University of Texas Press, 2016. Includes bibliographical references and index.
Identifiers: LCCN 2016000151
ISBN 9780292717794 (cloth : alk. paper)
ISBN 9781477310632 (pbk. : alk. paper)
ISBN 9781477309728 (library e-book)
ISBN 9781477309735 (nonlibrary e-book)
Subjects: LCSH: Aging in motion pictures. Motion pictures—United States.
Classification: LCC PN1995.9.A433 S53 2016
DDC 791.43/654—dc23
LC record available at http://lccn.loc.gov/2016000151.

doi:10.7560/717794

Nancy dedicates this book to
Shayne Pepper,
her husband and best friend.

From youth to old age, we'll always face the world together.

Tim dedicates this book to
Olivia Xendolyn,
his wonderful daughter.

We first enjoy youth and its searching for truth.
With age we achieve our own will to believe.

Contents

Acknowledgments

THE TWO OF US MET IN EARLY 2011, AT WHICH POINT Nancy was completing her dissertation on the subject of "elder kitsch" in American movies, and Tim had been working on youth representation for many years. Tim had previously proposed the idea for a book on older movie characters in 2006 to our acquisitions editor, Jim Burr, and we were most fortunate that Jim was patient and encouraging as we refashioned that initial concept into this coauthored volume. Further, we have enjoyed the enduring diligence and cooperation of Jim and his staff at the University of Texas Press, including our manuscript editor, Lynne Chapman; Molly Frisinger, assistant manuscript editor; and Sarah Rosen McGavick, editorial assistant.

We also thank our two external evaluators, Mark Gallagher and Maria San Filippo, who offered constructive critiques and beneficial suggestions for improvement of the manuscript.

Nancy would specifically like to thank her dissertation committee: Richard Abel, Yeidy Rivero, and Caryl Flinn, as well as her academic mentors Giorgio Bertellini, Sheila Murphy, Phil Hallman, Gaylyn Studlar, Maria Pramaggiore, Tom Wallis, Andrea Mensch, Devin Orgeron, Marsha Gordon, Joe Gomez, and Robert T. Self. Additionally, she is forever grateful for the support and feedback of many people, including Tony Adams, Kate Kane, Bob Ritsema, Wilfredo Alvarez, Cyndi Moran, Katrina Bell-Jordan, John Ross, Alan and Sarah Mace, Kevin Flanagan, Courtney Ritter, Nathan Koob, Zelina and Paul Brewer, Nora and Tommy McVittie, and Steven Byrd.

Tim would specifically like to thank the many friends who helped him in the evolution of this book through their provocative dialogues about aging issues on screen and in life: Richard Brown, Chris Boucher, Devin and Rachel Griffiths, Sara Hunicke Warren, Jon Kitzen, Chris LeBel, Ethan Lewis, Jon

Lupo, Gary Marcus, Diane Mullins, Elizabeth Patterson, Tom Scully, and Louisa Stein. Special thanks to Christopher Goodwin, who suggested our title. All these folks had direct impacts on his ideas, many of which have found their way into articulation on these pages.

Research from this project has been presented at conferences of the Society for Cinema and Media Studies, the Popular Culture Association, the Northeast Popular Culture Association, and the Popular Culture Association in the South. Tim extends his thanks to Mick Broderick and Antonio Traverso at Murdoch and Curtin Universities in Perth, Western Australia, who invited him to present early research at their "Interrogating Trauma" conference in 2008. Specific commentary related to this project has been published in the *Quarterly Review of Film and Video* and the *Journal of Popular Film and Television*.

Academic colleagues also shared stimulating ideas with us as we developed the manuscript, and we look forward to further dialogue with them as this area of study continues to mature. In this regard specifically, we thank Lester Friedman at Hobart and William Smith Colleges, Deborah Jermyn at the University of Roehampton, E. Ann Kaplan at Stony Brook University, and Linda Ruth Williams at the University of Southampton.

We would be most remiss if we did not name our own family elders who have had such positive influences on our entire lives. For Nancy, that is her parents, Tom and Judith McVittie; for Tim, his parents, Robert and Cecilia Shary.

Preface

IN THE 2014 HOLLYWOOD MEGAPRODUCTION *NOAH*, THE esteemed actor Anthony Hopkins tackles the role of arguably the oldest historical figure to ever appear in movies, Methuselah. In scripture, the grandfather of Noah lived until just before the great flood, dying at age 969. The movie, perhaps wanting to avoid narrative complications beyond the impending deluge itself, does not explain how Methuselah could have endured for nearly a millennium, whereas humans have historically tended to expire within a single century.

Age may be just a number, but consider at what point someone with the longevity of Methuselah may have been considered "aged" and you can appreciate our dilemma with defining the term. Only one reliably recorded human has ever lived more than 120 years (to age 122), perhaps a relatively juvenile age for Methuselah, yet well more than twice as long as the US life expectancy of 47 for those born in 1900.[1] At the same time, people born in 1900 who had lived past the age of 47 by 1948 were certainly not viewed as decrepit, and most still had many years of productive work and healthy living ahead of them; in fact, according to the 1900 census, nearly 70 percent of all men over 65 were gainfully employed.[2] Even though the *statistically* average person born in 1900 did not live past 50, the perception of "old age" in the last century was still more connected with cultural distinctions in appearance and ability than with the chronological age of a person. Indeed, determining the point at which age is "advanced" or when one becomes "aged" is a highly ambiguous and subjective process.

In approaching our study of aging in American cinema, we wrestled mightily with definitions of "aging" and "older" that we would apply to the characters in films we examined, just as we were often faced with characters whose ages within the films are not explicitly articulated. Whereas numerous cultural guidelines exist for measuring youth—by physical growth (infant to toddler to teenager), education level (preschool to elementary to high school), legal status (minor to adult), psychology (child to adolescent to young adult)—the guidelines for identifying older adults are not only indistinct but also largely inconsistent. Physical and psychological demarcations by age are blurred in later life, education and legal rights have few age restrictions, and even demographers disagree on when older populations become old.

If the cessation of employment—the start of retirement—could be an indicator of advanced age, that gauge has also been variable. Until 2002, Social Security in the United States allowed citizens to declare retirement and begin receiving full benefits at age sixty-five, but for those born between 1943 and 1959 (who will be turning sixty-five from 2008 to 2024), the same benefits are not available until age sixty-six. For citizens born in 1960 and later, the age is sixty-seven. Granted, the primary reasons for this two-year increase in the retirement age under Social Security are financial rather than statistical; the system is running out of money because so many Americans are living longer and claiming more benefits.

To consider some labor statistics, the actual age for retirement from full-time work for many Americans has been considerably lower than the age at which the government recognizes them as retired for Social Security benefits. While those still in the workforce have expected to retire at the age of sixty-five or older for many years, the average retirement age has been much closer to sixty, and did not reach as high as sixty-two until 2014.[3] One certain factor in the previous lower age of retirement included the inability of older workers to retain full-time positions in the workforce (for reasons including prejudice as well as declining health), yet in recent years factors such as financial needs and improving health have kept the aged working longer. In fact, after a steep decline in the older workforce throughout the twentieth century until the 1980s, the percentage of Americans age sixty-five and older with jobs (including part-time) has again begun rising, from 12.1 percent in 1990 to 16.2 percent in 2011, of which 44.3 percent worked full-time; thus, 7.2 percent of the population *older than* "retirement age" was still fully employed.[4]

The longer lives of citizens are another complication in understanding our broadly changing perceptions of older age. As Laura Carstensen explained in a recent report, "In less than a century, more years were added to life expectancy than all years added across all prior millennia of evolution combined."[5] To translate that dramatic development into specific numbers: Americans who reached the presumptive retirement age of sixty-five in 1900 could expect to live another twelve years, to age seventy-seven; by 1950, life expectancy for that same age population had risen to age seventy-nine; by 1980, to eighty-one; by 2010, to eighty-three; and the figure is still rising.[6]

The "twilight years" of life after retirement have thus been elongating, and the median age of citizens has been rapidly rising accordingly, from twenty-three in 1900 to thirty-eight in 2014—although just as twenty-three was not considered "middle aged" in 1900, few people today would label themselves as such at thirty-eight.[7] Consider that at the age of thirty-eight, very few Americans have had careers lasting more than twenty years, and most expect their careers to last at least twenty-five years more. Further, within that half of the population over thirty-eight in 2014, most people could reasonably expect to live over four more decades, into their eighties. Historically speaking, the middle age of the population has not been regarded as the middle age of life.

At the same time when American age levels were rising, the nation's largest advocacy organization for older citizens, the American Association of Retired Persons, which was founded in 1958, abandoned its full title in 1999. The group then became known simply by its acronym, AARP, signifying that its purview of "older citizens" was no longer limited to retirees. Further, AARP set an age minimum for membership at fifty, well short of the previously traditional retirement age, even if many Americans may deny they are of advanced age after just five decades.

Given these many conditions, we have been left with the inevitably judgmental task of determining the appropriate age range of characters we study. We tend to examine films in which protagonists are age sixty and older, based on the typical ages at which characters are retiring or pondering retirement and at which they have become grandparents. Since some characters confront relevant issues before this demarcated age, especially women faced with ageist attitudes in a sexist society, we have found ourselves occasionally considering the stakes of aging for somewhat younger characters when their *perceived* aged status affects their treatment within the narrative. Of course, identifying those characters who are of any specific age is often difficult, if only because so often characters' ages are not provided within the diegeses of films. We thus also study films in which arguably middle-aged protagonists substantially confront the prospect of being "older" through conditions such as impairment, loss of employment, or grandparental status.[8]

Notice that we focus only on protagonists and characters central to the plots of movies, and we are unable to examine many examples throughout history. This book is not meant to be a catalogue of every elder performance in American cinema, nor can we account for the thousands of films in which elder characters appear as secondary or background characters. We have included a filmography (appendix A) in which we list over one thousand films that we initially considered for this study due to their prominent discourses about aging. Even this list is not exhaustive, because of the sheer reach of older characters in Hollywood history, so we encourage further scholars to add to our research here.

Fade to Gray

Introduction

THE PROSPECT OF OLDER AGE CAN BE DAUNTING. AFTER all, almost everyone wants to live for a very long time, yet the idea of "growing old" is generally unappealing. This apparent paradox permeates our enduring quests for longevity and the preservation of youth, for we all want to enjoy life without the limitations that may arise with advanced aging. If one is fortunate enough to advance to an old age, however defined, an enormous range of primarily negative effects are assumed to await, such as bodily infirmity, mental deterioration, loss of friends, the indifference of family, waning pleasure, and painful death. At the same time, since humans now live longer than ever before and social structures are slowly developing to accommodate the needs and interests of older people, an altogether new appreciation for senescence—the condition of simply aging into the end of life—has been emerging.

Motion pictures were developed at the end of the nineteenth century, and have now outlived every human being on the planet. In being the dominant entertainment medium during the first half of the twentieth century, movies enjoyed a cultural relevance whose rapid growth and emotional reach were unparalleled in human history. That relevance had given way to television by midcentury and to the Internet by the end of the century; but into the twenty-first century, the media of television and the Internet continue to largely rely upon the same formal structure and psychological manipulation that even the earliest silent films of the 1890s employed. And given the durability of cinema for over a century now, it offers an ideal perspective on how to understand the representation of people who were born since it began.

This book endeavors to chronicle an analytical history of elder characters in movies by identifying the changing representations of aging, considering how the aged have been visually portrayed and dramatically performed, and,

Beryl Mercer plays the suffering and stoic Ma in The Public Enemy *(1931), who endures the indignity of watching her adult son Tom (James Cagney) slide into crime during the Prohibition era.*

most of all, looking at how they have been shown to embrace or endure experiences associated with longer lives. Such a chronicle could easily fill multiple volumes if every cinematic example were studied from every part of the world, but because of the dominance of Hollywood within the global movie market (for good and ill), and because of our own backgrounds, this work concentrates exclusively on American movies from the 1900s to the 2010s. Even within American cinema, the majority of *all* films made before World War II have perished with time. Thus, the bulk of this book will detail feature films made after the mid-1940s, and owing to the accessibility of examples and the thematic coherence of the chapters, many films will be given greater attention than others.

Like most industries, Hollywood began developing its products for mass consumption with the goal of ensuring the greatest profitability, and despite changes in the methods of production and sales, it continues to do so. As a consequence, the movie industry has not been required to portray life with complete realism, and instead tends to present a fantasy of life that entertains fundamental human ambitions such as the search for love, the accomplishment of goals, and the resolution of conflicts. Thus, any analysis of aging within the scope of dominant American cinema must begin with this disclaimer: the industry promotes an often *preferred* vision of life and, in the process, reveals an idealized vision of what elder movie characters might encounter. To that end, movies often indicate what their audiences perceive about and hope for the aged, a condition that effectively limits the depiction of real life.

Despite this efficient system of wish fulfillment, Hollywood has proffered a frequently negative image of older characters in movies, who are often assumed to fade into irrelevance, inactivity, or absurdity, compared with their younger counterparts. These images have yielded a sporadically malignant pattern of elder representation that has engendered ignorance or exploited intolerance. Our study identifies many harmful roles and proposes some of the social and political motivations for their persistence. It also gives some visibility to uncommonly authentic depictions of older characters that enable opportunities for better understanding and appreciation of the aged and the aging process.

A consequence of the Hollywood agenda for mass appeal is not only the underestimation of older characters, but also the marginalization (even exclusion) of those older characters who would fall into "minority" categories of the population at large. Accordingly, not only are older women represented less often than men, despite forming an increasing preponderance of the population as aging goes on, but characters of nonwhite races, non-European ancestry, queer gender identities, and lower-class wealth are also seen less often than representatives of the white Anglo heterosexual middle class, which has always constituted the majority of characters in Hollywood movies. We remained conscious of this throughout our investigation, though recognizing that an additional exploration of the inherent oppression that arises from sexism, racism, ethnocentrism, homophobia, and classism can be addressed only in relation to certain historical changes (such as wars and economic fluctuations) and themes (such as romance and health).

Unlike the dominant youth audience, which has yet to experience much of life, older viewers presumably come to their experience of movies with an established understanding of their lives. Yet more significantly, Hollywood, also unlike the youth audience, tends to largely ignore the interests of the older audience. After all, as people age, they attend movies at theaters in decreasing numbers, because most older people have diminishing disposable incomes and tend to spend less on media-based products, and thus they become a less valuable portion of the consumer audience that media industries rely on for consumption. By 2013, 20 percent of Americans were age sixty and over, yet constituted only 13 percent of the moviegoing audience; the average person in the same age group attended movies roughly one-third as often as the average person between the ages of eighteen and twenty-four.[1] American movie studios have been able to justify their preoccupation with stories about younger characters through this economic reasoning, yet via a more pernicious cultural reasoning, the movie industry continues to promote the idea that young lives are the most worthwhile, the most fulfilling, and even the most important.

In fact, America has been "aging" more than ever before, because people are living longer. As explained in the preface, the median age of American citizens increased by fifteen years between 1900 and 2014, and the percentage of the population age sixty-five and older more than tripled in that time, from 4.1 percent in 1900 to 13.3 percent in 2011.[2] This condition has resulted in numerous geriatric health concerns, such as the business of Medicare and the use of palliative treatments, and has become part of the political and cultural dialogue around geriatric capability as an increasing number of citizens extend their working careers and maintain a more visible presence in society. (Since 1985, the percentage of Americans working at age sixty-five and older has been increasing, after decreasing substantially throughout the earlier twentieth century.)[3] American movies remain relatively uninterested in these particular trends, except insofar as the expanding population of older people lends itself to familiar dramatic conventions, such as fighting illness and death, sustaining romance, and discovering one's sense of self—conventions applied to younger characters as well. The distinctions in movies about older characters are grounded in the evolved—but often still limited—cultural assumptions about what we perceive to be "old age."

The qualities that categorize aging characters naturally cover a spectrum of negative and positive traits: in the former realm, traits such as frailty, senility, and irritability, and in the latter realm, traits such as sagacity, serenity, and frugality (although even these qualities are often suspect). Certain stock character types persist throughout aging narratives—such as the curmudgeon who likes no one, the old maid who never finds a man to marry, and the sage who doles out wisdom—yet the variability and complexity of roles for older characters makes them rather difficult to label with consistency. In most arguments about dramatic characters throughout history, there has been a tendency to elucidate a taxonomy of consistent types, resulting in a stringent labeling that we find too prejudicial. We abandoned this inclination, so while we will often refer to certain recurring roles, our study proceeds overall as a thematic and chronological evaluation rather than a character classification system.

In addition, we realized that a single sustained thesis about the representation of aging, a possibly noble academic ambition, is not justified for the type of comprehensive study we hope to achieve here. After all, the history of the film industry's depictions of aging is not coherent or monolithic enough to offer a scrupulous structuring argument about these diverse roles. Because we are unable to be truly encyclopedic in scope, however, yet want to be critical of cultural perceptions as influenced by industry practices, we have employed a method that offers breadth and discernment by generally tracing the development of aging roles in movies through trends in stories and genres that those roles initiated. Thus, the chapters treat the progression of American cinema as a context in which images of aging have evolved, images that we have identified as the most prominent and salient within the medium.

Because of our different backgrounds as scholars, as well as the distinctive needs encountered when examining films from the distant past to the present, chapters in this book do not follow a single, all-purpose approach. The first three chapters draw upon Nancy's research and primarily detail the history of aging representation through the end of the studio era, taking a chronological approach and thereby placing shifts and trends in characterization in a historical and, to a lesser extent, an industrial context. The last three chapters, which draw upon Tim's research and also proceed chronologically, focus on influential topics that achieved their dominant realizations in aging depictions after the 1960s, and thus these studies are built on social trends and thematic developments related to older characters.

In chapter 1, we present an overview of representations of aging in early cinema through the 1920s, considering the way elder figures were most often employed as difficulties to be overcome by young protagonists. We further focus on the Great Depression and the 1940s, when older characters were positioned as figures to be both revered and pitied. Chapter 2 investigates representations of aging in the 1950s, revealing narratives in which anxieties about the cultural displacement of the aged were projected onto the plights of women (and a handful of male characters) facing down the enforced social irrelevance of late middle age. Chapter 3 applies the genre analysis used with melodrama in the previous chapter to horror and broad comedy beginning in the 1960s, exploring the ways in which older characters were transformed into objects of kitsch and derision. Chapter 4 surveys the generic tradition of road movies in relation to "elder odysseys" for aging protagonists, who were embarking on new missions of self-discovery in increasing numbers by the 1970s. Chapter 5 takes on the topic of romance, an often assumed or delicately conveyed aspect of otherwise common elder relationships (between the aged and with younger characters) that began to gain more expressive articulation toward the end of the twentieth century. Chapter 6 closes our study with the somber subject of death and dying, which has an understandable association with senescent characters, yet has been extensively repressed and complicated by social and industrial concerns, even as movies have entered the new millennium.

In Going in Style *(1979), George Burns, Lee Strasberg, and Art Carney play three retired widowers who rebel against expectations of the aged by pulling off a bank heist.*

Our overall approach examines widespread social attitudes by explicating individual films. On the macro level, we look at the perception of "older age" as a formalized and institutionalized cinematic category over the past century and more. This cultural manifestation reveals itself at the levels of the individual family, public policy, and media representation. As Andrew Blaikie writes, "In explaining the contemporary popular culture around aging, it seems logical that an approach which can embrace both large-scale transformations in social policy and micro-level shifts in commonsense understandings might be most plausible."[4] With this in mind, our project owes a debt to the type of approach taken by Michel Foucault in his work on categories such as madness and sexuality, or institutions such as the prison or the clinic, where analysis of macrolevel history and ideas are understood largely through instances at the micro level.[5] Since this project is both a social history and a media history, we are primarily interested in how the cultural category "older age" and the social formations that have emerged around it are represented through cinema, and how these representations have influenced and reinforced social ideas.

We thus consider aging through its attendant visual representation in movies, to include social and political factors such as the implementation of Social Security, postwar migration and suburbanization and the resultant shift in household membership, the expansion of nursing homes and assisted-living facilities, and contemporary debates about geriatric healthcare, euthanasia, elder abuse, and senicide. There are also related cultural factors, including generational conflicts and a wealth of media idealizing domestication, distinct gender roles, and the nuclear family. Industrial factors play a role, too, including the restructuring of movie studios after World War II, the growth and establishment of the television industry, and changing approaches to advertising, including the identification and targeting of newly conceptualized younger and older markets. Economic influences aligned with these industrial factors include the changing financial circumstances of nuclear family units and older Americans during recent decades that have engendered escalating consumerism. All these factors have continued to affect representations of aging in recent years, alongside advances in medical treatments that have resulted in prolonged life spans and the consequent growth of the older population, in both quantity and complexity.

Though age is one of the defining factors of lived experience and one's perceptions of self and others, it has been studied very little within a field that has done so much to consider other similarly defining concepts such as race, class, gender, and sexuality. Our project, therefore, aims to open up the discussion of ways in which age can be used as a lens to clarify our understanding of our cultural world and its media products. The topic of age in society is, of course, important to other disciplines, including sociology, history, gerontology, gender studies, cultural studies, and communication. Our hope is that this project may be useful not only as a means of constructing a conceptual framework within film and media studies but also as an example of how the interests of our field resonate beyond its borders to offer, in Richard Maltby's words (in another context), a way in which film studies can "matter."[6] In an effort to thus matter while also conducting our study most effectively, we focus our methodology on the textual and cultural analysis of movies exclusively, rather than attempting to account for the numerous other disciplinary concerns of aging.

Age is a particularly tricky concept in that it affects each and every one of us in quite different ways throughout our lives. It is a constant factor in understanding our own conceptions of self as well as our relationships with others. Aging studies is an area of research that has done much to cross the boundaries between scholarly inquiry and general interest, recognizing the oftentimes quite personal and affective aspects of the topic. Our hope is that this book ultimately contributes to that field and also presents scholarly material and analysis in a manner that can connect with a general readership. Our personal belief is that older age has been neglected in discussions within the sphere of popular culture, certainly relative to how much age affects our experience and thinking.

THE STUDY OF AGING IN CINEMA

Little attention has been devoted to the roles of older people in media, perhaps for the same reasons that so little media has been devoted to representing them: the older population does not spend as much time *or* money on media as younger people, and their roles tend not to interest many young people, who are the most cherished demographic of media promoters. The study of age imaging in general has emerged as a relatively new realm in film and media analyses, and has most often centered on the roles of children and teenagers.[7] We concentrate our concerns on representations of older age while recognizing that gerontology and public health policies for the aged have persisted as topics in culture at large and cannot be fully addressed within the scope of our approach. Our focus is on popular movie industry products, which tend to reach mass audiences: fictional narratives that convey perceived realities to the public about aging (even through exaggeration and distortion).

By comparison, much of the early attention to aging in media focused on work outside the popular realm. For example, *The Gerontologist* began publishing reviews of audiovisual materials about and for the aged in 1976, although it largely covered documentary films, and its notices were primarily aimed at a clinical readership. Hollywood movies remained at the fringes of the journal's radar until the 1980s, during the somewhat attentive years of the Reagan presidency. Robert Yahnke became the pioneering media critic for *The Gerontologist* at that time, publishing the 1988 catalogue *The Great Circle of Life: A Resource Guide to Films on Aging*, which thoroughly detailed nearly ninety short films made between 1964 and 1985, yet disregarded fictional features. Lack of interest in the popular depiction of the aged was further evident in the annual National Media Owl Awards, presented from 1984 to 1998 by the Retirement Research Foundation, which recognized outstanding media achievements on aging-related matters, but rarely honored any projects by major movie studios.

Feature films gained some academic attention by the 1980s in the first film studies book to deal directly with issues of aging in American film, Karen M. Stoddard's *Saints and Shrews: Women and Aging in American Popular Film* (1983). Stoddard looks at Hollywood depictions of middle-aged and older women from the 1930s to the early 1980s. She examines a number of recurring stereotypes (the witch, the saintly mother, the overbearing mother) through a feminist viewpoint, which places her in line with Molly Haskell and Marjorie Rosen in their broader 1970s studies of women in Hollywood movies, and her study operates very much as a companion to theirs.[8]

Historical studies dealing with age and the American family, such as Andrew Achenbaum's *Shades of Gray: Old Age, American Values, and Federal Policies since 1920* (1983) and Elaine Tyler May's *Homeward Bound: American Families in the Cold War* (1988), informed the field about larger social and historical changes affecting aging (Social Security, suburban migration, economic shifts, changing family composition, etc.). Achenbaum demonstrated the crucial relationship between legislation, social welfare movements, and economic changes, on the one hand, and cultural attitudes and social experiences around aging on the other. May's book offered a valuable conception of postwar American culture and social life through a skillful integration of statistical information, period studies, popular press materials, and media depictions that provided a comprehensive foundation for her arguments, as well as a compelling historical narrative. The balance between the individual historical artifact and the larger sociohistorical narrative demonstrated in a very practical way some of the balance we seek to achieve in our own approach.

Sociological studies on aging in cinema had emerged by the end of the 1980s with Andrea Walsh's essay "'Life Isn't Yet Over': Older Heroines in American Popular Cinema of the 1930s and 1970s/80s" (1989), an articulate consideration of four canonical films about aging characters; it challenged then-fashionable psychoanalytic perspectives with a sensitive critique of gender issues in older age. Bradley Fisher later offered a pedagogical view on understanding aging depictions in "Exploring Ageist Stereotypes Through Commercial Motion Pictures" (1992). Further work considering the use of elder images in film as teaching tools included Linda Ello's "Older Adult Issues and Experiences through the Stories and Images of Film" (2007). Tom Robinson then led a group in 2009 that conducted a content analysis of sixty teen movies (all made since 1980) featuring older characters; the results indicated a denigration of elders in movies directed at young audiences.[9]

In the 1990s, a number of aging studies exploring humanistic perspectives (predominantly literature based, though occasionally including the analysis of films) were published in Britain and the United States. While such writing tends to use filmic examples to further underscore arguments about literary or other cultural representations, there were occasional studies applied entirely to film. An illustrative example is Merry G. Perry's "Animated Gerontophobia: Ageism, Sexism, and the Disney Villainess" (1999), which applies to a different body of representations much of the feminist theorizing from Stoddard's work. Earlier in the decade, Susan J. Ferguson had published "The Old Maid Stereotype in American Film, 1938 to 1965" (1991), a similar catalogue of representations from a (slightly more cinematic) feminist theoretical perspective. In a revealing analysis of characters aged sixty and older, "The Mirror Has Two Faces" (2000), Elizabeth Markson and Carol Taylor detail the negative typing of aging women in American movies.[10] More recently, Deborah Jermyn edited *Female Celebrity and Ageing* (2014), which examines the contested status of stardom for Hollywood actresses. These kinds of works, though insightful, remain primarily film studies focused on gender rather than comprehensive studies of aging in cinema.[11]

Recently there have been attempts to more thoroughly explore the overlooked topic of older age in cinema.[12] One scholarly work expanding upon cinematic aging is Amir Cohen-Shalev's *Visions of Aging: Images of the Elderly in Film* (2009). In this concise monograph, Cohen-Shalev examines a dozen non-American films that take aging as a predominant subject, particularly those works of older filmmakers, whose "old age style" reveals "growing ambivalence and ambiguity" about aging, resulting in films that, unlike the work of younger directors, are "disturbing rather than peaceful, open-ended rather than providing a closure."[13] The study takes up films by "canonical" auteurs such as Ingmar Bergman, comparing earlier works (such as *Wild Strawberries*, 1957) to those made later in life (*Saraband*, 2003); other examples include Claude Sautet (*Nelly and Monsieur Arnaud*, 1996) and Akira Kurosawa (*Madadayo*, 1993). Giving some attention to relatively contemporary products like the Australian film *A Woman's Tale* (1991) and the British *Waking Ned Devine* (1998), Cohen-Shalev considers themes about the aged through an analysis of cinematic authorship in relation to age itself.[14]

Amelia DeFalco's *Uncanny Subjects: Aging in Contemporary Narrative* (2010) follows in the tradition of humanistic aging studies that include considerations of film without looking at that medium exclusively or situating analyses within a film-specific context. DeFalco uses theories of the uncanny to look at contemporary literary and filmic portrayals of aging. Through narrative analysis, she argues that such texts reveal the experience of aging as a process in which one's body and self become uncanny. She presents this as an especially modern conception of identity, as multiple and shifting, and as a representation of conceiving our own lives as narrative trajectories, influenced in no small part by the literary and filmic narratives dominant in our culture. Though the majority of texts examined by DeFalco are literary works, she does consider a handful of films, including the American *Requiem for a Dream* (2000), as well as the Canadian *Strangers in Good Company* (1990) and the British *Iris* (2001). DeFalco looks at how the sense of the aging body as uncanny contributes to a cultural treatment of the aged as "different" and to be feared, which has certainly influenced our arguments about the promotion of difference and dehumanization in what we term "elder kitsch."

Clint Eastwood, who at age seventy-eight directed and starred in Gran Torino *(2008) as a Korean War veteran with surprisingly sacrificial fortitude, has been a remarkably proficient auteur in his late career. Since turning sixty, he has directed twenty-one films, four of them after he turned eighty.*

Drawing heavily on disability studies, gerontology, and cultural studies, Sally Chivers's *The Silvering Screen: Old Age and Disability in Cinema* (2011) examines several high-profile films about aging and the aged, such as *Nobody's Fool* (1994), *The Straight Story* (1999), *About Schmidt* (2002), *Away from Her* (2006), and *The Savages* (2007). In reading these films, Chivers demonstrates how Hollywood repeatedly conflates representations of aging with representations of disability, presenting aging itself as the ultimate of disabilities, something of a horror. Her analysis touches on the double standard applied to aging actresses in Hollywood (such as Melanie Griffith), as opposed to aging male stars (such as Harrison Ford), and she examines insightfully the peculiar ways in which Hollywood has created a space on screen in recent years for aging action stars (particularly Clint Eastwood). While an early chapter surveys *Sunset Blvd.* (1950) and *What Ever Happened to Baby Jane?* (1962) as representations in which aging (the aging woman, in particular) is conflated with mental and physical disability, Chivers's focus is firmly on the contemporary period and films since the 1990s. The book is very much an argument against negative portrayals of disability on screen, here attaching disability to age, and an analysis of how recent films have sent mixed messages, both challenging and reinforcing such biases.

Following Chivers in further problematizing some of the dominant trends of aging representation, Pamela Gravagne argues in *The Becoming of Age: Cinematic Visions of Mind, Body and Identity in Later Life* (2013) not only for changes in the perception of older people on screen, but also for a comprehensive change in the cultural understanding of aging, using as test cases seventeen films made since 1990, most from outside the United States, including animated and documentary features. She elucidates a "narrative of decline" that is endemic to so many stories of aging, including the essentialist "biomedical" view, which reduces the body to a set of materials, and the social-constructionist view, which evaluates aging based on a political economy of meaning. She then introduces her hybrid theory of "agential realism," which disputes the decline narrative and disrupts the marginalization of elders who do not exhibit physical ability and mental acuity as the confirmation of their worth. She foresees how this approach "can allow us to denaturalize age, to uproot the pervasive assumptions about what is natural for certain ages and to see how these presumptions often violently limit our illusions about age and its lived experience."[15] Gravagne takes up gender politics, intimacy among elders, and Alzheimer's disease as portrayed in movies such as *Gran Torino* (2008), *Beginners* (2010), and *Away From Her*. She asserts that we should see "age as becoming," rather than as leading to dying, through an examination of four diverse films—including *Strangers in Good Company* and *The Straight Story*—that express positive future possibilities that aging offers to their protagonists, movies that "offer an implicit challenge to the assumption of decline, stereotypes of incompetence, and feelings of aversion that mass media images of the old generally convey."[16]

The strength of these books is, most simply, that they have further opened the conversation around age and cinema. Additionally, key theoretical arguments related to sexuality, identity, and mortality are pursued: vital foundational work for any aging study to build upon. What has been lacking so far is a study that examines representations of aging in films specific to Hollywood cinema throughout its history and across manifold cultural concerns. Our project thereby begins to sketch out the evolving depiction of "growing old" in American movies, historicizing these representations and tracing shifts in characterizations throughout the previous century and into the present.

FILMOGRAPHY AND TERMINOLOGY

As detailed in the preface, we considered thousands of films featuring older characters when building the filmography for our analysis, making subjective judgments about which films focused on issues about aging into the older years. We recognize that this is a crucial yet unavoidably flawed approach, because it does involve judgment. Our dilemma in identifying relevant films not only comments on the very ambiguity of being "old," but also sheds light on the difficulty of "aging studies" in general.

A recurring flaw in many studies of character representation is that authors are so selective in their inclusion of examples that they indicate personal bias, as well as reflect the bias of audiences. Many scholars are inclined to take a "greatest hits" approach to their topic, highlighting those films that won box office or critical acclaim, conditions that indicate some level of fame, yet do not validate the importance nor determine the influence of films in representing their given characters. In addition, this approach provides scholars a facile opportunity to winnow down their cited examples for study, particularly when the volume of possible films is too large to view, as with the present volume. Rather than relying solely upon critical or commercial success, we tried to bring to light the most relevant examples of texts within the time periods we cover, admitting that some inevitable amount of bias permeates our selections for commentary, yet endeavoring to be inclusive rather than exclusive.

We further recognize the inevitable attention that more recent films enjoy, if only because they are more accessible for study and more familiar to us as critics. Our analysis of films made before World War II is necessarily compromised by the shortage of extant examples to view, and some films made in the decades thereafter also remain unavailable.[17] This not only results in the aforementioned emphasis on more popular products (because popular films are most likely to receive wider media distribution in the years after their theatrical release), but also leads to a reliance on broader historical accounts of cinema in its first decades of existence. Thus, we have a better appreciation for social and industrial trends from decades ago, if only because they have become easier to understand with time, while we have a better appreciation of individual films from recent decades. Our chapters reflect this condition, since we examine many more films in later chapters, yet without the same benefit of time (and further analysis by other scholars in the field) that informs our study of earlier films.

The overall study progresses chronologically, although the ability to examine more films in recent decades compelled us to take on a thematic organization as well, which becomes increasingly pronounced as the chapters proceed. A thematic emphasis allows for more coherent analyses of certain trends and topics, and yet it further exposes an inclination toward more popular films and dominant subjects, which may not always be the most emblematic, given our comprehensive objectives. We thus ask for further latitude in our determination of pertinent concerns for this study.

Needing to construct a filmography from which to proceed, we began with meticulous plot searches in the Internet Movie Database (IMDb) and the *Catalog of Feature Films* from the American Film Institute. In the former, we searched by the following keyword terms: aging, elderly, grandfather, grandmother, nursing home, old age, old man, old people's home, old woman, retirement, senility, and senior citizen. In the latter, we searched by genre (elderly); subject (aging, aged men, aged women, aged persons, grandfathers, grandmothers, senility); and summary (the same keywords used for IMDb). Of course, these lists are subjective in their use of these terms, and many of the films listed under these headings did not fit our criteria. We ultimately arrived at a filmography of over 1,000 possible examples, as presented in appendix A, of which over 350 are discussed in the main text.

Our emphasis remains on films that significantly address topics *about* aging for protagonists, beyond merely featuring them as aged characters in supporting roles. Robert De Niro, for example, played grandfather characters in *Everybody's Fine* (2009), *Meet the Fockers* (2010), and *Grudge Match* (2013) who juggle concerns about their grown children. Yet many of his subsequent films, including *New Year's Eve* (2011), *Freelancers* (2012), and *American Hustle* (2013), did not focus on his characters within the context of a story related to their aging condition.[18]

The choice of language in a study about representations of aging has been a special challenge. The term "aging" is often used in an overly vague way. After all, we are every one of us "aging" all the time, making references to aging entirely relative. To describe "the aged" as a group has a bit more specificity, given an understanding that the people included in such a group are, to some extent, associated with the experience of moving beyond mere adulthood into older age. We have thus used references to "the aged" periodically throughout this work to connote a larger group of people for whom this is the case.

In considering the more specific language used when discussing particular representations or stars in this study, we tried to choose our terminology with care. Older age is again a variable category for our subjects, and often situational. For example, the Oscar-winning actors Dustin Hoffman and Anthony Hopkins were both born in 1937, yet the characters they have played in recent decades (and continue to play as they approach the age of eighty) have been considerably different in their age representations. With the exception of *Little Big Man* (1970), which Hoffman made at age thirty-three and for which he wore substantial makeup in two short scenes as a man over one hundred, he has yet to play a character that most people would deem "elderly"—even his new grandfather in *Little Fockers* (2010), made when he was seventy-three, defies traditional geriatric markers, appearing physically and sexually active, tan and fit, lucid and lively. Hopkins, on the other hand, convincingly

Anthony Hopkins garnered an Oscar nomination for his role in Amistad *(1997), believably portraying a historical figure who was more than a decade older.*

played the seventy-three-year-old John Quincy Adams in *Amistad* (1997) the year he turned sixty, and thereafter played many grizzled characters with declining mental capacity (*Hearts in Atlantis* [2001]; *Proof* [2005]; *Fracture* [2007]). More recently, he needed considerable makeup to play the younger eponymous director in *Hitchcock* (2012), who was age sixty-one in the story, whereas Hopkins was seventy-five. Hoffman continues to be presented in movies as a man of comparative middle age with no generational difference from the other adults with whom he interacts, while Hopkins has been comfortably playing the oldest character in movies whose casts view him as being close to senility, death, and even immortality (in *Noah* [2014] and the *Thor* franchise [2011, 2013, 2015]). Hoffman and Hopkins have both had very successful screen careers since they were in their twenties, so their audiences have not always had a perception of them as "older" character actors (as was the case with Charles Coburn, May Robson, Clifton Webb, and many others who did not have significant careers in Hollywood until their fifties and tended to play aged characters). Nonetheless, for a range of debatable reasons, including Hopkins abandoning hair dye in many roles after *Amistad* and Hoffman being inclined to play comic roles, the former has far more often been presented as older than his peers. In this and many other cases throughout our study, chronological age has much less bearing than contextual or situational age on perceptions of agedness.

We have therefore attempted to choose language reflecting the state of being part of "the aged" population that is inoffensive yet accurate. Referring to anyone as "old" can have a pejorative connotation that we want to avoid, and when possible we employ more precise nouns in labeling characters, such as retiree, grandparent, or septuagenarian. At times in this study, we refer to characters within the context of their stereotypical cultural representation and thereby employ adjectives common to a particular era—such as "old maid," "dotty," or "spavined"—which are intended to refer only to such historical characterizations.

Cultural euphemisms have developed over time to describe older people—venerable, long-lived, senior citizen, geriatric, senescent—yet the term "elderly" has developed a negative association with the very old. Most Americans would not identify themselves or others as "elderly" in their sixties or even seventies, especially if they are able-bodied and independent. Nonetheless, in identifying older characters for the purpose of this project, we have chosen in the majority of instances to use "elder" as a noun *and* an adjective. An "elder" is someone clearly positioned, whether through implication or stated status (retired, grandparent, over a certain age), to be of an older generation than other adult characters in a given film; "elder" also can describe the nature of older people distinguished from those who are younger, as in "elder romance." Further, "elder" has at least some respectability compared with other vague terms. This is perhaps not a perfect solution for the problem of terminology in this project, but it is the term that we feel best suits the needs of this study and best maintains consistency in meaning from usage to usage.

One of the rare films featuring a vibrant elder couple falling in love, Elsa & Fred *(2014) did not find an extensive audience despite featuring past Oscar winners Shirley MacLaine and Christopher Plummer in the title roles.*

We thus present this study of elder images in American cinema with respect for the population these movies portray, with a critical focus on how the film industry has developed these representations, and with a historical understanding of how American culture has evolved in its recognition of what being "older" really means.

CHAPTER ONE

Generational Conflict in Prewar Hollywood Film

When you're seventeen and the world's beautiful, facing facts is just as slick fun as dancing or going to parties, but when you're seventy . . . well, you don't care about dancing, you don't think about parties anymore, and about the only fun you have left is pretending that there ain't any facts to face, so would you mind if I just went on pretending?

LUCY COOPER (BEULAH BONDI) IN
MAKE WAY FOR TOMORROW (1937)

THE UNITED STATES EXPERIENCED AN UNPRECEDENTED increase in the population of citizens living past the age of fifty during the early twentieth century, primarily as a result of major advances in medical knowledge and public health. American society was still adjusting to this significant shift as the new medium of cinema became a dominant force. Representations of elders in movies then changed over time as social perceptions of aging changed in substantial ways. If we map American movie roles onto major moments of change in cultural notions of "the aged" during the first half of the century, clear trends and themes emerge.

In American cinema from its birth in the 1890s to the 1930s, older characters were all but entirely defined against younger characters. In these films, we see three clear themes: elders as hindrances, elders as helpers, or elders as recipients of help. In all three cases, the central narrative focuses on the distinction between the young and the old. Films such as *The Crab* (1917), *Old Lady 31* (1920), and *The Shepherd of the Hills* (1928) demonstrate that as elders became more numerous and commonplace in twentieth-century American life, their counterparts in cinema operated as a source of tension for the young, one more symptom of the nation's bumpy transition to modernity.

During the time surrounding the implementation of Social Security in the 1930s, a moment arrived when a culturally and bureaucratically recognized category of the American population known as "seniors" became clearly defined. Elder characters in Hollywood films during this period also often fall into three recurring types: saintly mothers, out-of-touch millionaires, and admirable pillars of the community. One important filmmaker that we examine as a case study of sorts during this period was Frank Capra, whose films not only were some of the biggest hits of their era but also featured elder characters prominently while striking an emotional chord with many viewers.[1] Films such as *Mr. Deeds Goes to Town* (1936), *You Can't Take It With You* (1938), and *Meet John Doe* (1941) not only stand in as representative of this period in the popular imagination, but also speak to concerns about the place of the elderly in the community. In addition to Capra's work during this period, we explore films such as D. W. Griffith's *What Shall We Do with Our Old?* (1911) and Leo McCarey's seminal *Make Way for Tomorrow* (1937) to further consider how the very prominent issue of the nation's (and the individual's) responsibility for our elders was negotiated.

The place of elders in American society underwent a dramatic shift in the wartime and early postwar years, when suburbanization and the rise of eldercare facilities begin to change the family configuration in important ways. We thereby discuss Capra's *Arsenic and Old Lace* (1944) and *It's a Wonderful Life* (1946) to note that shift before exploring postwar films further in chapter 2. Overall, this chapter demonstrates how cinematic representations reflected shifts in the cultural conceptions of family and community and the place of elders within these groups, and set the stage for the way that elder characters have been depicted on screen to the present day.

ELDER DEPICTIONS IN EARLY CINEMA AND THE SILENT ERA

Starting with the earliest American films, the relationships between elder characters and the young sometimes provide beneficial outcomes to both parties, but more often than not this difference is a source of conflict that must be resolved. When looking at the roles of elder characters in the initial fifty years of American cinema, meaningful and thought-provoking patterns of elder representation emerge.

While the lack of surviving films from the early period of cinema makes it difficult to analyze the representation of elders in cinema's first decades, catalogue descriptions and press accounts provide some interesting glimpses. In May 1902, for instance, the Edison Manufacturing Company released a

Carl E. Schultze's elder character "Foxy Grandpa," seen here in his comic strip incarnation, was popular enough in the early 1900s to spur stage and film adaptations in addition to such merchandising as banks, toys, and buttons.

film entitled *Naughty Grandpa and the Field Glass*, in which a gentleman uses a spyglass to secretly view a flirting young couple. When Grandma discovers Grandpa's voyeurism, she promptly punishes him by beating him over the head with the spyglass and breaking it. Thus, Grandpa is punished for behaving like a "dirty old man" and for deviating from the behavior socially prescribed to someone of his age.

In contrast are a series of eight films from the same period (1902–1903) that the American Mutoscope and Biograph Company released based on Charles Edward Schultze's newspaper comic strip *Foxy Grandpa*, with such descriptive titles as *The Boys Think They Have One on Foxy Grandpa, but He Fools Them* (1902) and *Why Foxy Grandpa Escaped a Ducking* (1903). Published in various incarnations from 1900 to 1918, the *Foxy Grandpa* comics feature the title character, a clever codger, constantly outsmarting and outwitting his two troublesome grandsons. Schultze's strip was popular enough to lead to reprintings in book form, an array of toys and memorabilia featuring Foxy Grandpa's likeness, and a Broadway show. The *Foxy Grandpa* films featured the star of the Broadway show, Joseph Hart, in the title role, and used the show's sets. Typical of films from the era, the *Foxy Grandpa* pictures are quite brief (under a minute each), revolving around simple plots and emphasizing the visual gag of the senescent man behaving youthfully. Unlike the old man in *Naughty Grandpa and the Field Glass* though, Foxy

Grandpa is not punished for his youthful antics but celebrated. While Foxy Grandpa in the comic strip is talented on numerous fronts, including acrobatics, engineering, and common sense, the American Mutoscope films necessarily focus on the kinetic visual of Foxy Grandpa's acrobatic and dancing skills. The scenarios feature the grandsons taunting Foxy Grandpa before being suitably shown up by his ability to dance, turn summersaults, and play the banjo. In this way, these short films of early cinema prefigure a film like *Jackass Presents: Bad Grandpa* (2013) from over a century later, in which the visual incongruity of elders behaving like young people is still a central, immediately familiar gag.

This particular type of comedic representation fell out of favor in Hollywood until it was resurrected in the 1960s (as discussed in chapter 3). The comedic presentation of misbehaving elders seen in *Naughty Grandpa and the Field Glass* and the *Foxy Grandpa* films appeared to fade away as films from the late 1900s to the early 1910s become longer and more dependent on narrative. Even though extant films from this era are difficult to access, the work of the esteemed director D. W. Griffith is worth examining because he notably featured prominent elder characters in his films.

Griffith's Civil War films of the 1910s, considered in-depth in Richard Abel's *Americanizing the Movies and Movie-Mad Audiences, 1910–1914*, often focused on the domestic side of war, telling tales of family melodrama that involved elder figures. *The Fugitive* (1910) and *The House with Closed Shutters* (1910) both present domestic dramas centered on sympathetic mothers of adult children involved, one way or another, in the war. In *The Fugitive*, a grieving Southern mother, whose son has been killed by a Northern soldier, ultimately allows the Northern solider to escape back to the North due to her empathy with his mother. *The House with Closed Shutters* involves a mother who protects her son's honor, allowing him to hide in her home, after his sister, cross-dressing as a Confederate man, took his place in battle and was subsequently killed.

Abel notes the "critique of Southern manliness" in these films, which perhaps helped make sympathetic presentations of the South palatable to northern audiences.[2] Similarly, in *His Trust Fulfilled* (1911), in which Griffith presents a sympathetic Southern male protagonist, he uses an elder "dutiful darkie" (played in blackface), undercutting any perceived "threat" from Southern masculinity or from race through the character's age and deferential status. In the film, a family is left under the care of their servant after the household patriarch is killed in battle. The old slave keeps careful watch over the family, saves the mother and children from Northern attack, and helps support them financially behind the scenes both before and after the war, allowing them to prosper rather than fail in white society.

Griffith's most explicit consideration of elders in American culture is *What Shall We Do with Our Old?* (1911), a social morality tale set in the contemporary period. Before we discuss this in length, however, it is worth first studying the roles of elder figures across the work of other directors from the silent era. While many older actors were employed in incidental roles, filling out the diegetic worlds of silent era films, a few trends emerge when we consider larger roles played by older actors in surviving works of the late 1910s and 1920s, as well as in catalogue descriptions of no-longer-obtainable films. The plot functions of elder characters within this period seem to be chosen from a fairly limited palette, the main themes of which are rooted in generational conflicts between the young and the old. As elders became more numerous and visible in American society, their on-screen presence was portrayed, in various ways, as a source of tension for youthful protagonists.

The first theme of sorts that can be seen in films from this era is that of the elder figure as a hindrance to a younger protagonist's happiness. In *The Rejuvenation of Aunt Mary* (1914; remade in 1927), a young man is disinherited by his wealthy Aunt Mary (Kate Toncray) after she receives word that he has behaved too exuberantly while at college. To win his way back into her affections and financial good graces, the young man and his friends put together an elaborate ruse to bring about a reconciliation. In the 1914 version of the film, the nephew falls in love with a wholesome girl while executing the ruse, and since Aunt Mary too is taken with this ideal young woman, she reinstates her nephew in her will, allowing him to marry and prosper. In the 1927 version, the young people reunite Aunt Mary (May Robson) with a lost great love of her youth; suitably cheered, she reinstates her nephew, allowing him to move forward with his life as a man of means once more.

Pay Dirt (1916) features Mollie McConnell as Moll, an elder woman in a mining town who has become notorious for her gambling habit and uncouth ways. When it is revealed to the townsfolk that Moll is the mother of the handsome "easterner" (Henry King), his wealthy fiancée abandons him. The reputation of his mother, initially an embarrassment, becomes now a hindrance to the man's financial and romantic future. In the end, however, the departure of the wealthy fiancée turns out to be a positive event, since it allows a less status-obsessed and better-suited young woman to catch the man's eye and, eventually, win his hand in marriage. *A Girl Like That* (1917) similarly deals with the consequences of a disreputable older parent causing difficulty in an adult child's life. Nell (Irene Fenwick), the daughter of an ailing former bank robber, is desperate to procure funds to pay for her father's medical treatment. Nell is coerced into helping her father's former business associates rob a bank. In the process of the long con, she obtains work at the bank as a stenographer and falls in love with the bank manager. When Nell has a change of heart about aiding the criminals in stealing from her new boss, her father is shot and killed in retaliation. She agrees to complete her role in the con, but when the bank robbers are in the vault, Nell sounds the alarm, saving her love interest from robbery and avenging her father's murder in the process.

Elder love interests also pose a threat to the happiness of young protagonists. In *Pots-and-Pans Peggy* (1917), the title character, played by Gladys Hulette, is unhappily betrothed to a wealthy older gentleman while in love with her family's chauffeur, who is age appropriate but not financially appropriate in the eyes of the young woman's mother. The chauffeur beau eventually exposes the elder love interest as a spy who has been getting close to Peggy in order to obtain important war documents from her father. Only once the aged spy is exposed and removed from Peggy's life can she be free to marry her true love, who is now a hero to her parents and her country. *The Price She Paid* (1917) features another woman forced to marry an important man many years her senior for financial stability. Once the young woman is able to divorce herself from her cruel, aged husband (also revealed late in the film to be a bigamist), she embarks on a new life in Paris, finds true love, and establishes herself as a world-renowned pianist. *A Hoosier Romance* (1918) features not one but two older men wreaking havoc on the romantic life of a young woman. Colleen Moore plays an Indiana farmwoman, Patience Thompson, who is at the mercy of her cruel father's whims. Although she is in love with a noble young farmhand, Patience is forced by her father into an engagement with an aged associate of his. Only an elaborate scheme orchestrated by sympathetic townsfolk, which sends both older gentlemen off on wild-goose chases when they are led to believe that Patience has fled, allows her to find happiness and to marry her age-appropriate lover. In *The Rose of the World* (1918), a woman who believes that her husband was killed in the war remarries unhappily to an older pompous lord. It is eventually revealed that the woman's first husband was not killed, much to the woman's distress. Her second husband is reluctant to dissolve their marriage, also much to the woman's distress. Eventually, the long-lived lord chooses not to stand in the way of true love and frees his young wife to be with the man she loves.

When elder figures stand in the way of younger characters' happiness, however, this obstructiveness is not always intentional. In *Welcome Home* (1925), for instance, an older man moves in unannounced with his son and daughter-in-law, disrupting their way of life. The crusty man's continual demands, obnoxious friends, and obliviousness cause a strain on the young couple's marriage until the wife threatens to leave her husband if his father does not find another place to live. The retired man goes to visit his friends at a rest home and takes a liking to it. When it is revealed that his son and daughter-in-law are expecting a child, the soon-to-be grandfather recognizes that he is standing in the way of the young people's happiness and agrees to move into the old-age home with his peers, thus literally moving out to make way for the next generation.

The second theme of conflict between elders and younger generations is a somewhat more positive one: films in which elders aid younger people in some fashion, helping save or redeem them, thus operating in the service of the younger characters' narratives. In *The Heart of Ezra Greer* (1917), an older man strives to reunite his daughter with the father of her illegitimate child. Working as a butler to the younger man, the wise father works to instill a sense of responsibility and decency in him, eventually helping him become a model husband. In *The Man of Mystery* (1917), a deformed and aged man is healed and rejuvenated through the magical properties of Italian lava. Using his newfound healthy body, the man exposes a plot of international conspirators, saving his country. International intrigue also plays a part in *Miss Robinson Crusoe* (1917), in which two aging spinster aunts work not only to bring two young lovers together, but also to help the pampered young man assert his masculinity by safeguarding secret government documents from violent foreign agents. *Grumpy* (1923) likewise includes an elder who becomes involved in intrigue. A retired lawyer (Theodore Roberts), known as "Grumpy" for his crotchety ways, uses his lifetime of experience and clever logic to unravel a diamond heist mystery, saving a young woman who was unwittingly made a patsy.

In a darker vein, *Money Magic* (1917) features an aged man who makes the ultimate sacrifice to help a young person. Haney (William Duncan), a mine owner in very poor health who is married to a much younger woman, journeys to the East Coast with his wife, befriending a young man along the way. It becomes clear to Haney over a period of time that his wife has the kind of romantic connection with this younger man that she does not have with Haney. Eventually, Haney decides that he can no longer be a burden to his wife and a hindrance to her finding true love and happiness, so he climbs a mountain, knowing that the exertion will likely be too much for his weak heart. His resulting death allows his wife to inherit his fortune and frees her to pursue happiness with the younger man. Continuing in this more melodramatic territory, *The Natural Law* (1917) also features an older man who realizes his younger wife is in love with a man her own age. Howard Hall plays Dr. Webster, who refuses to give his wife an abortion after she is impregnated by this younger man. Instead, Dr. Webster tests the young man's character by informing him that the pregnancy has indeed been terminated. When the man is outraged and threatens Dr. Webster, the doctor is satisfied of the young man's morals and helps arrange a marriage between the two.

Deception is another means by which an elder figure can work behind the scenes to redeem or better the lives of young people. In *Rich Man, Poor Man* (1918), an older man forges documents in order to give a young woman a chance at a better life, making her appear to be the long-lost granddaughter of a millionaire. While this duplicity leads to some troubles, it ultimately betters the lives of both the young woman and the cantankerous millionaire. *The Shepherd of the Hills* (1919; remade in 1928) features an aging shepherd who seeks to atone for the sins of his son who abandoned a young woman pregnant with his child. Without revealing his true identity, the shepherd becomes employed by the woman's father. In this position, the older man works to redeem and reform his son, showing him the error of his ways and guiding him to take responsibility. The shepherd also has a helpful effect on the young woman, her family, and other people in the rural village, inspiring them with his wisdom and outlook.

The third theme of generational conflict apparent in these silent era films reverses the second: an elder figure is saved or redeemed in some fashion by a younger person. In *The Crab* (1917), a bitter old man adopts a spunky young girl who warms his heart despite his gruff exterior. When the man is accused of abusing the girl and is taken to court, the girl takes the stand in his defense, and her loving descriptions of the elder man's kindness not only redeem him in the eyes of the court and the public, but also help the aging man embrace his good side and be a "crab" no more. Similarly, in *God's Crucible* (1917), a bitter older man has his faith in humanity restored by an unlikely friendship with a small boy, leading to a reconciliation between the man and his estranged adult son. Along the same lines, in *Winning Grandma* (1918), a young girl softens the heart of her money-obsessed grandmother, indirectly leading to a family reconciliation. Curiously, such warm bonds and changes of heart seem to occur only when there is more than a generation between the parties involved. In these films, it is not adult children "saving" their parents by reminding them of humanity's goodness; it is young children who act as intermediaries between the geriatric and the middle-aged.

While stories of loveable children restoring a youthful outlook to cynical elders through simple innocence and goodness are interesting to consider, the two most prominent themes from this period were elders being a hindrance to young people's happiness and elders using their better sense and greater life wisdom to help younger people. These three recurring patterns speak to the complicated relationship between American culture in the early twentieth century and the aged. From 1900 to 1940, the number of Americans reaching the age of sixty-five or beyond tripled, from just over three million to nine million.[3] This increase in older citizens led to a large number of elders needing medical or physical care, along with financial provision; but at the time, very little institutional support was in place and there were few historical models to follow. The question of how to deal with this newfound social "problem" was one much debated in the public and legislative spheres. It was also, on occasion, a source for consideration in the cinema.

Two interesting exceptions that break away from the loose thematic categories so many of the other films fall into are D. W. Griffith's *What Shall We Do with Our Old?* (1911) and John Ince's *Old Lady 31* (1920). These films are important to single out because they address the economic difficulties faced by many aging people in America during this period, difficulties that social welfare advocates were seeking to have addressed on the federal and national levels. Griffith's film employs the director's signature melodramatic style. It begins with an intertitle proclaiming that the film was "founded upon an actual occurrence in New York City," thus underscoring the validity of the social problem depicted. The story concerns an aged carpenter with an ailing wife. The carpenter loses his job, along with all the other older workers at his place of employment, after a new foreman "weeds out the old hands." Unable to find other work because of his obvious age, the carpenter and his wife exhaust their savings and find themselves on the brink of starvation. The aging carpenter is arrested when, in desperation, he attempts to steal food to feed his wife. The judge takes pity on the venerable man in court, however, dropping the charges and then giving the man some money himself. Accompanied by sympathetic police officers and a grocer's basket full of food, the man returns home, only to find that it is too late and his wife has died. Unable to console him, the police officers leave the man grieving over the body of his wife. A final intertitle reads, "Nothing for the useful citizen, wounded in the battle of life."

Old Lady 31 approaches similar economic problems from a comedic perspective. After losing their life savings on bad stock investments, Abe and Angie Rose (Henry Harmon and Emma Dunn) use their last $100 to secure Angie a place in a women's rest home. Knowing they will likely never see each other again, the couple says their goodbyes at the gate to the home. The other women residents take pity on them and agree to help Abe stay on at the rest home with his wife, disguised as "Old Lady 31." Surrounded by the women residents, however, Abe eventually feels smothered by their attentions, and escapes from the home. Later overcome by guilt, he vows to return to his wife. Before doing so, he finds out that the stock they invested in did not become worthless after all, and instead of returning to while away the rest of his days with his wife in the rest home, he rescues her and they buy back their house to retire as they have always lived.

Both films are unique for the period as instances in which the social and economic realities facing American elders are not only acknowledged but also considered. The comedic mode of *Old Lady 31* allows for a wish-fulfillment fantasy answer to the problem, while *What Shall We Do with Our Old?* acts as a dire warning to the viewing public about the dangers of ignoring the issue. The economic circumstances facing elders in the twentieth century were brought up again in films like *Make Way for Tomorrow* (1937) and *No Place to Go* (1939), which tackle the matter within the new context of the Great Depression and the passage of the Social Security Act.

THE NEEDIEST AMONG US

The period surrounding the passage and implementation of Social Security in the 1930s marks a turning point in America: its elders became formally demarcated as a separate class of citizen, requiring large-scale governmental assistance financed by its younger generations. Of the many demographic groups affected profoundly by the Depression, older Americans were among those hardest hit. Along with impoverished children, the plight of elders left destitute was one of the areas of concern most frequently depicted in the media. Examples of this can be seen not only in photographs and newsreels, but in written descriptions as well. Throughout the 1930s, a common sight in major newspapers was a section devoted to "the neediest among us." These sections contained short descriptions of individuals or families (usually identified by first names or initials only), the hardships they had endured, the exact amount of money that could help them get back on their feet, and the specific charity where such funds could be directed. Widows and elders were common subjects.

One profile, published in the *New York Times* on January 1, 1933, describes Mrs. P, aka "Case 395." Mrs. P, according to the article, had spent the last seventeen years toiling at cooking and cleaning positions in order to support her invalid husband. The year prior, things had begun to look up, since Mrs. P's husband had improved to the point that doctors suggested he might be capable of walking again. "And then," the article reads: "At the age of 53, she broke down; high blood pressure forced her to give up her toil. Her husband, now 60, is still too crippled to earn a living and probably never will work again. Their savings are now gone and they were hungry until outsiders learned of their distress. Rather than let the neighbors learn that they had no food, Mrs. P would boil an onion for hours to deceive them with its savory odor. But the time came when she had to confess her destitution and ask for help."[4] The case immediately following that of Mrs. P is entitled "Last Days of an Old Mother," detailing the story of a seventy-two-year-old doorman who dropped dead of a heart attack, leaving his ninety-four-year-old invalid mother and her sixty-year-old caretaker daughter without any insurance, pension, or means of support.

Such stories undoubtedly appealed to the sympathy of the American public and helped inspire large-scale support for the establishment of some type of federal pension plan. As part of his New Deal, President Franklin Roosevelt signed the Social Security Act into law in 1935.[5] Despite heated public and political debate over the specifics of the program (many of the same arguments have continued nearly unchanged into our current day), Social Security was expanded and went into widespread effect in 1939.[6]

Notwithstanding the Great Depression, the 1930s are often viewed as a golden age of Hollywood cinema, associated with some of the most revered films and stars of the studio era. Though Hollywood was not immune to the effects of the Great Depression and struggled in the early years of the economic crisis, the years between 1934 and 1945 represented the peak period of movie ticket sales in American history. During this era of regular moviegoing, Hollywood cinema was a crucial element, along with radio and periodicals, of many Americans' media consumption. Moreover, as Tino Balio writes, "As a central social institution, Hollywood ranked as the third-largest source of news in the country, surpassed only by Washington and New York . . . This fascination with the movies revealed itself not only in the public's preoccupation with the lifestyles of the stars, but also in the presumed power of the movies as a socializing force."[7] It is this power as a "socializing force" that makes American cinema of the period a particularly interesting subject when we consider the change in social position that elder figures underwent during the political battles for, and implementation of, Social Security. Films not only help shape the fashions and trends of their time, but also reinforce or even present models of "acceptable" behavior and dominant values, so Hollywood is certainly an important place to look when considering how Americans of the time were being instructed, however intentionally or overtly, to conceptualize their elders.

In films of the 1930s, older actors' roles can generally be grouped into three recurring types: saintly mothers, out-of-touch millionaires, and admirable pillars of the community. Such types are informative for understanding the patterns established for elder roles in the golden age of Hollywood, as well as for sowing the early seeds of what would become elder kitsch or, perhaps, the representations from which it was a notable diversion. The first of these categories, which Karen Stoddard explores in some depth in *Saints and Shrews: Women and Aging in American Popular Film* (1983), portrays older women, in this case, almost exclusively mothers, as "saints." A well-known representation of this type is Ma Powers, the virtuous, unconditionally loving mother of gangster Tom (James Cagney), played by Beryl Mercer in *The*

Public Enemy (1931). Such characters, Stoddard argues, are symbols of the goodness and old-fashioned values from which youth such as Tom strayed. These "saints" are also notably powerless, though theoretically admirable for their righteousness. Stoddard writes, "A close analysis of the character of Ma Powers may well suggest that the power of the pedestal diminished for women whose backgrounds moved them far away from the middle-class, WASPish ideal; Ma, an aging immigrant, could only stand by and watch the disintegration of her family within a culture of which she could never truly be a part."[8] While Stoddard attributes this movement away from the middle class to Ma's immigrant status, it can just as easily be attributed in part to widowed Ma's generational shift from "the middle" to a more vulnerable and dependent elder class. Ma is economically dependent on her sons but also socially removed from the rapidly changing world (one of crime, corruption, and changing morals) to which they endeavor to adapt.

The representation of the saintly parent was not limited to widowed mothers. In *Make Way for Tomorrow*, we see the parents of adult children, the husband and wife Barkley (Victor Moore) and Lucy (Beulah Bondi), presented as figures of moral superiority and sympathetic spirit, as well as victims of their children's behavior and of the changing times. While not criminals of the James Cagney standard, the children of the saintly parents in *Make Way for Tomorrow* are characterized in nearly as negative a fashion, shown to be selfish and lacking in empathy, materialistic and short-sighted.

Based on a popular contemporary novel and stage play, both titled *The Years Are So Long*, *Make Way for Tomorrow* speaks quite clearly to the public discourse and concerns that would lead to the passage and implementation of Social Security during the 1930s. Barkley and Lucy are left in financial turmoil when Barkley is forced out of a job due to his age. Their home goes into foreclosure, and the two are split up, each sent to stay with one of their children's families in different parts of the country. Much of the film dramatizes the couple's attempts to carry on their affectionate relationship through letters and telephone calls while their children complain about the burden of caring for their parents. By the end of the film, Barkley is to be shipped to California to stay with yet another of his children, and Lucy is confined to a women's nursing home on the East Coast. It is made clear that after one comedic and sentimental afternoon spent revisiting the locations of their honeymoon in New York, the couple do not expect to ever see each other again. At the end of the film, their children too come to this realization and chastise themselves for their selfish behavior, though they seem unwilling or unable to change this outcome now that their decisions have been set in motion, closing the film on a tragic note.

The adaptations of the Edna Ferber short story "Old Man Minick," pro-

Max (Maurice Moscovitch) jokes about the younger generation and reminisces about old times with the convalescing Barkley (Victor Moore) in Make Way for Tomorrow *(1937).*

duced twice by Warner Bros. in the 1930s, as *The Expert* (1932) and *No Place to Go* (1939), tell a similar story of a saintly parent treated poorly by his unlikable son and daughter-in-law when he comes to live with them. In both films, the elder man (played by Charles Chic Sale and Fred Stone, respectively) quickly finds that he is not wanted or appreciated in the home of his son and social-climbing daughter-in-law, making friends instead with an impoverished young orphan boy and some friendly aged men who inhabit a nearby rest home. Tensions escalate between the older man and his son and daughter-in-law to the point that he uses his savings to buy a place at the rest home for himself and the orphan boy, whom he adopts. Unlike the institution awaiting Lucy in *Make Way for Tomorrow*, the rest homes in these pictures are presented as positive places, promising generational camaraderie; but, it should be noted, unlike Lucy and Barkley, the older man in these films has the financial independence to buy his own happy ending.

A similar divide of generations and values characterizes the second category of elder representation common in 1930s films: out-of-touch millionaires. Just as Beryl Mercer might be seen as the quintessential saintly mother actress of the period, Alice Brady might be the ideal representative of Hollywood's mindless moneyed matron. This seems evident in films such as *My*

Man Godfrey (1936), in which she plays the empty-headed and judgmental matriarch of the wealthy Bullock family, or *Mama Steps Out* (1937), in which Brady plays a similar, though more likable, bored and frivolous matriarch. While the age of Brady's characters may signify their "out-of-touch-ness" and removal from modern concerns and morals, much as do the age and Old World ways of a saintly mother like Ma Powers, this out-of-touch-ness is not exclusively tied to their age. The cruelty in such comedic roles centers around class issues rather than age—only upper-class elders are open to humiliation and scorn, and their upper-class children, such as Mrs. Bullock's snobby daughter, played Gail Patrick, are equally buffoonish. Lower-class elder figures, such as Godfrey's older tramp friends, are presented instead as humble and "good."

This association of goodness with powerlessness (economic and otherwise) continues in the third category of popular elder representation: admirable pillars of the community, holding families of all kinds together. Examples of this type of representation can be seen in *Make Way for Tomorrow*, in the characterization of an older German immigrant couple that Barkley befriends. Owners of a general store in the small town where Barkley has been sent to live, they are shown to be equal and enthusiastic partners in the enterprise. The store serves as a hub within the community, in no small part because of the efforts and friendliness of the German couple. It is this couple that draws Barkley out of isolation, giving him a reason to leave his child's home, to talk to people outside his family, and to take part in life, despite being separated from the companionship of his wife and the purposefulness of employment. They also take care of Barkley when he falls ill, seeming to do a better job than both the young town doctor and Barkley's family. Yet a contrast is drawn between the German couple and Barkley and Lucy, who, though they have a similarly intimate and affectionate marriage bond, are experiencing their own community (their family) being torn apart by the actions of their children. The German couple have autonomy and purpose in their larger community—and consequently, *feel* younger—whereas Barkley and Lucy lack purpose and are wholly vulnerable to the whims of younger people.

Such depictions, however, are not limited to dramas or melodramas but can, like the out-of-touch millionaires, be seen frequently in comedies as well. This type of representation takes on its full form in the films of Frank Capra. While Capra's films of the era have their fair share of "saintly mothers," they also very deliberately specialize in representing elders as "pillars of the community." In the remainder of this chapter, we use Capra's work to examine this particular representation and its changing public and critical response from the 1930s to the mid-1940s, revealing a prevalent conception of elders throughout the period.

SOLID PILLARS IN UNSTABLE TIMES

Capra's films, from *The Younger Generation* (1929) onward, contain a number of elder characters. Although many can be categorized by some of the representations outlined above, at times they also seem to work against these types. For the classic "saintly parents" role, we can look to *The Miracle Woman* (1931), which features Beryl Mercer playing troubled Barbara Stanwyck's pious and admirable saintly mother. We can also look to *The Younger Generation*, a transitional part-talkie that deals pointedly with the divide between an upwardly mobile first-generation Jewish American, Morris Goldfish (Ricardo Cortez), and his immigrant parents. Morris is an ambitious businessman who is ashamed of the Old World ways of his parents. He Americanizes his name to sound less Jewish, disowns his sister out of fear that her recently jailed husband will bring the wrong kind of attention to the family, and disregards his parents' wishes and advice, viewing his own very "American" and modern way of thinking as better than theirs. At the climax of the film, Morris becomes embarrassed by his parents' old-fashioned dress and behavior while out with his love interest and her parents. He berates his parents in Yiddish, unaware that his love interest's father understands the language. His potential father-in-law scolds Morris for speaking to his parents so rudely and forbids his daughter from marrying someone with so little respect for his elders.[9]

While out-of-touch millionaires turn up as well—in the highbrow banker character Anthony Kirby (Edward Arnold) in *You Can't Take It with You* (1938), and in the wealthy men whom Longfellow Deeds (Gary Cooper) consorts with in New York after receiving his unexpected inheritance in *Mr. Deeds Goes to Town* (1936)—it is the pillar-of-the-community elders who are central to the Capraesque portraits of America and its communities. Though the stories in his films almost always center on youthful stars like Gary Cooper, Barbara Stanwyck, Jean Arthur, James Stewart, or Cary Grant, contemporaneous reviews consistently commended the work of each film's entire cast, often noting that no one actor could be singled out from such a successful group effort. It is these ensemble casts, so central to Capra films, that feature older actors in a remarkable array of parts. Among those who appeared frequently in Capra pictures, covering a variety of roles, are Lionel Barrymore, Edward Arnold, Spring Byington, Beulah Bondi, H. B. Warner, and Samuel S. Hinds. Capra's rotating cast of elder characters help furnish the diegetic worlds of his pictures with the sense that his characters exist within a "real" world, populated by a recognizable community, not simply a world constructed of photogenic youth. In these films, characters hold jobs for years, live in the same houses all their lives, and share a history with the people around them. Elder figures are not merely limited to "color" or flat, "kindly grandmother" roles, but instead have their own pursuits and plots—in some cases, as in *You Can't Take It with You* and *Arsenic and Old Lace* (1944), they become more central to the story than the supposed hero or heroine.

These characterizations of older people in Capra pictures allow them to become more than simply "elder figures." Within a single picture such as *Mr. Deeds Goes to Town*, there are a variety of representations of older age—the dotty and naïve but sweet Faulkner sisters (Margaret McWade and Margaret Seddon); the clever housekeeper (Emma Dunn) who works for Longfellow Deeds but communicates on an equal level with him and teases him; the pompous Freud-like Austrian psychiatrist (Gustav von Seyffertitz) called in to testify regarding Deeds's sanity, who is later called out as a childish doodler; and the judge (H. B. Warner), who insists upon proper courtroom protocol but later is revealed to be sympathetic to the eccentric Deeds, declaring him "the sanest man who ever walked in this courtroom." And this is not to mention the thousands of older men who show up at Deeds's home to apply for the farm plots he has decided to give away. Though they are referred to in the film only as farmers, it seems a notable choice of casting that not one of them appears to be a day under fifty. These aging men are the sympathetic heart of the film, exhibiting humility, pride, and quiet desperation in the face of the Great Depression. They bring out Deeds's altruistic side, inspiring him to give away his millions, and they show up to protest in Deeds's behalf at the courthouse when the rest of the public has turned against him. In the second-to-last scene of the film, Deeds is literally carried away by a sea of cheering gray-haired men.

The senescent vitality displayed in the scene above is not unique. Capra's elder characters, unlike those portrayed in many 1930s media images, such as Mrs. P and her invalid husband in "Case 395," are often lively, spirited, and active. Stuffy Anthony Kirby in *You Can't Take It with You* complains throughout much of the film of his stomach ailments and mentions that he used to wrestle in his youth, but brushes off the suggestion to demonstrate some of his old moves. Later, after being seduced by the carefree philosophy of Grandpa Vanderhof (Lionel Barrymore), Kirby dances, plays the harmonica, and picks up a younger brute, spins him around, and slams him to the ground. This idealized portrait of geriatric verve extends even to the

In You Can't Take It With You *(1938), Grandpa Vanderhof (Lionel Barrymore) and Anthony Kirby (Edward Arnold) create juvenile delight with their harmonica duet.*

realm of nonfictional infirmity. Lionel Barrymore was troubled enough by arthritis during the making of the film that he was filmed walking on crutches throughout the picture. Within the film, this is explained away not as the result of a physical disorder associated with aging, but as the result of Grandpa Vanderhof having slid down the banister with his granddaughter and broken his leg—fun-loving, youthful indulgence.

The vitality of elders in these films is representative of the vitality of the community, a central part of Capra's diegetic social value system. What is more remarkable than these idealized portraits of happy, healthy elders is that they are not excluded from the community or cordoned off as separate within it. Rather, like the youthful eccentrics and dreamers around them, the elders are no different from anyone else. This ties into the films' historical moment by not only offering a bit of attractive fantasy in place of the sad reality of many elders during the Great Depression, but also by offering an appealing, idealized representation of an extended family at a time when economic devastation was making desertion commonplace and forcing many people into shared living situations with relatives or neighbors.

Capra's films represent not only extended families of relations, as in *You Can't Take It with You* or *Arsenic and Old Lace*, but also de facto extended families among groups of characters in shared workplaces, neighborhoods, and residences. Communities become *like* family, with all the attendant responsibilities of the individual to the group. This was a crucial ideal in the context of the 1930s, appealing in the way that it countered mass disillusion and strife with the message that Americans could make things better at least locally, even if not nationally, by helping one another and treating strangers as if they were family. Consider again the "neediest among us" features mentioned earlier: in such presentations, overwhelming problems become reduced to the stories of individual people, arousing sympathy, often through family descriptors like "widowed mother" or "fatherless child." Much the same is witnessed in *Mr. Deeds Goes to Town* when Deeds is drawn in by the face of one destitute farmer and is inspired to give away his millions to help others who are hurting.

The importance of the individual's membership in and responsibility to his community is seen again and again in Capra's films, as in *Mr. Smith Goes to Washington* (1939), when Jefferson Smith (James Stewart) filibusters himself to the point of collapse in order to save land intended for a scout camp, or in *Meet John Doe* (1941), when the public demonstration of desperation by John Doe (Gary Cooper) inspires millions of ordinary citizens around the country to form John Doe Clubs, which, without any government intervention or support, help the needy in their communities. One of the most blatant expressions of this sentiment comes when Doe gives a rousing radio address, inspired, it should be stressed, by Ann Mitchell's (Barbara Stanwyck) tales of her "old man." On national radio, he declares:

> We've all got to get in there and pitch. We can't win the old ballgame unless we have teamwork. And that's where every John Doe comes in. It's up to him to get together with his teammates. And your teammate, my friend, is the guy next door to you. Your neighbor—he's a terribly important guy, that guy next door. You're gonna need him and he's gonna need you, so look him up. If he's sick, call on him. If he's hungry, feed him. If he's out of a job, find him one . . . Yes sir, my friends, the meek can only inherit the earth when the John Does start lovin' their neighbors. You better start right now. Don't wait till the game is called on account of darkness. Wake up, John Doe. You're the hope of the world.

Such inspirational, second-person address is echoed in advertising for Capra's films, which extends the communal sensibility beyond the screen and into the audience. Ads for *Mr. Smith Goes to Washington*, which feature portraits of twelve cast members (not just the romantic leads, and including several gray-haired characters) arranged like a halo around a framed portrait of Frank Capra, declare that Capra has created "his most stirring human spectacle" out of "the hearts of its people, the very soil of America."[10] One series of ads for *You Can't Take It with You* features a similar portrait arrangement, promising: "You'll love them all."[11] Another reproduces an image from the last scene of the film, in which the whole extended Vanderhof-Sycamore-Carmichael clan, having adopted the Kirby family as well, is gathered around the dinner table, heads bowed in prayer. The text below this image reads: "If our picture makes the world just a little better place to live in, that's all we ask. As for the rest . . . we leave it up to YOU."[12]

In all his films from this period, Capra presents communities made up, by choice and circumstance, of very different individuals, emphasizing the importance of the community to the individual, and vice versa. A crucial textual element, though, is that all the heroic young leads of Capra's films of this period credit the examples of community elders for their dedication to community and their belief in inclusion and responsibility to others. Jefferson Smith is inspired by the work of his deceased father, and Longfellow Deeds credits his deceased parents for having looked after their local community long before he took up the responsibility and expanded it to the whole nation. John Doe is inspired initially by the sentiments of his girlfriend's father and then is further touched and spurred to action by the example of the John Doe Club members, many of whom are elder figures.

Fittingly, the most prolific community builder of all is Grandpa Vanderhof in *You Can't Take It with You*. Vanderhof, voluntarily retired for thirty years, has created within his New York brownstone an eclectic extended family. His family includes his daughter (a playwright), her husband (a fireworks manufacturer), their daughter (a ballerina), her husband (a southern candy maker and admirer of the Communist Party), the other granddaughter (a stenographer), an African American cook and her husband (who is on relief), an elderly toymaker, another aged man (whose occupation is unclear), and a Russian dance instructor. All live together, along with a litter of kittens and a pet crow, in apparent harmony. Outside the brownstone, everyone in the neighborhood (a multiethnic, multigenerational, multiclass mixture) addresses Vanderhof as "Grandpa" and looks to him as the community patriarch, asking for advice and reassurance. When taken to jail, Vanderhof befriends the drunks, encouraging them all to join him in a rendition of "Polly Wolly Doodle"; in the courtroom, the packed audience is made up of Vanderhof's friends, who spontaneously collect the bail money needed to return him to their community. The judge, another elder figure, remarks at one point to the bailiff, "I didn't know anybody had so many friends."

The emphasis on friendship, particularly across generational and class lines, is key to the vision of an ideal family-like community expressed within these films, with elder figures at the heart. Grandpa Vanderhof has developed his values and ethics through decades of experience, and with the intent of sparing others from making the same mistaken value judgments he made in his youth (working thirty years for a company and believing "that was all there was"), he works to spread what he has learned and to put his re-centered values into action as a socially active and politically conscious father figure in his community. Other elder figures follow suit—in *Meet John Doe*, Ann's mother is continually off to look after the children of sick members of her neighborhood, spending the little money that she is given from her daughter's income on their care; in *Mr. Smith Goes to Washington*, the jaded senior senator, played by Claude Rains, is shaken from his years of cynicism by the heartfelt actions of his contemporary's son, Jefferson Smith, and those of the preadolescent Boy Rangers.

Younger adults like Jefferson Smith, Longfellow Deeds, Ann Mitchell, and John Doe develop their ethics in large part from listening to their elders, respecting their wisdom and learning from their experience. The younger adults then carry on such ethics in their actions, spreading much-needed benefits within their community. It may not be possible for the elder figures to accomplish such actions on their own, it seems, but the younger adults credit the smaller-scale examples of their elders with being inspirational and foundational to their own actions. Their close relationships with elder figures are often a major feature that defines such characters, suggesting that their values come from a particular familial source. Additionally, children pass in and out of scenes, interacting with members of all generations, such as the Boy Rangers, who rally their state and then the country to support Jefferson Smith, or the immigrant children in *You Can't Take It with You*, who teach Tony Kirby (James Stewart) and Alice Sycamore (Jean Arthur) to do a dance called the Big Apple, which is in turn performed by Anthony Kirby and Grandpa Vanderhof—the inclusion of children completes a complex system of influence and exchange among those from different generations and social classes within the community. Care for the community must be taken on by all kinds of community members in order to be successful, and this value of shared responsibility and concern is kept alive through both action and instruction. In short, everyone has a part to play and must play it because of their responsibility to everyone else.

But the portraits of family and community are more than merely idealized. In true Capraesque fashion, the films actively feed into nostalgia, and did so even at the time. Characters refer to the works and deeds of prominent eighteenth- and nineteenth-century elder statesmen—Benjamin Franklin, Thomas Paine, Abraham Lincoln—and when, as commonly happens, characters join in song, their choices are straight out of traditional American songbooks. Everyone in New York seemingly sings along to "Polly Wolly Doodle" at some point, and in *Mr. Deeds Goes to Town*, Babe Bennett (Jean Arthur) and Longfellow Deeds break the ice over a "Swanee River" duet, ending, it should be noted, with a final line longing for "the old folks at home." The nostalgic factor is important in the context of elders, the family, and the community. As far back as 1922, Abraham Epstein singled out the ills of modernity as partly responsible for the numbers of elderly who found themselves without a familial safety net: "Conditions of impotence in old age are augmented still further by the break up of the family unit in modern society. With increasing rapidity, home-ties and family solidarity are being weakened and broken by the mobility so essential to modern industrial development. . . . And as a result, one finds that the only source which secured sustenance and bare comfort to old age, in an earlier society, has disappeared for a great many. We, therefore, send these unfortunate, in our laissez-faire fashion, to the unfriendly poorhouses to secure the care and comforts available."[13]

By offering the exact opposite, Capra's pictures play to this distrust of mobility and the threat of individuals left rootless and without family. Characters sing the virtues of small towns and small-town life, expressing distaste for city life. Longfellow Deeds spits on Times Square, Babe Bennett speaks of her desire to go back to the small town where her mother and family still live, and Grandpa Vanderhof, though he lives in New York City, has managed to create his own small-town-like community on his block and has three generations of family rooted in his brownstone. All these sentiments, combined with the representations of ideal families and communities, sell the idea of a "better" time when family members stuck together rather than deserted one another and when, if one was hurting, the community could be counted upon for support. They hark back to the days of the Elks and the community chest but neglect to address the reasons why such institutions had to be replaced. They present a lovingly detailed and warmly attractive Norman Rockwell–like image of community revitalized and reanointed with authority. Included in this image are portraits of elder figures, who are likewise given back their vitality, authority, and respect within their communities. In the 1930s, when 25 percent of the working population was unemployed and many more were forced to depend on charity and government relief, older Americans were not the only audience members who might have found this fantasy appealing.[14] The restoration of respect for elders, even within the confines of a handful of comedic films, is symbolic of the restoration of respect for the nation at large.

ELDERS IN THE NUCLEAR ERA

If so much of the success of Capra's films in their time was dependent on, as Robert Sklar puts it, Capra's status as "a unique creator of entertainments that gave Americans a pleasing and convincing image of themselves," then one must wonder what changed in the 1940s to make the images that Capra continued to present no longer quite so pleasing or convincing.[15] One major factor to take into account, of course, is the US entry into World War II. As millions of able-bodied men left to fight, domestic environments were radically affected. For example, while opinion polls throughout the 1930s showed that 80 percent to 90 percent of the public disapproved of married women holding jobs, only 13 percent objected in 1942.[16] The reason behind this change was simple—during the Depression, a married woman holding a job was perceived as just another contributing factor to the unemployment (and disgrace) of able-bodied men. During wartime, however, jobs were not scarce, but able-bodied men were. It was a woman's patriotic duty to perform a man's job if she could and keep the economy rolling.

A similar public change of heart seems to have taken place regarding America's elder citizens. As Andrew Achenbaum documents, one of the arguments that helped influence Congress to pass the original Social Security Act was that it would encourage more elders to retire, thus opening up jobs for some of the masses of unemployed younger adult men.[17] Yet the many limitations on eligibility for Social Security before its 1939 expansion helped discourage a large wave of voluntary retirements from occurring. Once the expansions of 1939 began to go into effect in the early 1940s, such retirements might have become more likely, but the switch to the encroaching wartime economy again delayed such an occurrence. Achenbaum writes: "Data collected by the Social Security Board indicate . . . that the gradual but long-term decline in labor force participation rates among men over sixty-five was interrupted by the needs of the wartime economy. Officials noted that skilled workers postponed retirement and deferred benefits under Title II's insurance provisions. Some previously retired workers rejoined the work force."[18]

Achenbaum notes that despite the intentions of some Social Security supporters who wanted it to be used by employers to impose mandatory retirement at age sixty-five, such actions were delayed by wartime needs: "The overwhelming (even if short-term) need for skilled and unskilled employees during the war made the aged a far more valuable resource than they had seemed in the midst of the Great Depression. Since the law did not require them to stop working, older workers behaved like younger members of society. Those who had skills and talents to offer contributed to the patriotic cause as they saw fit."[19]

Older Americans who stayed home but who were part of formal or informal extended families presumably found themselves with a renewed sense of responsibility and social contribution, for children were commonly left in the care of other family members or neighbors as women took up their patriotic duty to join the workforce. Elaine Tyler May notes, "Public funds were not allocated for day care centers until 1943, and even then, the centers provided care for only 10% of the children who needed it."[20] Without assistance from governmental entities, elder relatives and neighbors often stepped in to fill this need.

Despite the continued value of older workers and extended family members during the early war years, domestic media encouraged a focus on the prosperous years that lay ahead, when such communal efforts would no longer be necessary. May's historical study, *Homeward Bound*, details a number of propagandistic efforts, some supported directly by governmental funding and others through the output of private institutions closely attuned to the government's sentiments, that promoted the securing of a happy future—not a return to prewar life—as the purpose of all domestic and military war efforts. Visions of this happy future, perhaps designed to transport American fantasies as far from the prewar Depression as possible, repeatedly emphasized that once Americans won the war, they would be free to marry, have many children, and move out to a brand-new home in a nonurban paradise. There was a peculiar mixture of the lure of the modern with the nostalgic, as was heard in one government-sponsored ad that aired frequently on radio during 1942, in which a young man proclaimed that the war effort was about "young people, like us": "About love and gettin' hitched and havin' a home and some kids, and breathin' fresh air out in the suburbs. About livin' and workin' decent, like free people."[21] Statistics show that Americans during the war were marrying younger and having children earlier and in greater numbers than they had in the previous four decades, despite the disruptions of men leaving for war and women leaving for the workplace. Though earnings by those who remained in the workforce during the war years were higher than any time in recent memory, discretionary spending remained fairly flat. When polled, many bank depositors indicated that they were saving their money to spend on "future needs" and the home. There was even a popular market for "dream home" scrapbooks in which consumers could record plans and ideas for their future homes.[22]

Governmental policies following the end of the war helped make these dreams attainable in some form to many Americans. Responding in part to the massive shortage of housing faced by returning veterans and their eagerly expanding young families, programs like the Veterans Administration and the Federal Housing Authority offered guaranteed low-interest mortgages to veterans, and provided incentives and backing to real estate investors and employers who developed land outward from congested city centers. More American families became homeowners in 1946 than in any time prior.[23] Such opportunities were not equally available to all Americans, however, or even to all veterans. GI Bill benefits were not extended to female war veterans, and though they nominally included male African American veterans, they were not guaranteed the same federal loan insurance as their white counterparts. Redlining policies largely kept even affluent African Americans confined to urban areas, where industries were rapidly closing up shop and heading for the government-subsidized expanses of the suburbs.

Also among those largely excluded from this migration of American families were elders. Following the return of the veterans, many employers began to impose again, in a number of ways, mandatory retirement policies. A new class of "retirees," with their own means of adequate, though not often generous, finances, resulted from myriad factors: the combination of Social Security expansions put into effect before the war, older workers' savings from the employment-rich war years, a new market for supplemental retirement plans, and changes to labor laws that allowed employers to offer pension benefits in lieu of wage increases. Additionally, Andrew Achenbaum notes that the original Social Security Act, Title I, prohibited residents of poorhouses from receiving benefits, but did not mention residents of "rest homes," thus indirectly financing a boom in the construction of private geriatric care facilities.[24]

Increasingly, the nuclear family was promoted as the "normal" or even ideal family structure. The architecture of the new suburban tract homes seemed designed with only young nuclear families in mind. The typical three-bedroom–one-bath Cape Cod or ranch did not encourage occupant flexibility in the same way that rambling farmhouses and Victorians, or even cubby-hole-rich bungalows, had. The ideal postwar American family was young, independently homesteaded, and luxuriously isolated on its "ranch" spread. Houses like those in Levittown, promoted for suburban life after the war, were often designed around spacious, private yards, demarcating the play territory of children and featuring picture windows from which housewives could keep an eye on them. Socializing outside the home seems to have been designed into the layout of such neighborhoods as something that should happen only with deliberate effort. This meant socializing with neighbors only by choice, of course—one of the selling features of suburban over urban living environments—but the same applied to relatives and elders.

The question of the defined familial space of grandparents and other elders was so clearly in a transitional state that the sociologist Belle Boon Beard put together a study in 1949 entitled "Are the Aged Ex-Family?" In this essay,

Beard muses, "If elderly couples and grandparents are not families or members of families, what are they? Obviously they were once considered members of families. When and how did they lose their family status? At what age or under what circumstances do people become ex-family?"[25] She seeks to answer this question through a survey of contemporary sociological studies of the American family, noting over the course of her survey that elders are seldom mentioned in such studies; when they are, they are almost uniformly mentioned as inconveniences or as burdens that growing numbers of families felt they should not be expected to bear. Most interesting is Beard's exploration of the changing definition of "family" and its exclusion of anyone beyond a two-generational level of parent and child. Though the term "nuclear family" had been in use for some time among anthropologists, it had not come into popular or even sociological field use at the time of Beard's paper.[26] She points out that terminology had changed—elders had previously been included in the more general term "family," though it no longer seemed to encompass them: "Some authors call this the 'natural' or 'biological' family. In order to include grandparents or other older relatives, one must use such a term as 'extended family' or 'great family.' No one has defined precisely the point at which a parent ceases to be a member of the family and becomes an 'extension' of the family. . . . 'The family' has apparently come to be synonymous with marriage and the rearing of children."[27]

That this change in the meaning of "family" and the status of elder relatives was noteworthy enough to be of interest to sociologists points toward the idea that along with the many other large-scale changes affecting so many Americans in the postwar years, there were also shifts in the cultural conceptions of family and community and the place of elders within these groups.

It was in this transitional period of redefinition and reimagining that Frank Capra released his two commercial feature films of the mid-1940s. Their content shows an interesting negotiation of values regarding family and community, and together they offer an explanation of, and some points for consideration regarding, the shifting values of Americans at this time, particularly around perceptions of elders.

Arsenic and Old Lace (1944) is in many ways an atypical Capra film in relation to the others already discussed. The film, produced for Warner Bros., was the first one that Capra made after his many years with Columbia and his last project before joining the Signal Corps, where he devoted his attention to the production of the film series "Why We Fight," a US propaganda and military recruitment tool. Capra had completed *Arsenic and Old Lace* in 1941, although the film was not released until 1944, because a contractual agreement with the producers of the stage play required the film to be held for release until the play had finished its run on Broadway. The film was released

Aunt Abby (Josephine Hull, center) and Aunt Martha (Jean Adair) watch eagerly as one of the lonely old men becomes a potential next victim in Arsenic and Old Lace *(1944).*

by a studio other than the one Capra was famously associated with, during a time when he had been off the scene for three years, and advertisements promoted it less as a Frank Capra picture than a vehicle for Cary Grant, though Capra's name remained above the title. It was also, despite the presence of the two actresses largely credited with the success of the play on Broadway and popular character actors Raymond Massey and Peter Lorre, *not* sold as an ensemble. The tone of the comedy, as well, is different from the humane social comedy of Capra's post-1935 work—this picture plays much more as broad farce. In some sense, the film is a return to the screwball comedy style of Capra's *It Happened One Night* (1934), although it does directly address the problem of what to do with unwanted and uncared-for aging members of society.

At the center of the picture is Mortimer Brewster (Cary Grant), a theater critic who moonlights as a writer of books on relationships and is famous for his many antimarriage, pro-bachelorhood publications. As the film opens, Mortimer has had a change of heart and, undercover in sunglasses and a hat, married the girl next door (literally), Elaine Harper (Priscilla Lane), daughter of the local minister. Eager to depart on his honeymoon and start his new life with Elaine, Mortimer returns home to share the news with his two elder aunts, Abby (Josephine Hull) and Martha (Jean Adair), who raised him and his two brothers and who apparently still oversee the household. Abby and Martha are, according to the neighborhood beat cops, pillars of their community through the self-initiated works of charity they perform. These include taking the children of ill or overworked mothers to the pictures and, most notably, inviting lonely older men into their home for a good meal and some conversation. Such elder figures at first seem to fit easily into Capra's established diegetic America. Like Anne Mitchell's mother or Longfellow Deeds's father, they perform beneficial roles in the community despite being otherwise overlooked, and like Grandpa Vanderhof, they are respected and beloved by their neighbors. All the same, Abby and Martha are revealed to be quite different when Mortimer discovers that when they invite susceptible older men in for dinner, they poison them and bury their bodies in the cellar.

Confused at Mortimer's horrified reaction, Abby and Martha patiently explain their rationale. The first "lonely gentleman" who came to visit died at the table of natural causes. The expression on his face struck them as so peaceful that they decided, "If we could help other lonely old men to find that peace, then we would." The film successfully pokes fun at the Capraesque messages of loving thy neighbor and looking out for the community, so familiar from his previous pictures, and this may have provided an additional level of humor for audiences, who showed their appreciation for *Arsenic and Old Lace* at the box office. Such speculation is difficult to confirm from reviews of the film, though, which praise it for its humor but don't explicitly parse out why it is funny. Much of the humor lies in how it unexpectedly reverses what appears to be a charitable community activity by transforming "sweet old ladies" into warped, murderous figures who view their poisoning of aged men as "a mercy"—and yet the film keeps everything "light" and safely in a farcical mode. That this was presented to the public as a Frank Capra picture may merely have added another amusing or ironic layer.

The film may have connected with the public also for its deconstruction of the image of the ideal, likable extended family at a moment, near the end of the war, when American interests seemed to be switching from the problematic, stuck-together extended families of the present to the idealized nuclear families of the future. In addition to the burden of figuring out what to do with his aunts, Mortimer must deal with his two brothers: Teddy (John Alexander), who has been living peacefully with Mortimer and his aunts despite his belief that he is former president Teddy Roosevelt, and Jonathan (Raymond Massey), a violent serial killer who returns to the family home while hiding from the law. Mortimer grapples with the increasingly difficult and bewildering situation, all the while pining to run off with his new spouse.

Yet Mortimer's responsibilities to his extended family members prevent him from leaving on his own pursuits until he makes sure that his aunts and his two troubled brothers are properly looked after. The solutions that Mortimer finds seem utterly suited to the nuclear era. Jonathan is handled most easily: he is arrested and, presumably, sent off to spend the rest of his days incarcerated, perhaps awaiting execution. After much wheeling and dealing with the relevant officials, Mortimer manages to have Teddy committed to Happy Dale, a sanitarium. Notably, when the cab driver refers to Happy Dale as a "nuthouse," the director of the sanitarium corrects him: "We prefer to call it a 'rest home.'" This semantic exchange acts as a giveaway for the solution to the problem of Mortimer's aunts and their care. Fearing that Teddy will be lonely without his family, Abby and Martha request that they too be sent away to the Happy Dale "rest home." Within a single twenty-four-hour period, Mortimer's entire problematic extended family has been successfully sent away and out of sight. Finally, as an unintentional parting gift of sorts, Mortimer's aunts inform him that he is not actually related to any of them—he is adopted, and his entire birth family is dead. With this statement (and his jubilant reaction to it), Mortimer is absolved of all responsibility for this extended family and freed to go off and pursue his own nuclear family if he desires. The last scene of the film shows Mortimer joyfully carrying his bride over the threshold of her home, symbolically beginning their new nuclear life. What is to become of the bodies in the basement is never mentioned. Those "lonely old men" are not related to Mortimer and therefore, it seems, not his problem.

While the reversal of the Capraesque presentation of "family" in *Arsenic and Old Lace* is unexpected, its portrayal of generational relationships and elder figures is also surprising. Rather than learning from his elders or even communicating with them as adults, Mortimer is clearly more knowledgeable about the workings of the world, and his aunts are characterized as naïve. A similar relationship involves the older beat cop, who is training a younger officer to take his place. While the younger man is played as being a bit foolish for misinterpreting countless signals of what is really going on in the Brewster home, the older is even more buffoonish, having missed the killings for years. Whereas elder figures in previous Capra films might have passed their wisdom on to younger generational figures, here they stand to pass on only dangerous naïveté.

The portrayal of the aging aunts in *Arsenic and Old Lace*, however, is the most curious one in the film. On the one hand, they intentionally commit murder twelve times. On the other hand, as they explain it, they had a perfectly logical rationale for doing so and performed a service to the community rather than a grievous act. The fact that they face no consequences for having bodies buried in their basement seems, to some extent, to validate their belief that they have not actually hurt anyone. Like so many Capra characters, they are eccentrics. But when eccentrics like Grandpa Vanderhof or Longfellow Deeds are shown doing good for the community, they do no harm. Whether Abby and Martha can be classed as "lovable eccentrics" in the same fashion or should be considered something akin to dementia personified—walking social problems—is an unsettling question raised by the film.

There is something similarly unsettling in the portrayal of elders in Capra's first film to be made after the war, *It's a Wonderful Life* (1946). Within a story about a young family man appears the bitter, greedy Mr. Potter (Lionel Barrymore); the bumbling, forgetful alcoholic Uncle Billy (Thomas Mitchell); Mr. Gower (H. B. Warner), a pharmacist who is so incapable of controlling his emotions following the news of his son's death that he nearly poisons a sick child; and the literal angel Clarence (Henry Travers), who is so bad at his job that after eighty-nine years he still has not received his wings. There is also, in great contrast to elder characters in earlier Capra films, a startling acknowledgment of the frailties of senescence. Peter Bailey (Samuel S. Hinds), the father of the protagonist, works himself to illness and dies of a heart attack. Destitute, insane Mr. Gower is mocked by the local townspeople, literally kicked to the ground. Lionel Barrymore, whose real-life infirmity was given a playful gloss in *You Can't Take It with You*, is pushed in a wheelchair throughout *It's a Wonderful Life*, his affliction openly attributed in part to his age. These are not, by and large, fantastical portrayals of older people.

Generational interactions are also presented with more shading. It is twelve-year-old George Bailey (Bobbie Anderson) who points out to Gower that he has prepared lethal medicine for the sick child, only to receive a beating for his insolence before Gower realizes the boy is right and tearfully apologizes. Potter fails in his attempts to forge a fatherly relationship with Peter Bailey in order to secure power over his savings and loan, and fails again when he attempts the same with the adult George Bailey (James Stewart) many years later. George becomes openly frustrated with his small children and yells at them, even making his daughter cry; a neighbor remarks to George and his wife (Donna Reed) with disgust, "Youth is wasted on the young," expressing disappointment as well as a generational divide. At the height of his desperation, George lashes out at his elders, calling Mr. Potter a "warped, frustrated old man" and Uncle Billy "a silly old fool." Nonetheless, the younger George grew to have quite a close relationship with Gower, and his love and respect for his father is clear when he defends him from insults by Potter at a board meeting; further, in a quiet exchange over dinner, George as a young adult tells his father, "You're the best man I know."

Rather than any of the town's elder citizens, George becomes a pillar of the community through his generous management of the savings and loan, yet he is weighed down with responsibilities. The greatest instance of this occurs when Uncle Billy's forgetful oversight results in the loss of an $8,000 deposit, which George must account for. Unwilling to abandon his business and familial responsibilities, and foiled by the nefarious Potter, who discovers and steals the missing money, George decides that only his suicide and the life insurance policy that will be redeemed upon his death can save them. In this case, it is the community, not George's dependent family, that sacrifices to fulfill its responsibility to him. Folks in town are heard in voice-over calling on God to rescue George spiritually and seen on camera contributing their own money to rescue him financially.

The messages about family and community in *It's a Wonderful Life* are, upon scrutiny, somewhat mixed. The film paints a rather grim picture of an individual driven to desperation and suicidal rage by the pressures of community and familial responsibilities. Yet the ending of the film finds George even more tightly enclosed in community life, after he has been divinely manipulated to appreciate it rather than find it oppressive. Joyous over this development, the whole community joins in singing "Auld Land Syne," a traditional folk ballad with roots in an eighteenth-century poem. In contrast to Capra's hallmarks of nostalgia and communal empathy, this ending may have promoted a suspicious view of wartime promises for the future.

It's a Wonderful Life celebrated this nostalgia just as Americans were becoming more interested in the prospect of moving forward. After World War II, Capra made pictures that relied on the same ideas (albeit with less certainty) that had worked so successfully in the prewar culture, but America had changed. Like so many members of the previous generation, Capra was quietly cast aside from the main thoroughfares of cultural activity. It does not seem coincidental that several films produced in the early postwar years, which we discuss in the following chapter, such as *Sunset Blvd.* (1950), *All About Eve* (1950), and *Limelight* (1952), explicitly address the disappearance of elder figures from society and the problems associated with showing aging faces in entertainment. Capra's presentations of the active, community-integrated elder already appeared dated at this point. It was as if, having "solved" the problem of the indigent aging population and the Great Depression through governmental schemes and the collective efforts of World War II, Americans in general, and American popular culture in particular, were eager to move away from such concerns and focus on the dream of the nuclear family and its independent, modern home.

Although the focus may have shifted, anxieties about aging in America, the place of elders in society, and increasing generational divides, did not disappear with the implementation of Social Security. Rather, such anxieties persisted, manifesting in curious ways on screen.

CHAPTER TWO

The Sensational Specter of Aging

Wake up, Norma. You'll be killing yourself for an empty house. The audience left twenty years ago.

JOE GILLIS (WILLIAM HOLDEN) TO NORMA DESMOND (GLORIA SWANSON) IN *SUNSET BLVD.* (1950)

On May 2, 1947, a brief piece appeared in the *Los Angeles Times* with a headline that proclaimed, "Film Officer of P.T.A. Tells Opportunity: New Audience of 35,000,000 Seen for Adult Pictures."[1] While this statement is likely based on somewhat exaggerated claims, it is also not nearly so astonishing as it may appear at first glance. For one thing, the body of the article reveals that the head count of this "new audience" was based, apparently, on an estimate of the number of American citizens who chose not to be regular film attendees. This number of non-moviegoing Americans was indeed large and of great interest to the film industry, which was suffering a sharp decline in attendance. While some of these supposed thirty-five million new customers were never likely to attend films for a variety of reasons (poverty, infirmity, language barriers, racial barriers, and so on), a good number were viewed as potential customers. Whereas some potential filmgoers had simply never become regular attendees, others previously had been active filmgoers, a group that would come to be referred to during this period as the "lost audience."

The second part of this newspaper headline that may seem surprising is the contention that this potential audience of thirty-five million would be lining up for "adult pictures." If we understand the label "adult" in the sense that is now familiar—namely, as a euphemism for pornographic films—this 1947 headline may raise some eyebrows. But that is not the case. Rather, the term refers to pictures that appeal to mature and sophisticated audiences, not juvenile audiences. Such pictures may even be perceived as striving for something beyond mere entertainment, closer to art, as the content of this newspaper article goes on to show. The PTA officer, Mrs. Lee B. Hedges, working in conjunction with a study of media and popular culture conducted by Stanford University, had been appointed to survey potential new audience members and to find out why such people were not active cinema attendees. At the completion of her survey, Mrs. Hedges concluded that this large potential new audience stayed away because the pictures Hollywood was making did not appeal to them. The sheer number of potential audience members being overlooked, she reported, "would justify an effort on the part of producers to make better films as an art and become adult in subject matter."[2]

Mrs. Hedges's conclusions were no anomaly. They were, in fact, part of a distinct moment in postwar cinematic history in which the idea of the "adult" film occupied an important part of the public discourse. In this chapter, we look to this discourse as a manifestation of the growing generational divide that occurred during the postwar years. This discourse reveals a debate between critics, academics, educational groups, members of the public, and the film industry itself as they struggled to define "adults" as a separate audience from the general public, and one that desired entertainment that spoke to their own interests. Exacerbating the struggle within the industry throughout the postwar years was a conception of the American audience that divided it into separate groups along generational lines and perceived maturity. The discussion surrounding "adult" films and the "adult" audience thus revealed not only a moment of potential artistic promise but also increasing social division and flux, much of it centered on anxieties regarding aging.

In *Melodrama and Meaning: History, Culture, and the Films of Douglas Sirk*, Barbara Klinger draws attention to the widespread use of the term "adult" in the promotion of films during this period. She examines this use of "adult" specifically within the context of selling films of a singular genre, Sirkian melodrama: "As the case of *Written on the Wind* will demonstrate, Universal-International's exhibition practices made these connections by creating, on the one hand, a generic identity for melodramas as 'adult' films in order to capitalize on increasing trends toward sexually explicit representation in the media. On the other hand, exhibition presented melodramatic style as a veritable wonderland of consumer fantasies and goods to appeal to the post–World War II affluent mentality."[3]

While Klinger makes the connection between the use of "adult" as a euphemism for the boundary-pushing sexual content of postwar melodramas, this does not account for the way in which "adult" was employed in the discussion and promotion of films that did not have sexuality as a central or even secondary subject. (The association of "adult" with the sexual subject matter of women's pictures of the 1950s certainly resembles the more contemporary understanding of the term, an important point dealt with at the end of this chapter.) This use of "adult" as a signifier encompassing a broad variety of film types (dramas, comedies, and Westerns as well as romantic melodramas) is crucial to our overall argument.

In short, the discursive formation of adult films in the late 1940s and 1950s reveals a bold line of generational distinction within the content of films as well as within the broader culture, which could be seen in contemporaneous discussions of Hollywood product. Such a distinction was negotiated within these discussions, as well as through representations of aging figures struggling with changing generational roles. While the previous chapter examines early instances of the generational conflict that began to show up in Hollywood cinema during and after the implementation of Social Security, this chapter looks at how these generational conflicts played out during the early postwar period. By then, American society had worked through the trauma of the war and the financial division and physical separation of elders from families. These films, though, depict a culture where those "discarded" aging figures—the "ex-family" citizens that Belle Boon Beard wrote about in 1949—continue, problematically, to exist.

AN AUDIENCE LOST

To begin examining the discourse around adult films and perceived audience maturity, one must first look to the economic troubles facing Hollywood studios in the immediate postwar years. As Douglas Gomery has documented, "The fall in theatrical moviegoing in the United States began in the latter months of 1946 and continued steadily downward through the 1940s and into the 1950s."[4] This drop in attendance was of great financial concern to the studios, aggravated further by the Paramount Decree in 1948, the Supreme Court decision that forced the studios to sell their interests in movie theaters, thereby disrupting the vertical integration (in which studios controlled everything from production to exhibition) that ensured corporate profits. The lost audience was also, of course, devastating to theater owners, who suffered the greatest financial repercussions from declining ticket sales.

The lost audience, however, was not solely an industry concern. The term pops up regularly in popular-press articles throughout the period, and by 1951 the industry crisis was newsworthy enough that *Life* magazine ran a feature on the loss of attendance and revenue, and consequent theater closings.[5] In this and other sources, two ideas became constant: Hollywood was facing a

In Sunset Blvd. *(1950), Norma Desmond (Gloria Swanson) makes sexual advances toward the younger Joe Gillis (William Holden), which are presented as both darkly comedic and horrific.*

potentially catastrophic drop in movie attendance, and this was due, in varying ways, to the industry's miscalculations of what the audience desired.

While popular accounts have attributed this historical decline in attendance to the rise of television as an alternative entertainment, Gomery points out that "the decline in admissions at the theatrical box office was greater from the 1946 to 1950 period than from 1950 to 1960."[6] Since televisions did not start becoming widely owned products in American homes until the early 1950s, other factors must account for the decline. For Gomery, much of the loss can be attributed to changes in Americans' spending habits and priorities. Although overall American income and spending rose during the postwar period, much of this spending was put toward domestic purchases people had not been able to make before or during the war. These included buying and furnishing new houses, purchasing and operating automobiles, and expanding and outfitting families to levels never before seen in the American middle class. As waves of Americans migrated from cities to suburbs, they moved away from urban neighborhoods and downtown centers where movie theaters had previously been popular destinations for entertainment. As Lynn Spigel's study *Make Room for TV: Television and the Family Ideal in Postwar America* skillfully illustrates, entertainment in suburban America tended to be concentrated within the home. Advertising and women's lifestyle magazines heavily promoted the purchase of pianos, record players, game tables, and later, of course, televisions to keep entertainment and families centered in the home. All these factors contributed to the phenomenon of the lost audience.

With reference to contemporaneous writing, there was an additional (and, certainly, related) factor that also figured into the loss of audience: age. "The members of the lost audience," Geoffrey Wagner writes, "that influential portion of our population who are deserting the cinemas, have been analyzed as the more mature of us; their average age is thirty-five."[7] The polls and statistics in *Hollywood Looks at Its Audience*, a study by Leo Handel support this. Lack of attendance among the very oldest potential patrons could, Handel speculates, be assumed to result from such patrons being older than cinema itself and thus not having developed the moviegoing habit in their youth. Among those who made up the first generation to grow up with the cinema, however, Handel points to a drop-off in attendance coinciding with age: "According to an estimate by Dr. J. S. List, a consulting psychologist, a fifth of the nation's theatergoers cease to be regular patrons when they reach the age of forty. List contends further that 75 per cent of the patrons are lost to the industry when they reach sixty, and 98 per cent when they reach seventy. He sees the cause for this diminishing market in the lack of understanding of adult tastes on the part of the producers, and the failure of the exhibitors to cultivate this section of the public."[8]

This "lack of understanding of adult tastes" was deemed the primary culprit by many of those writing about adult audiences' abandonment of the cinema. Handel concludes: "In general, the findings seem to indicate a misconception on the part of some producers who feel that they have to 'play down' to the lowest intellectual level to make a motion picture a financial success."[9] In the mainstream press, a Pittsburgh newspaper columnist expressed similar sentiments in a less academic fashion: "The number of Hollywood movies I have seen is vast and my opinion of them is that about 95 per cent of them have a mental age of not over eight."[10] Similar expressions can be found throughout film reviews of the time, which complain about an immaturity that seemed to mark much of the Hollywood product.

In *The Great Audience* (1951), Gilbert Seldes makes this notion a centerpiece of his argument. He begins by pointing out, "No other manufacturer of a mass-consumption commodity—cigarettes, soaps, cereals, motorcars—has deliberately cut himself off from the larger part of his market. Why have the movies done so?"[11] He elaborates, noting that Hollywood films' plots, tropes, and morals are skewed to a youthful outlook on life that decreases in relevance for audience members as they attain more life experience: "As Americans pass through the stages of courtship and begin married life, as they go to work, break from the protection and discipline of their parents, and begin to establish families of their own . . . the image of the hero, the throb of passion, the myth of success, as conceived by the movies, are no longer needed; and as time goes on they become unacceptable."[12]

Seldes's argument, reinforced over the course of several chapters, is that not only were Hollywood producers losing potential income by presenting material irrelevant to this audience, but also, by doing so, they were actively damaging the audience that remained. Seldes laments a future "nation of teenagers" conditioned by the media to hold youthful values throughout their lives, to never mature in their worldviews because they had seen no accurate representations or valuations of that maturity. He assigns blame not just to the film industry but also to American popular culture en masse. Seldes warns against the threat of these developments:

> Nothing in the popular arts suggests to people of thirty or forty that they can safely read a book, discuss politics, bother about juvenile delinquency, go on a picket line, demonstrate against picket lines, serve on a jury in a civil suit, earn a living, or write a letter to the editor—all of these things and a thousand others are the stigmata of maturity and must be practiced in secret, if at all. The eternal juvenile takes no part in the life of the community and has no resources of his own; to the aging who wants to be as like him as they can, he offers other occupations.[13]

While Seldes's fears may appear alarmist when shifted from a mere criticism of Hollywood film to dire warnings about the future of the American public, they reveal genuine concerns and anxieties brought about by the rapid, sweeping social and cultural changes occurring in the immediate postwar period, particularly those changes involving the shifting of generational roles.

Though not carrying out their arguments on so grand a scale, several prominent film critics of the time expressed similar discontent with the perceived immaturity of Hollywood film. Two critics in particular, Bosley Crowther of the *New York Times* and the critic(s) writing as 'Mae Tinee" in the *Chicago Daily Tribune*, made continual references to Hollywood's failure to address adult audience members.[14] In a typical piece, Tinee praised the film *14 Hours* (1951) as rare "proof that our own motion picture industry can produce a product worthy of mature attention if the public will permit."[15] Crowther, meanwhile, had such an interest in the topic that he appeared before a panel of educators in New York to speak about how "television and motion pictures show the same tendency of catering too much to the juvenile mind," and to advocate for "the 'specialization' of motion pictures to appeal to various segments of the population, instead of the traditional emphasis on mass appeal."[16]

Seldes, a cultural critic who published frequently in periodicals like the *Atlantic* and dabbled in writing for Broadway and adapting Shakespearean plays for the screen, had a vested interest in the kinds of films being released to the American public, as well as in the kinds of media that same public was conditioned to seek out and support. Critics like Crowther and Tinee were similarly invested in films for which there was an intelligent and discerning audience, such as the kind of audience interested in reading their critiques. Crowther developed a reputation for perhaps being overly invested in these debates. Letters to the editor in the *New York Times* and even articles by Crowther's fellow critics made frequent reference to his curmudgeon status and constant harping on Hollywood's assumption that its audience was immature. It is worth noting that Seldes, Crowther, and Tinee had been publishing for several decades by this time and fell well within the bounds of the lost audience for which they advocated. But they were certainly not in sparse company.

THE FORMATION OF "ADULT FILMS"

It can be difficult, particularly in retrospect, to comprehend the specific attributes tied to the label "adult" as it was applied (and understood) by these critics. Some qualities linked with the term, however, can be found in reviews of films praised as "adult." A review of *Daisy Kenyon* (1947), for example, contains the following: "The dilemma of this woman is very disturbing and very real; it is also very commonplace, or would be if it had not been written, directed and performed with a sensitivity rare in Hollywood creation. . . . [The film has] a script of extraordinary depth and compassion. . . . Otto Preminger has directed it with comparable taste and intelligence. . . . [It is] thoughtful and adult."[17] A review of *All My Sons* (1948), an adaptation of the Arthur Miller play, reads: "'All My Sons,' at the Palace, is a finely-made, adult and engrossing film. Written with integrity and acted with skill, it is a picture for the discriminating. . . . The film makes virtually none of the customary attempts to relieve its tone; 'here,' says the film, 'is our story.'"[18] In these reviews, the quality "adult" seems to be linked with particular notions of realism, sensitivity, complexity, and good taste. Other reviews similarly praised adult films as "sophisticated," "subtle," and "intelligent."

Seldes gives a more elaborate explanation that seeks to explain the definition from which he and his fellow critics are working. Following an extended comparison between the relative maturity and immaturity of foreign versus domestic releases, Seldes explains:

> The single mark of maturity, stamped like a seal of approval on all the pictures I have mentioned, sunny or somber, is this: the story develops in humanly acceptable terms; even in farcical situations the actions are credible although we could never have predicted them; and the threads of the serious stories are woven logically into their complete pattern. Moreover, the characters are men and women, individuals not types; their motives are understandable, and the fictions in which they appear are stories not myths . . . They are not escaping from our human predicament, they are only relating the myth to our times.[19]

This interest in a particular kind of realism is coupled with a sense that a film's makers have assumed a certain level of intelligence in their audience, which does not need to have character motivations or plot points overly explained. And yet much of what Seldes describes as the mark of an adult film could presumably be applied to any high-quality picture. How do we differentiate the particular qualities that mark a picture as "good" because it is "adult"?

One way may be to look at how adult films were discussed according to what they were not. Crowther, writing in 1951, gives us some idea of what was *not* appealing to this adult audience, on behalf of whom he advocates: "There has been some discussion lately of Hollywood's general neglect of the so-called 'over 30' audience—the audience, that is, which one assumes is more interested in literate, adult subjects than crooners, cowboys, cover girls and crime. And in these contributive discussions, the point is frequently made that Hollywood should give more attention to the wooing and the winning of this group—this large group of people over 30 who have money, maturity, and minds."[20]

"Crooners, cowboys, cover girls and crime" would seem to encompass a great number of popular Hollywood films of the time, from Bing Crosby vehicles and Roy Rogers pictures to the gritty, violent dramas that would later be grouped under the category film noir and lauded for their complexities. In a review of *The Adventures of Hajji Baba* (1954), Tinee describes it as an "often ludicrous costume picture which has all the old tried and true ingredients: plenty of scantily clad girls, a buxom princess in disguise, a daring young Berber who woos her." She ends with the explanation, "It's the sort of motion picture that adults may find pretty rough going, but teen-agers inhale as happily as they do popcorn."[21] Once again, the lines drawn between a good film and bad film, between sophisticated and not, are generational. Curiously, though, the aspect of frank sexuality here, in the references to "scantily clad girls" and "buxom princesses," are markers of the nonadult, demonstrating that sexuality per se was not a marker of the adult film, as Klinger would argue, but that the treatment of sexuality could mark a film as utterly juvenile rather than adult. This unsubtle treatment of sexuality, with flesh on display for presumably (in the critic's opinion) no purpose beyond that of titillating spectacle, reads as both juvenile *and* old-fashioned. In this respect, calls for adult pictures were appeals not so much for the entertainment styles and sensibilities of the past (or of the generations that dominated the entertainment industry of the past) as for something more "modern." The adult picture was a modern take on cinema, but it required the sophistication acquired through age and experience to be appreciated.

An emphasis on novelty seemed to be a good part of what critics (and presumably audiences) were seeking. The novelty, however, did not come in the form of spectacle or technical innovations, at which Hollywood excelled. Rather, it came from seeing qualities different from those with which Hollywood had been heavily identified and which audiences had seen many times during years of regular attendance. Tinee points out in her *Hajji Baba* review that despite the film's young stars and lavish Cinemascope presentation, it was the kind of film that "might have been made 20 years ago."[22] In the review quoted above, Crowther discusses two films that he sees as part of Hollywood's attempts to capture the attentions of the adult audience by simply featuring stories about middle-aged characters, but failing in this endeavor by presenting the stories in a juvenile Hollywood-esque fashion. "Certainly," Crowther writes, "the over-30 audience is entitled to more respect for its experience and its intelligence."[23] Such a complaint harks back to historians' arguments that a large part of the social devaluation of elders in the twentieth century came about because of the country's rapid mechanization and industrialization, which made flexibility and adaptability more useful qualities than experience. Experience was a quality increasingly devalued by those in power, whether they were employers or the producers of cinematic products.

These debates about age and sophistication—and about whom "good" media products should aim to please and entertain—reveal the tensions surrounding aging and its changing status during this period. The American anxiety—nightmare, even—in the postwar age was to be stuck in the past, to be reminded where we had been rather than urged to look forward to what we were destined to become. The films of this period point to this anxiety of aging, of growing old, of no longer being the bright future but rather the dark past. As we see in the films analyzed in the remainder of this chapter, a number of 1950s pictures grappled with this issue, depicting a culture striving to move forward while the "old" problematically continued to linger, standing in the path of "progress," whether that was manifested in the forward momentum of upwardly mobile young couples and families, Cold War politics, glamorous young actors and screenwriters trying to make names for themselves, or young cowboys and oil tycoons conquering the American frontier. Such films bear witness to an intriguing moment in which characters with "money, maturity, and minds" struggled against stepping aside to make room for the ascent of "crooners, cowboys, cover girls and crime."

COMPETING FOR THE ADULT MARKET

In a discursive formation, a phenomenon must not only be present to be talked about, but talking about the phenomenon, in many ways, makes it more visible. Hollywood was not unaware of the discourse surrounding adult films and the general distaste of older audiences for its products. Susan Ohmer's *George Gallup in Hollywood* (2006) illustrates the powerful role that polling and audience-preference surveys, particularly those performed by George Gallup and the Audience Research Institute, began to occupy in 1940s Hollywood. Much of the research Ohmer details is referred to in the works by Handel, Seldes, and Wagner cited above, indicating a certain pool of shared information both within and outside the industry. As Ohmer illustrates, such information was interpreted in a number of ways in order to serve different purposes and interests, but as the reality of the lost audience became increasingly clear, the information contained in such studies grew more significant and difficult to deny. It was also likely that the film industry did more than simply read the same research accessed by these critics—some within the industry likely also read the criticism itself. Crowther and his fellow critics may not have held sway over the industry and the culture to the extent they wanted or imagined, but they expressed their ideas on a large public platform, which would not have gone unnoticed. Handel's work represents a more concrete example of this critical discourse receiving industry

Well-meaning Ellen (Thelma Ritter) attempts to be helpful without disrupting the marriage of her son (John Lund) and daughter-in-law (Gene Tierney) in The Mating Season *(1951).*

attention. In addition to its content revolving in large part around the same surveys examined by the industry, Handel acknowledges the assistance of, among others, Howard Dietz, vice president of MGM; Jay A. Grove, a former head of sales development for MGM; and another MGM employee, Thomas W. Gerety, whose position is unspecified. The release of Handel's book—despite its status as a work of social science put out by an academic press, presumably for a scholarly community—was noteworthy enough to merit a small article in an industry journal, the *Hollywood Reporter*.[24]

In looking at the subject matter of several adult pictures released by the studios during this period, as well as in examining how Hollywood experimented with promoting and exhibiting such films, it becomes clear that a potential audience market was recognized and briefly courted. Among the adult pictures released by the studios during this period are several that deal directly in their texts with the difficulties of aging in contemporary society as well as with growing generational divides and conflict; these include *The Mating Season*, *My Son John*, *Forever Female*, *Sunset Blvd.*, and *All About Eve*.

In *The Mating Season* (1951), Thelma Ritter stars as Ellen McNulty, the widowed mother of a successful man who has newly wed a high-society girl. Ellen, the proprietor of a failing restaurant, receives word of the wedding just as her attempts to keep the business afloat have come to an unsuccessful end. Using the last of her savings, she plans a surprise visit to the newlyweds as a distraction while she figures out how she will support herself and where she will live. Her daughter-in-law, Maggie (Gene Tierney), mistakes Ellen, aged and unfashionably clothed, as a housekeeper sent over by an agency. Not wishing to embarrass her daughter-in-law or reveal the working-class background from which the new husband hails, Ellen takes on the role of the housekeeper (as well as the accompanying wages and room), convincing her reluctant son to help keep up the ruse. Hijinks ensue until eventually all is revealed and the newlyweds welcome Ellen to move in permanently as a member of the household.

In addition to the main points of the plot, Ellen's concerns about being a burden to her son, and her desire to make herself of use while taking up residence in his home, speak to the uneasy social place of an elder in a modern, nuclear setup. Her skeptical reaction to the materialism of her son's life adds to the generational conflict and tension of the broader story. While the story of an elder out of place in the home of the younger generation is not so far removed from the plot of a film like *Make Way for Tomorrow*, it is given a new spin in *The Mating Season*. Ellen has the means to be independent—she has run her own business and proves competent as a professional-quality housekeeper—but she chooses to live with her son and his wife, which is presented as a novel and unusual situation. The burden of dependency does not create dramatic tension; rather, class and generational difference turn the engine of the plot.

In the notorious drama *My Son John* (1952), the director Leo McCarey harks back to his work on *Make Way for Tomorrow* in his sympathetic portrayal of two aging parents who come to recognize that their adult son is a fervent member of the Communist Party. Although dealing with the hot contemporary topic of the communist threat and the fear that "they walk among us," the majority of the film concentrates on the drama of the parents, Lucille (Helen Hayes) and Dan (Dean Jagger), in coping with the cultural gap that has opened between them and their son John (Robert Walker). John, who "has more degrees than a thermometer," returns to visit his parents after a very long time away. They are put off and hurt by the attitude he brings back with him, one of scorn for his parents' old-fashioned patriotism and devotion to their church. He is condescending and treats his parents—otherwise upstanding and respected citizens in their community, active members of the church and the American Legion—like children. Toward the end of the film, when Lucille sides with her conscience and country and tries to turn her son in to the FBI, he claims that she is a mentally unstable old woman and attempts to have her institutionalized to protect himself. The film ends

In My Son John *(1952), Lucille (Helen Hayes) and Dan (Dean Jagger) are torn between admiration for the accomplishments of their son (Robert Walker) and horror at his leftist political leanings.*

on an unsettling note: the parents are devastated by what has become of the child they raised, and John, momentarily reconsidering his choices after finally listening to his mother, is murdered by a fellow party member. McCarey's film is notably alarmist, not only in its portrayal of the communist threat, but also in its conflation of that threat (and its attendant callousness, icy intellectualism, selfishness, and inhumanity) with the generation ascending to social dominance.

In *Forever Female* (1953), Ginger Rogers stars as an aging Broadway star, Beatrice Page, desperately still trying to play "twenty-nine." The film revolves around Beatrice, who, since divorcing her age-appropriate producer Harry (Paul Douglas), has continued to star in his plays and remain friends with him while dating a series of much younger men. Stanley (William Holden), an up-and-coming playwright, befriends Beatrice and Harry; the latter agrees to produce Stanley's first play, a drama about an adult woman struggling to break away from her powerful mother, provided that Beatrice plays the daughter. Stanley reluctantly agrees, and during preproduction embarks on an affair with Beatrice. Meanwhile, a comedic sequence of aged actresses brought out of mothballs to audition for the mother role commences, and Stanley meets an aspiring young actress, Sally (Pat Crowley), who attempts to romance him and convince him that the role of the daughter will work only if played by an age-appropriate actress. The play eventually opens with Beatrice in the role of the daughter, to little success.

Though Harry warns Beatrice that her relationship with Stanley is a joke, stating, "You've played comedy enough to know when a thing is funny," she accepts Stanley's proposal of marriage. Before they can wed, though Beatrice leaves Stanley to embark on her yearly solo trip abroad. While she is away, Stanley begins to second-guess their relationship, and one night Harry takes him on a trip to a secluded cabin in upstate New York. There they find Beatrice with graying, undone hair, no makeup, and frumpy clothing, taking part in such unglamorous activities as sculpting pottery and rocking on the porch. Resigned to the fact that Harry has revealed her secret yearly getaway, she explains to Stanley that this is the only place where "for two months a year, I can be my age." When Stanley asks why she can't be her age all year, she explains:

> You ask an actress to give up being twenty-nine? When you're an older and wiser playwright, Stanley, and you write a part for a woman of thirty-four or thirty-five or even forty, you'll find that the actress will come to you and say, "Why does she have to be thirty-four or thirty-five or even forty? Why can't she be twenty-nine?" It's such a wonderful age. Can you blame us for lingering and lingering and lingering? And then finally having to be dragged through . . . And it isn't only in the theater—look at the audience sometime. It's full of twenty-nines.

After learning of Beatrice's true age and feelings, Stanley agrees that breaking off their engagement is for the best. They decide to continue with the play, only with Beatrice in the role of the mother and Sally as the ingénue, and do so to great acclaim. The film ends with proper generational order restored: Stanley is paired up with Sally, and Beatrice is back together with the age-appropriate Harry.

The positioning of Beatrice in *Forever Female*—as the aging diva unwilling to cede the stage to the younger generation—is of particular interest because it is of a piece with a number of film portrayals from the early 1950s that focus on a plot in which an aging female star confronts her own social and professional irrelevance. In *Forever Female*, Beatrice eventually comes to accept this fact with a modicum of grace. In two much better-known pictures of this period, though, *Sunset Blvd.* (1950) and *All About Eve* (1950), this negotiation of generational dominance and shifting social place is much more fraught. Released almost back-to-back, these two films seem to be speaking directly to this generational conflict between Hollywood and its aging audience members, and serve as interesting case studies of potential attempts to recapture this particular part of the lost audience. On the surface, the films have some remarkable similarities. Each features as its central character an aging actress involved with a more youthful man and struggling against having become (or being in the process of becoming) irrelevant to the worlds where they formerly reigned.

In *Sunset Blvd.*, Gloria Swanson plays Norma Desmond, a former silent film star who has been almost wholly isolated in her Hollywood mansion since the coming of sound pictures, yet begins a delusional attempt at a comeback. This comeback effort is accelerated when Norma meets a down-on-his-luck young screenwriter, Joe Gillis (William Holden). Norma hires Joe to edit a screenplay retelling the story of Salome, which Norma plans to have Cecil B. DeMille direct, starring herself. Within *Sunset Blvd.*, the generational and gendered power dynamics of the period are reversed: Norma holds an incredible amount of power over Joe. She pays off his debt collectors, provides him a room in her mansion, and gives him a salary (far higher than he had been making as a struggling screenwriter) to edit her pet project. This reversal of power, seen in Joe's financial dependence on Norma, is the opposite of the setup in a film like *The Mating Season*. Joe is not only emasculated by his lack of power in their relationship but also displaced as a young, able-bodied man, dependent on an aged woman for income and support. Such a reversal, underscored by Norma's romantic advances toward Joe, is presented as perverse. Joe is openly uncomfortable with the situation, voicing his disgust with himself and exhibiting repulsion toward this older woman in power; Norma is presented as an unnatural, ghoulish femme fatale.

Norma's unusually powerful situation is steadily undercut throughout the film. The fan letters she receives daily are revealed to be written by her devoted manservant and ex-husband (Erich von Stroheim), who supports her fantasy of social relevance rather than allow her to face the truth that she is no longer a person of consequence in contemporary society. She is not allowed the dignity of upholding any mystery in her beauty routine, which is presented as a horror show that involves peculiar rituals and devices and that requires herculean efforts to maintain her face and physique. Her power as an experienced star and a wealthy woman are undermined by her frequent bouts of theatrical melancholy and failed suicide attempts, revealing a desperate need for attention and overwhelming insecurity. Norma's only regular company, beyond her manservant, are "the waxworks," a trio of fellow Hollywood has-beens (including Buster Keaton, Anna Q. Nilsson, and H. B. Warner) who meet occasionally to play cards, and a pet monkey that, at the start of the film, has died, leaving her devastated. Norma's monkey and waxwork friends aren't the only things presented as immobile and isolated from the contemporary moment—the opulent furnishings of Norma's mansion are frozen in the era of the Roaring Twenties, her acting style is consistently implied to be passé, and even the titular street on which the action of the film takes place has implications of death and stars gone dark.

Norma's choice to cast herself in the role of Salome for her comeback is a plot element designed to emphasize Norma's delusion, since Salome was a seductive, foolish young woman. It is also a symbolic choice—Salome orders the head of John the Baptist brought to her on a platter as an act of revenge; in *Sunset Blvd.*, Joe ends up dead through an act of revenge by Norma. When Joe announces at last that he is going to desert Norma, leaving her in a position of no power over anyone, she shoots him in the back in a fit of rage. After murdering Joe, Norma is tricked into bringing herself downstairs to the police (presumably, to be arrested and institutionalized) by being told that Cecil B. DeMille and her adoring public are waiting for her to come out and perform her Salome. Driven by her desire for attention and importance, Norma makes her famous staircase descent, informing DeMille that she is ready for her close-up.

All About Eve is also a film about one generation usurping the social power of the previous generation, though its protagonist, Margo (Bette Davis), is not delusional about this or even in denial, as Norma was. In contrast, Margo is all too aware of this inevitability, her bitterness about its approach marking her within the film as an ill-tempered diva. Like *Sunset Blvd.*, *All About Eve* opens near the end of the story and then backtracks to demonstrate how things got to that point. We are introduced to Margo, a Broadway star all too aware of her increasing age and the approaching loss of favor in the eyes of the public and casting directors. She is at the peak of her power, commanding star roles and dating a handsome younger director. In a moment of pity, Margo invites a down-on-her-luck, worshipful fan named Eve (Anne Baxter) to be her assistant, despite the fact that Margo's maid and aged confidant, Birdie (Thelma Ritter), does not trust the young woman. Over the course of the following year, Eve turns out not to be as innocent as originally believed; rather, she is cunning and deceitful, playing the part of endearing ingénue while gradually undermining Margo, scheming to use the older star as a means to achieve Broadway success.

As Margo becomes aware of Eve's ulterior motives and true nature, she struggles to reassert her own authority, but is chastised by those close to her in her personal and professional lives, who believe the aging actress is merely acting out of insecurity, paranoia, and jealousy. The ageist (and sexist) nature of this treatment of Margo by those who supposedly know her best reaches its highest articulation when Margo's younger director-lover breaks off their relationship, only to find himself seduced by Eve, who is poised to become the new darling of Broadway. Margo has been, both personally and professionally, replaced by a younger model. Although Margo and her lover reconcile and decide to marry, Margo's career stagnates. She continues performing in the same show while Eve schemes her way into roles originally intended for Margo, and they serve as the launching pad for her ascension as Broadway's new star. Though the film ends with no redemption for Margo's career, many of her friends and colleagues return to her side, realizing her wisdom. In a cynical twist in the final moments of the film, some element of karmic justice seems to arrive as Eve befriends a worshipful young fan, who rapidly insinuates herself into Eve's life as an assistant of sorts. The fan-assistant is shown helping an exhausted Eve to bed and then secretly trying on Eve's award-show gown, implying another inevitable generational coup.

Both *All About Eve* and *Sunset Blvd.* revolve around matters uniquely relevant to adult audience members—these are not the problems or difficulties of youth—but also uniquely of interest in the context of Hollywood's supposed catering to an increasingly juvenile audience. Depictions of the indignity of aging in a modern world where there are always vivacious youths ready to replace the world's former stars satirize aging not only in modern society but also in Hollywood. The films present a portrait of Hollywood's treatment of aging both on and off screen. It seems strangely appropriate that, in the race for the Best Actress Oscar that year, Swanson and Davis were singled out as the two favorites for the prize. There was much coverage and media speculation over which grande dame would take the trophy, but both were beaten out by twenty-nine-year-old Judy Holliday.

The presence of these experienced actresses, along with other older stars such as von Stroheim and Keaton, may have appealed to an older audience that had grown up with such stars and possibly felt a stronger connection with them than with younger stars. Additionally, there may have been some revival of interest in stars of Hollywood's earlier eras. As Douglas Gomery points out, beginning in the late 1940s and carrying on into the 1950s, pre-1948 titles (for which residuals did not have to be paid) were sold to television and subsequently aired often.[25] Additionally, as Christine Becker's work *It's The Pictures That Got Small: Hollywood Film Stars on 1950s Television* (2008) details, the early years of television regularly featured older Hollywood stars in new programming. Many stars with active studio contracts were forbidden from appearing on television until the mid-1950s, so these older stars brought a level of prestige to the fledgling industry, which in return offered them roles and exposure they were unable to obtain elsewhere. Davis was still a viable and prolific actress, but had been, at that point, a Hollywood star since the mid-1930s and was certainly past the peak of marquee stardom. Gloria Swanson's heyday, like Norma Desmond's, had ended with the coming of sound, though she appeared sporadically on film into the early 1940s. Notably, she was the host of an early television show, *The Gloria Swanson Hour*, in 1950, the same year that her *Sunset Blvd.* costar Buster Keaton also began hosting a weekly television program. Such stars may have been viewed by the television studios as welcome bait for the desired adult audience, promising not only the novelty of older stars on screen but also producing nostalgia, harking back to earlier eras when both the stars and their fans were at the peak of their social relevance.

The print advertising campaigns for both pictures fit clearly with this narrative of selling adult films. While print ads that appeared nationwide for *All About Eve* were fairly unremarkable, using pull quotes from critics and centering on Davis's still-bankable stardom, they marketed the film based on prestige and implied sophistication, particularly those ads that ran toward the end of 1950, which touted the film as a serious Oscar contender.[26] The film was marketed to exhibitors and industry members in this fashion more explicitly; in a notable example, a ten-page spread in the *Hollywood Reporter* on October 18, 1950, advertised the film through full-page reprints of its critical reviews.[27] That critics loved the film meant that it should satisfy the adult public's craving for more challenging, intelligent fare.

The advertising for *Sunset Blvd.* took a different approach, emphasizing the youth-age divide in the film. Ads that ran in multiple papers throughout September 1950 featured a knotted filmstrip dividing the ad space diagonally. On one side was an image of Swanson looking enraged and imposing; on the other side, an image of Holden and his age-appropriate love interest, Nancy Olson, embracing—explicitly drawing a line between old and young.[28] Other variations of this ad included text that read: "*Sunset Boulevard* is the story of young Joe Gillis, a Hollywood writer. It is also the story of Norma Desmond, a glamorous movie star . . . and of young Betty Schaefer [Olson] who loved Joe with all her heart."[29] Another variation, which dropped the signature knotted-film-strip motif, instead placed images of Swanson, Holden, and Olson in a diagonal line (Swanson at the top, Olson at the bottom, Holden in the middle) with text that read: "When a woman as experienced and rich as Norma Desmond gets her clutches on a man as heedless as young Joe Gillis . . . nothing can save him but a lovely girl like Betty Schaefer."[30]

The contrast between generations was underscored more visually in trade ads for the film's premiere, which featured the images of Swanson, Holden, and Olson separated by the knotted film strip, but in this instance the images were placed inside a drawing of an hourglass, with Swanson (and her association with the ravages of time) bearing down on Holden and Olson.[31] Since Olson's role is fairly small within the film's plot, the consistent inclusion of her in the ads, the emphasis on conflict between the younger couple and Swanson, and the use of descriptive terms like "young," "experienced," and "girl" made age and the generational divide key selling points. The idea of Swanson as a deranged figure of menace, keeping the young and naïve Holden in her "clutches" and apart from good "girl" Olson, is somewhat different from the reality of the film's content: Olson is a street-smart Hollywood screenwriter and a fairly minor character, and Holden is sarcastic and grim, using Swanson for her money. In these ads, age and generational conflict were stirred up and inflated for the purpose of selling the film.

A look at the exhibition of *Sunset Blvd.* and *All About Eve* reveals experimentation perhaps intended to attract a more "adult" or mature audience. As Handel surmised in 1950, "Moviegoing is essentially a social activity, and young people are more likely to band together for the purpose of entertainment. Then, for movies one has to leave the house, which probably becomes more distasteful as one grows older."[32] The early exhibition strategies for *Sunset Blvd.* and *All About Eve* may be viewed as possible attempts to draw those older people from their homes for the purpose of seeing adult films, to make the experience more appealing and less "distasteful." One way to make such an excursion worthwhile is to make the film screening appear to be an event, to build a sense of exclusiveness around it. Before its official New York City premiere in August 1951, *Sunset Blvd.* had twenty-one private pseudo-premieres.[33] Over the course of seven months, Paramount's publicity department kept a waiting list of interested "important names," and when this list reached around seventy-five names, a screening was held, complete with director, screenwriter, producers, and stars in attendance. During the last three months before the premiere, Gloria Swanson was dispatched around the country for a "three month exploitation tour" in a prerelease promotion for the film.[34] Following the actual premiere, the film was trucked around the country for a series of fifteen engagements in cities such as Des Moines, Buffalo, Jacksonville, and Indianapolis before opening its proper first-run release.[35]

In the early exhibition history of *All About Eve*, we see a different attempt to draw attention to the experience of attending the film. In August 1950, Twentieth Century–Fox announced plans to enforce a "scheduled performances" policy in which tickets for all screenings of *All About Eve* at every theater that booked the film had to be purchased in advance, and no one would be allowed to enter the auditorium after the screening had begun.[36] Additionally, the film would be screened only as a single bill. According to Fox, "The average larger theatre would have tickets on advance sales at the box office, at ticket offices, drug stores, etc. The tickets would have a different color for each show and would have the date and starting time of the performance printed on them."[37] The plan, which received quite a bit of coverage, was justified on the basis of allowing screenwriters to be "freed of many restrictions."[38] Presumably, this implied that screenwriters would no longer need to write such simplified plots or characterizations that the film could be easily understood by patrons entering at any point during a screening, a clear attempt by Fox to emphasize the value of the film as an art form rather than a commercial product.

This policy was tied to the quality of *All About Eve*, too. A Fox promotion reads: "When we first saw *All About Eve* . . . we became aware that its utter fascination and charm were immeasurably due to the fact that we were seeing it the only way it should be seen—from the beginning."[39] Despite the publicity, however, by the end of the film's premiere run at the Roxy in New York City, it was announced that the remainder of *All About Eve*'s run would follow normal exhibition practices, that is, patrons could enter after its start time and without buying advance tickets. The "scheduled performances" practice was deemed unsuccessful: "Confusion arose because of the public's deeply ingrained habit of going to a movie at any desired hour, when most convenient or on impulse."[40] It seems wholly intentional that the practice of "scheduled performances" ultimately attempted to turn the filmgoing experience into something resembling a night out at the legitimate theater, an activity presumed to be frequented by those who, to use Crowther's description, had "money, maturity, and minds." Practices like those applied to *Sunset Blvd.* and *All About Eve* worked to differentiate these films from other Hollywood output, as well as to differentiate the filmgoing experience from that associated with youth audiences at drive-ins (an increasingly popular venue) and local theaters.

These films and the strategies employed to promote and exhibit them can be viewed as a kind of "adultsploitation." During the same era when many filmmakers attempted to lure audiences in by exploiting the idea of "youth"—in the form of juvenile delinquents, bobby-soxers, and, eventually, wayward teens and rock and rollers—Hollywood experimented with exploiting the idea of the "adult" as both subject matter and experience. This notion of "adultsploitation" is revisited in a more garish "agesploitation" form in the psycho biddy pictures and elder kitsch roles that followed. We discuss those films of the 1960s, with a focus on genre, in the next chapter, but there is one popular genre of the 1950s that we must examine first, for its adult depiction of the tension of aging during this era's climate of concern about youth and progress: the melodrama.

In All That Heaven Allows *(1955), Cary (Jane Wyman), a widow, flirts with the younger, working-class Ron (Rock Hudson), causing scandal in her upper-class neighborhood.*

GENDER AND GENERATION IN MELODRAMA

In the postwar years, melodrama experienced what many scholars now describe as a golden era in Hollywood. Though the genre had always had a presence in American cinema, particularly during its first decades, the 1950s saw the genre flourish artistically, critically, and popularly. The best-known examples of such films are those of Douglas Sirk: luscious Technicolor melodramas made for Universal, such as *Magnificent Obsession* (1954), *All That Heaven Allows* (1955), and *Imitation of Life* (1959). In addition to Sirkian melodramas and Nicholas Ray's similarly auteurist melodramatic output, however, a number of other high-profile "mainstream" films of the era also have strong melodramatic components and share in the conventions of the genre, including what Thomas Elsaesser defines as "family melodramas," like *Giant* (1956) or *My Son John* (1952), and sophisticated "adult" films like the previously discussed *Sunset Blvd.* or *On the Waterfront* (1954) and *East of Eden* (1955). While these films cross into any number of loose generic categories—film noir, social problem films, and even Westerns (*Johnny Guitar*, 1954)—

they all overtly demonstrate characteristics of melodrama. These include excessive expressions of emotion, an overt moralizing quandary, and a character at odds with the society that surrounds him or her.

That the melodramatic mode operated so strongly in Hollywood during the postwar period perhaps could be related to the era's cultural fixation on morality, repression, and even a popular fascination with Freudian psychoanalysis. Scholars such as Christine Gledhill have discussed the function of the melodrama in American society, particularly during the genre's postwar heyday, as presenting a cathartic manifestation of the Freudian "return of the repressed" within the safe confines of an entertaining Hollywood film.[41] In this sense, resentments, anxieties, and desires repressed by the era's emphasis on public conformity to social performances defined more narrowly than in previous decades (stricter gender roles, greater emphasis on patriotism and capitalist or consumerist displays, etc.) bubbled up and found expression through the emotional excesses of such films. Their attraction, then, came from offering a cathartic release otherwise rarely available without the risk of breaching social propriety.

According to Barbara Klinger, the melodramas of the postwar period (particularly the films of Sirk) blossomed in part because of their inclusion under the umbrella of the adult film, which offered a way of viewing sensational topics under the cover of an adult label and, therefore, supposedly made them sophisticated. In her examination of Sirk's *Written on the Wind*, Klinger ties this notion to the argument that it was a filmic expression of the "return of the repressed," which attracted viewers during this period:

> What I am arguing here is that during the 1950s such a "culturally specific" construction of generic identity for *Written on the Wind* and other melodramas occurred. It occurred through affiliation with a transitory "local genre"—the adult film—forged by a mixture of institutional and social factors. This generic frame selectively activated filmic elements, such as psychosexual and romantic conflicts, tormented characters, and erotic performances, to foster an ideological identity for the film which was commensurate with the era's strong emphasis on sexual display. This climate, underwritten by a renewed heterosexual fervor in the anticommunist, post–World War II years, created a voyeuristic audience ethos focused on the objectification of women and a lurid sensationalizing of social problems and human relationships.[42]

In this sense, the melodrama, along with melodramatic conventions apparent in more "mainstream" films and other genres, experienced a decade or so of popularity because of a confluence of industrial, social, and cultural factors as well as, perhaps, related psychic needs on the part of the moviegoing public.

An important element, however, was that so many of these melodramatic films featured plotlines focused on the difficulties of an aging person (usually a woman) who had to struggle with her changing role within society. Sirk's *All That Heaven Allows* finds the protagonist, an upper-middle-class widow, falling in love with her much younger working-class gardener and facing resistance and shunning from her social circle and her adult children as a result. Sirk's *Magnificent Obsession* features the two leads from *All That Heaven Allows* (Jane Wyman and Rock Hudson). Wyman again plays a widow, Helen, attracted to Hudson, a young surgeon named Bob. Helen has been left financially vulnerable by her late husband, a highly respected local doctor, and then, after staying true to her husband's memory and her prescribed social role by rejecting the advances of the disreputable Bob, she is struck by a car and blinded. Helen's situation continues to deteriorate as she is told her blindness is incurable; she retreats from local society and grows increasingly isolated and ill. Helen essentially disappears from the narrative until it is time for her to return, through a device by which the newly redeemed Bob can complete his transformation into a worthy member of society. He performs risky brain surgery on Helen, curing her illness and blindness. Thus Helen, we are led to believe, may be able to reintegrate herself into society and again take on her role as the noble widow and steward of her late husband's legacy.

In both these films, age and its attendant vulnerabilities are used to underscore the pathos of the melodramatic plotting. While neither deals directly with a truly geriatric woman, they rely on a still-attractive-but-past-her-box-office-prime actress to portray the difficulties and anxieties of women who are being shifted out of their previously central social roles and starting down the path toward senescence. From a practical perspective, the casting of Wyman and the focus on the concerns of the aging woman (widowhood, disability, an empty home) can be seen as deliberate choices made by the studios in their attempt to appeal to the same older audience members whom they sought for their mainstream adult pictures. Additionally, the circumstances of the older, established woman provide a useful plot device, offering novel obstacles to be overcome (compared with the conflicts of traditional younger heroines) and stricter social boundaries to confine the characters, an advantageous element to melodramatic conventions. As Thomas Schatz writes, such films "involve the courtship of an older woman, invariably a widow or divorcee, whose adult status and established familiar role minimize the possibility for flight from her repressive environment."[43] In melodrama, the greater the social constrictions, the greater the dramatic value and, theoretically, the greater the potential for psychic release.

If adult films, particularly the melodramas that Klinger would include under that umbrella, rely on timely and currently sensational topics for material, we can understand the plight of the aging woman as fitting neatly into the social context of the period. There was, for one thing, a new isolation of elder Americans brought on by the social and political factors previously outlined. The plotlines of these films are infused with anxiety about seemingly inevitable isolation, whether through community shunning, blindness and disability, or simply from the expectation that an older woman should stay inside her empty nest with only her television for company and entertainment. One way or another, the threat of losing a public role, purpose, or place looms.

Additionally, such plots are timely and sensational in that they encourage a desire to witness a woman (particularly an older woman, who, as Schatz points out, is even more restricted than her younger counterparts) transgress the ever-tightening social boundaries placed on her during the postwar years. While such a transgression may be disruptive or upsetting in lived reality, film—the emotionally excessive and cathartic melodrama especially—keeps it confined to a hypothetical world while still providing a vicarious thrill for the viewer. These films portray a fantasy along with the pathos. In addition to the consumerist fantasy of Sirk's characteristically excessive mise-en-scène, the plots act out a kind of wish fulfillment in which the threat of isolation and vulnerability brought on with aging is thwarted. The older woman ends each picture having managed to escape the confines of her previous social position, sidestep the pending threat of isolation, and reach a point of new and renewed confidence and self-actualization. That this escape so often comes about through the necessary intervention of a virtuous (and younger) man reinforces not only the strict gender roles of the era but also the generational power dynamic. It is not the wisdom of the experienced that leads to ultimate contentment, but the unorthodoxy and bravado of the young. Such dynamics keep the fantasy from becoming, perhaps, too fantastic and from presenting a culturally distasteful portrayal of a woman with too much power or ambition.

As we can see, when examining representations of elder figures in film during the postwar period, the topic of gender and sexuality cannot be ignored. Beyond the representations addressed here, there is, of course, the well-known trope of the "silver fox," a dashing, worldly, older male lead, usually presented as an object of admiration to both sexes and paired romantically with a younger, very attractive actress. The availability of such roles to older stars appears to have depended most importantly on gender; actresses like Bette Davis, Joan Crawford, and Ginger Rogers were certainly as famous in their box-office heyday as Gary Cooper, Cary Grant, or James Stewart, yet

Davis, Crawford, and Rogers found no female equivalent to the silver fox on offer in their later years. Instead, in films like *All About Eve*, *Forever Female*, and *The Best of Everything* (1959), they play aging women forced to reckon with the decline of their power to attract and influence those around them, and forced to ultimately accept a diminished role in their worlds in order to find contentment. The existence of the silver fox role may be understood as a holdover of the traditional economic power that an older man theoretically amassed over his lifetime, his money a symbolic stand-in for virility. By the same token, the nonexistence of an equivalent role for older actresses can be understood as a holdover of the crone, her loss of fertility symbolically associated with the loss of attraction. (We explore the topic of May-December romance in chapter 5.)

With few exceptions, elder representations that do not fit the silver fox role were segregated by genre and gender: older women were featured in melodrama and horror, and feminized older men took on the comedic roles. In horror and comedy, the notion of an elder figure possessing and acting upon sexual desires is met with, respectively, revulsion and mockery, a dichotomy that we explore further in the following chapter. In melodrama, however, we find a curious space in which an older woman is allowed to have and express her sexuality without being presented as either a monster or a joke. Unlike films in which the sexuality of an older woman is either wholly absent or employed for shock value, postwar melodramas offered an acknowledgment that an older woman might indeed possess sexual desires and sexual attractiveness, which were validated by the (usually younger) men around her.

In regard to gender in melodrama, while women dominate in the elder-character plotlines of postwar films, we do still see representations of male elder characters, not usually in women's weepies, but in other melodrama-inflected films popular at the time. Two of the most famous melodramatic portrayals of older men in this period are those of Ethan (John Wayne) in the Western *The Searchers*, and Bick (Rock Hudson, wearing gray face) at the end of the family melodrama *Giant*, films released to good box office and critical acclaim in 1956. For both these characters, sexual desire and romance are referenced but treated as concerns of the past. Instead, each is focused on being the leader of a family on the western frontier, unwilling to cede power or authority to young men close to them. Ethan and Bick are presented as highly capable, experienced figures, but—and this is what marks these films as firmly of the postwar period—the value of their experience and capability is undercut by their inability to fit in with the popular cultural attitudes around them. In each case, they espouse racism, which is clearly presented as outdated and as a cause of distance from younger generations. Each of these

Ethan (John Wayne) struggles to relate to younger men like Brad (Harry Carey Jr.) in The Searchers *(1956), as he further struggles with the changing times and morality of the post–Civil War West.*

men is ultimately forced to face their bigoted views and overcome them in isolated acts to keep their families together and save patriarchal face before they relinquish control to the younger generation. Like the older women of melodrama, Ethan and Bick are forced to leave their previous places in society rather than carry on where they are no longer necessary or relevant. For Bick, this means stepping back from his role as head of the family oil empire and enjoying his dotage as a sedentary grandfather; in Ethan's case, the film literally closes the door on his image as he walks away from civilized society.

Regarding the golden age of the melodrama, Thomas Schatz notes the contradictory impulses at the heart of the genre: "The melodrama reached its equilibrium at the same time that certain filmmakers were beginning to subvert and counter the superficial prosocial thematics and clichéd romantic narratives that had previously identified the genre. No other genre films, not even the "anti-Westerns" of the same period, projected so complex and paradoxical a view of America, at once celebrating and severely questioning the basic values and attitudes of the mass audience."[44]

In examining these representations of the aging in melodramatic films of the postwar period, we can clearly witness a questioning of contemporary social attitudes toward elders and the ways in which such attitudes limited the social experience available to the aging population. Rather than offering solutions to what is clearly presented as a frightening and undesirable reality, or issuing calls to change, however, these films ultimately conform to the role of genre pictures, as detailed by Judith Hess Wright.[45] Melodramatic representation in the postwar era clearly shows that social irrelevance awaits the aging. It draws on its audience's anxieties about this situation and offers emotional relief through its excessively emotional viewing experience. Ultimately, though melodrama acknowledges the unappealing social realities of its aging audience, the only escape that it offers is a fantastic one.

It is no coincidence that the drop-off in the popularity of melodrama as a formal Hollywood genre coincided with the rise of camp in American popular culture. On the production side, as we have seen, though Hollywood made attempts to attract older audiences throughout the 1950s, such strategies were largely abandoned in the 1960s, and adult films and melodramas formed a large part of this jettisoned stock. This was in large part due to the continued decline of the studios, which were usurped at the box office by independent producers and distributors. The youth audience became a primary focus in Hollywood as the baby boomers came fully of age as a cultural and economic force. Melodrama largely disappeared from the silver screen, though it continued on in the ever-popular soap opera formats (beginning in radio and carrying on to thrive in television) and, later, in made-for-television movie formats.

On the cultural side, the baby boomer generation during this period is often presented as one for which irony was a much-prized sensibility. Melodrama, with its excesses of emotion and sentimentality, its calls on the audience for sympathy and empathy, and its reverence for social order, became rapidly read as outdated and old-fashioned in an age of mass camp and irony. Yet as Thomas Schatz points out above, and numerous scholars have argued in retrospect, melodrama, under the cover of its strict genre conventions, questioned the status quo, an activity that became a central tenet of a large portion of the baby boomers' culture in the 1960s. As melodrama faded from the silver screen during the early 1960s, it took with it the unique space and audience that it offered the aging female star.

Although many of the elder characters in the films of this chapter would hardly be classified as more than middle-aged today or late middle-aged by the standards of the era, such films had an impact on later representations of aging. Our analysis reveals an entertainment industry moving away from prewar and wartime strategies of mainstream audience appeal and toward niche demographics, influenced in large part by shifts in the advertising industry, by internally commissioned research, and by significant shifts in Americans' social environments. This discourse suggests that a specific aging public was starting to feel that their entertainment needs were going unmet by Hollywood at a time when critics, academics, and people within the industry were warning against the "juvenilization" of American film.[46] All this coincided with the initial breakdown of the studio system and the rise of the independent producer; those changes, along with the weakening Production Code which had operated as the censor of moral maturity, allowed for the expansion of many representations on screen.

The moment also spoke to a larger social fracturing along generational lines. The young and the aging no longer were viewed as part of the same mainstream popular culture—and seemingly no longer viewed themselves that way—but instead moved further apart socially as well as spatially. In American cinema, this meant that representations of "older" characters were altogether different from those of the dominant population, wherein youth was becoming the norm. At the box office, even as the youth market became increasingly valuable, the range of on-screen roles for older characters was simultaneously finding new sophistication and exaggeration.

CHAPTER THREE

The Horrific and the Hilarious

*[*Lady in a Cage*] adds Olivia de Havilland to the list of cinema actresses who would apparently rather be freaks than be forgotten.*

TIME, JUNE 19, 1964

BY THE LATE 1950S, AMERICAN POPULAR CULTURE WAS beginning to undergo a change from the production of mass entertainment, envisioned as appealing to the broadest audience possible, to one more demographically varied, with media consciously designed to attract narrower, niche audiences. By far the most prominent group targeted was the youth market, specifically the teenagers and young adults of the baby boom generation. As Thomas Doherty writes regarding this youth audience: "In the 1950s, market research firms began to document a peculiar trend in consumerism, one that in the 1960s would become a commonplace of American life: teenagers were often the opinion leaders for the rest of the culture. . . . Although creators of entertainment had always paid some attention to the youth market, the demographic realities of the 1950s encouraged them to consider it as never before. Henceforth teenagers would have a major, sometimes dominant, voice in determining the nation's cultural diet."[1]

While Hollywood was still very much in the business of turning out big-budget productions with the broadest possible mainstream audience in mind, such as *20,000 Leagues under the Sea* (1954), *Around the World in 80 Days* (1956), *The Big Country* (1958), and *Ben-Hur* (1959), films specifically designed to attract the youth market became increasingly central to American cinema, particularly in the independent productions that began to seriously challenge the old studios' supremacy in the marketplace. In this chapter, our analysis moves from looking at big pictures, designed with a mass audience in mind, to examining smaller pictures restricted to the confines of "low" genres, such as low-budget horror films and broad teen-centric comedies produced by specialty outfits such as American International Pictures (AIP). This mirrors in some ways the changing Hollywood industry of the 1960s, in which the massive culture machine of the old studio system and its tent-pole production approach began to be usurped culturally and financially by independent film companies aiming squarely for the youth market.

Something quite interesting occurs in these genre pictures, though, that had long-term effects on the representation of elders in Hollywood cinema. In these horror and comedy films aimed at youth audiences, elder characters are, surprisingly, not only present, but also represented in ways that, with the possible exception of *Sunset Blvd.* (1950), had not often been seen previously. These representations became even more intriguing in the cultural and political context of the 1960s, carrying on the tradition in genre pictures of addressing social issues in ways that are often much more direct than those afforded by more mainstream productions. Highly generic films have customarily been viewed by the public at large (and, until recently, by many cultural critics) as less "important" or worthy of extended examination than those less dependent on generic formulas. Because of this low-culture ghettoization, such films have often been allowed to fly under the radar, and this inconspicuousness has allowed them to address controversial topics more directly than other films that are more highly scrutinized and less bound to the conventions that set genre films apart as less "real" and therefore less "serious."

In this way, genre pictures have come to be viewed as unique spaces in which one can witness the anxieties of particular cultural moments being addressed often overtly and spectacularly. Regarding the unique social position that genre pictures hold in addressing (and soothing) a society's cultural anxieties, Judith Hess Wright writes: "These films came into being and were financially successful because they temporarily relieved the fears aroused by a recognition of social and political conflicts; they helped to discourage any action that might otherwise follow upon the pressure generated by living with these conflicts. Genre films produce satisfaction rather than action. Pity and fear rather than revolt."[2]

Just as one can unpack American anxieties about communism by examining postwar science fiction films, or about civil rights by examining postwar Westerns, so too can we use genre as a window into anxieties about aging in an increasingly youth-focused postwar culture in which the young nuclear family was the center of all things, and white middle-class adolescents were the tastemakers for the culture at large.

It is also important to consider genre pictures in this era simply because such films became a refuge of sorts for aging stars during the disintegration of the studio system. Genre pictures in the 1950s and 1960s often took advantage of available, slightly tarnished (whether by age, scandal, or inactivity) stars to boost the films' cachet or the audience's interest. Additionally, genre films, which often reached into the contemporary arena for new material to enliven their conventions, used these stars in texts that addressed social fears about aging, and the sexual and cultural obsolescence it portended. Having considered this in 1950s melodrama, we now focus on horror and comedy, wherein aging became quite curious during the 1960s.

THE HORROR OF AGING

Traditionally focused on fantastical (and male) creatures such as vampires, mummies, or werewolves, the horror genre underwent a change following the surprising box-office success of Alfred Hitchcock's *Psycho* in 1960. Many of the horror films that followed in the wake of *Psycho* demonstrate a notable deviation from fantastical monsters, focusing instead on horrific "normal" people: those whose traumatic experiences and quirks of psychology leave them dangerous and deranged. As Robin Wood writes about the genre, "One might say that the true subject of the horror genre is the struggle for recognition of all that our civilization *re*presses or *op*presses: its re-emergence dramatized, as in our nightmares, as an object of horror, a matter for terror, the 'happy ending' (when it exists) typically signifying the restoration of repression."[3] If one considers this shift in the genre's monsters reflective of a shift in the horrors that the culture needed to repress, some thought-provoking issues are raised, particularly within the series of films featuring aging women, which became its own prominent subgenre throughout the 1960s.

Following the popularity of *Psycho* and *What Ever Happened to Baby Jane?* (1962), a series of pictures featured older actresses in grotesque roles, what some horror enthusiasts have dubbed "psycho biddy" films and what Peter Shelley christens the "Grande Dame Guignol" subgenre of horror in his survey of these pictures. In describing the character of the grande dame or psycho biddy, he writes:

> The grande dame as unstable antagonist may pine for lost youth and glory, or she may be trapped by idealized memories of childhood, with a trauma that haunts her past. She is akin to Miss Havisham in Charles Dickens's novel *Great Expectations*, her adult life wasted as she

> rots away in her unused wedding dress in her room. Like a ghost, the grande dame cannot rest until the unbalance of the universe is corrected. A refusal to accept reality and the natural process of life exemplifies the fear of aging and death, and implicitly a fear of women.[4]

Beyond a general anxiety about women, a perennial undercurrent of the horror genre throughout its history, this subgenre reveals anxieties specific to the culture of the period and its shifting social environment. These films, along with other post-*Psycho* horror pictures, are in keeping with the postwar era's fascination with psychology and Freudian analysis, putting less emphasis on the notion of external monsters (whether aliens, werewolves, or communists) and more on how modern society produced members who are themselves monsters of a different sort. The increased emphasis on the dangerous, easily corrupted, or damaged individual psyche reveals discomfort with the contemporary world and its society of increasing isolation. The post-*Baby Jane* trend of psycho biddy pictures literalizes those fears in the body of the aging woman. There is horror in her isolation, horror in the fact that she is allowed to operate in twisted fashion without outside intervention, and, most of all, horror in her transgression of generational roles. These characters embody anxiety about the roles that society dictates to older women, and the horror elements come about when these women rise up in defiance of those roles. In keeping with Robin Wood's summation of the horror film as a genre, by the end of each film, these women must be rendered submissive, a repression of the cultural discomfort her presence creates. Reinforced by the sheer number of such films made during the 1960s, this representation of elder figures became degrading, transforming older, once sexually desirable female stars into dehumanized objects.

Shelley points to Capra's *Arsenic and Old Lace* (1944) and Wilder's *Sunset Blvd.* as precursors of this subgenre. *Arsenic* is different, however, in being a farce and, therefore, diluted by comedy. Its elder female protagonists are presented as desexualized and, therefore, nonthreatening (though still homicidal). Additionally, their characterization is clearly marked as well meaning and humanistic rather than horrific. *Sunset Blvd.*, with its overtly gothic elements and ghoulish presentation of Gloria Swanson and her sexuality, is a more direct forerunner to the psycho biddy films of the 1960s, though it operates within the melodrama–adult drama genre rather than horror. In this sense, it fits into the group of adult films released in the early 1950s about fading female stars, including *All About Eve* (1950), *The Star* (1952), and *Forever Female* (1953). These films present aging women struggling against the redefinition of their place in society, but this struggle is not one of malevolent defiance; at worst it is pitiable, at best, relatable. Though *Sunset Blvd.* offers

The grotesquely childlike Jane (Bette Davis) builds sandcastles while her disabled elder sister, Blanche (Joan Crawford), lies captive in What Ever Happened to Baby Jane? *(1962).*

the least empathetic of these representations, it is a far cry from the outright hostile representations of the psycho biddy horror cycle.

What Ever Happened to Baby Jane? is worth examining in some detail for the audacity of the treatment of its star, Bette Davis, as well as for the fact that it created the mold in which the subsequent psycho biddy pictures were cast. The plot revolves around the later lives of two sisters, one a former child star in vaudeville, Jane (Davis), the other a former star of 1930s Hollywood, Blanche (Joan Crawford). Blanche's career was cut short after Jane hit her with an automobile in a jealous, drunken rage, putting Blanche in a wheelchair for the remainder of her days. Following this backstory, the main plot of the film picks up in the present-day 1960s. The sisters share a home where Blanche, confined to an upstairs bedroom, is dependent on Jane and a part-time housekeeper for food, care, and contact with the outside world. Jane, who has long been lost in the past, obsessed with her childhood fame, is becoming increasingly unstable; as a consequence, Blanche puts a plan in motion to sell their longtime home, move to a smaller house with the housekeeper, and have Jane permanently institutionalized. Jane, having caught wind of the scheme, becomes motivated to rekindle her childhood stage act in order to have personal and economic independence from her sister and avoid institutionalization. In her pursuit of this, Jane hires a younger man, Edwin (Victor Buono), to be her musical accompanist. Desperate for the money, Edwin ignores the obvious delusions of Jane and her awkward sexual advances, and he encourages her incongruous performances of childish songs in little-girl costumes. While pursuing attempts to rekindle her childhood fame, Jane works to keep Blanche unaware of the situation, cutting off her communication with the outside world by intercepting her mail, removing the phone lines in her bedroom, and firing the housekeeper.

As the film progresses, Jane's treatment of Blanche becomes increasingly villainous—she kills Blanche's pet bird and then serves it to her for dinner, bringing her nothing else for days until she then offers up a cooked rat as an alternative, leaving Blanche in a weakened, starved, and terrified state. Jane fends off others who attempt to inquire about Blanche's well-being, impersonating Blanche on the telephone to her doctor and accountant, lying to the neighbors, and, finally, murdering the housekeeper when she threatens to call in the police. Eventually, Edwin alerts the police, and Jane kidnaps Blanche and goes on the run. A short time later, the two are found on a public beach. The film ends with the police rescuing Blanche while Jane, pleased to have an audience, performs her childhood stage routine for a group of gawking teenage beachgoers before, presumably, being arrested and institutionalized.

In Jane and Blanche, we see characterizations of older women that were repeated in many subsequent films and became, by default, some of the predominant representations of elder figures on the big screen during this time (and, in reruns, on the small screen thereafter). In the character of Blanche, as Sally Chivers has pointed out, we initially see a representation of the proper aging woman, since Blanche is pleasant and grateful for the assistance she receives, even though she asks for relatively little, keeping to her room and apart from the rest of the world.[5] She is seen reminiscing about the past without trying to relive it or cling to the identity of her younger self. Above all, she is passive. This is, of course, complicated by the late plot revelation that Blanche caused her own paralyzing accident and later blamed it on her already mentally unstable sister, thus undermining her representation in the story as the epitome of the proper aging woman and proper aging star. Throughout the majority of the film, though, Crawford plays the aging woman as a figure of ultimate vulnerability, dependent on the kindness and intervention of other, younger people, and in constant danger because of her physical limitations, isolation, and status as someone easily forgotten about by the larger community. This vulnerable elder representation appears periodically throughout the copycat films that followed *Baby Jane*'s success.

Davis's Jane, by contrast, is the true psycho biddy: psychotic and unpredictable, a nightmare vision of a woman refusing to pass quietly into the proper performance of senescence. Davis's makeup in the film, in contrast with the restrained, natural look of Crawford or the aged but still glamorous look of Swanson in *Sunset Blvd.*, is heavy and distorting. The makeup exaggerates the age of Davis's face, creating deep wrinkles and shadows, resulting in a grotesque, melted-mask-like visage. Her costuming, on the other hand, emphasizes the horror of her age through incongruity, growing progressively more juvenile as the film goes on, relying on the uncanny absurdity of a grown woman, much less an elder woman with the face of a monster, in a little girl's pinafore and hair bows. The character personifies what Chivers, borrowing a concept from Mary Russo, refers to as the "scandal of anachronism," the disruption caused when a member of society plays a role socially assigned to a different (usually younger) age group.[6] In Jane, this scandal is not merely a faux pas or a cause for pity—rather, it is an outright threatening transgression. Jane is physically and sexually aggressive, sarcastic and cruel, alcoholic, violent, mentally unstable, and subject to overpowering rages of childish jealousy. She operates as a self-destructive danger to herself and those around her.

By the end of the film, however, Jane has fled the private confines of the mansion and is rendered much less powerful. The threat of her anachronism is diminished in public space, and confronted by figures of authority (the police), as well as by the mass gawking of teenagers, she is made powerless and disgraceful. This also emphasizes a last key element of the psycho biddy films: overt generational tension. Often this is expressed in a psychotic older woman's attack on a younger protagonist; even in *Psycho*, Norman Bates (Anthony Perkins) inhabits the role of the older woman who tormented him psychologically and uses this role to attack the young female protagonist. *Baby Jane* may be most famous for its biddy-on-biddy violence, especially featuring two well-known Hollywood rivals, but lesser plot points involve Jane's aggression toward the younger maid and the young mother and daughter next door, as well as Edwin's repressed horror at Jane's sexual advances. In the closed-off and unnatural world of her home, Jane rules with frightening power and horrific anachronism; in the public space, dominated by order and, more importantly, youth, she is returned to her "proper" social place as a pitiable and, crucially, mockable elder.

After *Baby Jane*, a number of other films employing aging stars in similar roles were released, consolidating the psycho biddy as a popular trope and providing a steady stream of representations of elder figures as inhuman, threatening, and laughable. Davis and Crawford appear in a number of such films. These include *Dead Ringer* (1964), in which Margaret (Davis) kills her widowed identical twin sister, takes over her identity and wealthy lifestyle, and then is sent to prison after evidence arises that Margaret's sister had murdered her late husband in order to be with her younger lover. *Strait-Jacket* (1964) features Crawford as Lucy, a woman who was institutionalized after murdering her husband and his mistress with an ax but has returned home to her young adult daughter, Carol (Diane Baker). A series of ax murders are at first pinned on the unstable Lucy but are eventually revealed to be the work of Carol, who, in a *Psycho*-esque twist, was driven insane by her mother and began committing the ax murders while wearing a wig and clothing reminiscent of her mother. Carol is then institutionalized, and Lucy, in order to take care of her, has herself admitted to the same institution. *Hush . . . Hush, Sweet Charlotte* (1964) again casts Bette Davis as an unstable recluse, Charlotte, and again sets her against a same-generation rival, Miriam, played by Olivia de Havilland. Charlotte and Miriam duke it out via a series of depraved acts, ultimately ending with Charlotte's murder of Miriam and subsequent institutionalization. In *I Saw What You Did* (1965), Crawford does not have the lead villainess role, but she plays the part of a sexually threatening and mentally unstable older woman, Amy, attempting to blackmail a younger neighbor, Steve (John Ireland), into marrying her. Amy ends up murdered by Steve as a result.

The Nanny (1965) features Davis as a nanny beloved by her employers despite their young daughter having drowned while in Nanny's care. Nanny is not beloved, however, by her other young charge, Joey (William Dix), who was blamed for his sister's death despite his insistence that Nanny was responsible. The child is pitted against Nanny in a series of increasingly terrifying events until eventually Nanny is caught attempting to drown Joey as well. She is punished accordingly, presumably with institutionalization. In *Berserk!* (1968), Crawford plays Monica, the owner and ringleader of a circus in which a series of performers have died in elaborate fashion during their acts. Monica is suspected to be behind the deaths, which have resulted in excellent ticket sales and packed shows. When Monica partners up in romance and business with a much younger man, Frank (Ty Hardin), Frank's jealous former lover murders him and attempts to murder Monica as well. The younger rival is struck dead by lightning, and surprisingly, Monica survives to continue on as head of the circus, though with the problematic relationship with the younger man, perhaps more threatening even than her potential status as a serial killer, eliminated.

In all these films, the older woman is continually presented as problematic in her unwillingness to obediently adhere to her prescribed social role. With the exception of *Berserk!*, the films are uniformly resolved by killing off the problematic aging woman or handing her off to an institution where she can be safely kept away from society and presumably warehoused until death.

Other aging actresses starred throughout the decade in a number of films that fit within this subgenre, including Olivia de Havilland (*Lady in a Cage*, 1964), Tallulah Bankhead (*Die! Die! My Darling!*, 1965), Barbara Stanwyck (*The Night Walker*, 1965), Miriam Hopkins (*Savage Intruder*, 1968), and Ruth Gordon (*Rosemary's Baby*, 1968; *What Ever Happened to Aunt Alice?*, 1969). With the exception of Bankhead in *Die! Die! My Darling!* and Gordon in *Rosemary's Baby*, these actresses play victims rather than terrorizers, more akin to Crawford in *Baby Jane* than Davis. In these roles, the woman is often isolated and vulnerable, subject to the whims of dangerous, unstable younger people. If the portrayals of the malevolent psycho biddy represent the horror of the older woman unwilling to accept her changing role in society, these victim roles appear to take on the anxieties of isolation and vulnerability expressed in the aging-women melodramas of the 1950s and, within the new genre context, to literalize their horror.

Linda Williams argues that "body genres," horror in this case, are essential to our conception of the relationship between the audience and representation on screen, in part because of the way those representations elicit physical response in the viewer.[7] She posits that with horror cinema, the scream and the shudder are involuntary physical responses prompted in the viewer, revealing a physiological and emotional connection between the viewer and the bodies and faces on screen. These films constantly present characters marked physically and psychologically by "age" and place them within a generic context that, as Williams argues, encourages intense moments of viewer identification. This is important in considering how representation can affect the way a culture becomes trained to respond to certain "types," in this case, those marked as elder figures. Sally Chivers further highlights this importance in discussing *What Ever Happened to Baby Jane?*

> Because so many members of the audience imagine aging inscribed on their own bodies, a sense of troubling horror emerges from the disjunction between what they had learned to expect from these starlets and the realization of the stars' aging psychical forms as per the frightening logic: if even Hollywood stars age, then so too must we (*memento obsolesci*, as it were). This horror then ironically allows the audience members to distance themselves from the process.[8]

On how this distancing operates, she adds:

> Collectively [these films] try to make aging femininity out to be so frightening that it is almost not to be feared. That is, by exaggerating the characters' self-delusions the films encourage audience mem-

> bers to think that just as they could never be quite as beautiful as the young Crawford, Davis, or Swanson, so too their old age could never be quite so horrifying.[9]

In other words, the performances and characterizations within these films are so over-the-top as to render the "biddies" less than recognizably "real," so removed from the reality of lived life as to be something less than human. The psycho biddy cycle of films renders the aging women at their core as monstrously "othered" objects.

This dehumanization and objectification of the elder figure sets the stage for another generic representation, the comedic trope that we are terming "elder kitsch." This trope presents elder figures as a source of amusement, juxtaposing their obviously aged physical appearance with youthful activities, behavior, and statements. Such comedic presentations have become pervasive in contemporary popular culture, employed to advertise soft drinks, candy bars, and amusement parks, but their origin appears to lie in the mass camp sensibility of youth-oriented Hollywood comedies of the 1960s. At the moment when "old age" was becoming a distinctly different cultural category, this shift was often negotiated through the elder kitsch trope, which we explore further in the following section. The relationship between these comedic representations and the horrific representations of the psycho biddy movie cycle, however, cannot be overstated.

To understand this connection, it is crucial to consider the cross-genre space that the psycho biddy films occupy. These films borrowed actresses and narratives from 1950s melodrama and put them in a horror context, and the resulting combination was easily read as camp. Particularly during this historical moment, so dominated by youth culture and attitudes, when irony and skepticism were directed toward "anyone over thirty," this enjoyment of older stars within a camp context was quite different from the straightforward entertainment, gravitas, or nostalgia such stars were invited to offer through their previous performances. *What Ever Happened to Baby Jane?* can be seen as a meeting point between melodrama, horror, and comedy, a vital moment when the audience was presented with the tragedy and the horror of being "old" in postwar America, but learned to deflect it with laughter.

Although the aging woman held the prominent representation of the psycho biddy during this period, there were a fair number of elder male representations in the horror genre at this time as well, even if they were notably desexualized and, as a result, presented as far less sinister and disturbing. One of the films mentioned above, the Roman Polanski–William Castle collaboration *Rosemary's Baby* (1968), is noteworthy because it was not only a main-

Pajama Party *(1964) features Buster Keaton as the dirty old man Chief Rotten Eagle, here opposite the buxom Helga (Bobbi Shaw).*

stream, fairly pedigreed production, but also because it was egalitarian in its inclusion of threatening elder figures. Sparring off against the ingénue, Rosemary (Mia Farrow), Ruth Gordon and Sidney Blackmer, as Mr. and Mrs. Castevets, are particularly sinister in that they work to present themselves as lovable and harmless elders seeking to take care of Rosemary like a granddaughter. It is gradually revealed, of course, that the Castevetses, along with a cabal of fellow elders, are secretly aligned with the devil. They use their sweet, doting appearance as a cloak for their activities, arranging to have Rosemary drugged, raped by Satan, and forced to birth his spawn.

Elder male actors appeared in a number of more traditionally "low" horror films during this time as well. While aging female stars like Bette Davis, Joan Crawford, and Olivia de Havilland were moving from the respectable realms of the adult film and melodrama in the 1950s into the realm of horror with the psycho biddy cycle of the 1960s, a handful of older male stars were also part of a peculiar generic migration during this period. These stars, including Vincent Price, Boris Karloff, and Peter Lorre, had, during the golden era of the studio system, been mostly associated with their star turns in horror films. In the mid-1960s, however, Price, Karloff, and Lorre became familiar faces to teen audiences through their numerous appearances in campy teen comedies produced by American International Pictures. This was where the connection between the camp horror of aging stars and the camp comedy of aging stars became most explicit.

ELDER EXPLOITATION IN YOUTH FILMS

AIP was formed during the period of upheaval in Hollywood following the Paramount Decree in 1948. Like many other independent outfits, AIP took advantage of newly opened exhibition opportunities to distribute independently produced low-budget films aimed at a teen market. Initially focusing on exploitation fare, like *The Fast and the Furious* (1955) and *Girls in Prison* (1956), AIP worked closely with exhibitors and teenage focus groups, determining what stars, titles, and scenarios were most popular and then planning upcoming productions based on this information.[10] In this fashion, AIP became a reliable B-movie distributor, regularly releasing films exploiting teen interest in juvenile delinquency, hot rod racing, and rock and roll, as well as a number of horror pictures featuring traditional monsters placed into a teen-friendly setting, such as *I Was a Teenage Werewolf* (1957) and *I Was a Teenage Frankenstein* (1957).[11]

In the early 1960s, AIP released a series of horror films based on the work of Edgar Allen Poe, directed by Roger Corman, and starring Vincent Price. Intended to compete with the popular British Hammer studio's horror films of the time, *The House of Usher* (1960) was notably more sober than other AIP horror pictures, such as *Attack of the Giant Leeches* (1959), and used Price's earlier stardom as a marker of legitimacy. Following the success of *House of Usher*, AIP released six more Corman-Price films between 1961 and 1965, including *Tales of Terror* (1962), *The Raven* (1963), and *The Masque of the Red Death* (1964). As part of the same formula, other actors from Price's golden-era cohort, including Peter Lorre, Boris Karloff, Lon Chaney Jr., and Basil Rathbone, were cast in these subsequent films. Although the Poe pictures start off as straight horror films, they gradually become campy and farcical, culminating in the release of a parody of the series, *The Comedy of Terrors* (1963), starring Price, Lorre, Karloff, Rathbone, and Joe E. Brown. Just as female stars who would never have been in horror films in their heydays were presented during this later period as something scary (or at least horrifying), male stars previously associated with being scary were presented as funny. Both cases demonstrated the use of stars' previous fame to add legitimacy to cheap films, but more importantly, the status of these aging stars was undermined, setting them up as something to be laughed at.

This shifting of older actors into roles that acknowledged their previous stardom by making fun of those personae, positioning them as incongruously absurd in a "knowing," contemporary context, was represented in AIP's entry into broad, campy comedy with the successful "Beach Party" films, beginning with *Beach Party* (1963). *Beach Party* features two teen stars of music and television, Frankie Avalon and Annette Funicello, along with parties on the beach, cross-promotional musical performances, and, oddly, a cameo by Vincent Price. The beach party pictures that AIP released frequently over the next several years were notable for their self-aware, consciously campy approach. While they may have begun as an attempt to cash in on the then-popular *Gidget* films (which started in 1959), which focused on a teen girl surfer and her fellow California beach teen friends, the beach party films dropped the father-daughter relationship at the heart of the *Gidget* pictures and the accompanying sentimentality. The beach party films are flip and over-the-top, trading wholesome athletic teens for buxom bikini girls and centering on farcical plots featuring mad scientists, motorcycle gangs, and mermaids.

The biggest difference between the beach party pictures and the *Gidget* films, though, is the wholesale removal of parental presence. The teenagers of the beach party films—which continued with *Muscle Beach Party* (1964) and *Bikini Beach* (1964)—exist in a world devoid of the complications and limitations associated with parents and school, a world of endless summer populated by teenagers in beachwear and teen musical performers like Little Richard, Leslie Gore, and "Little" Stevie Wonder. Into this teen world pop occasional nonteen stars like Paul Lynde or Don Rickles and, like Price, older stars of the teens' grandparents' generation: Lorre, Karloff, and Rathbone make frequent appearances, as do Elsa Lanchester, Dorothy Lamour, Francis X. Bushman, and Buster Keaton. These older figures do not act as parental presences at all, appearing to be fully a part of this teen-centric world of beach parties and shake shacks. Nor are they grandparental; rather, they perform as simplified, one-note versions of their previous star personae, kitsch objects for the amusement of the kids.

The stars are still clearly presented as anachronistic, relics from an older period, but within the campy, comedic context of the beach party films; they are not presented as people whose longevity and ties to another era are to be appreciated. In these instances, it is all about the anachronism and its ridiculous incongruity. Keaton, for example, in films such as *Pajama Party* (1964), *How To Stuff a Wild Bikini* (1965), and *Beach Blanket Bingo* (1965), operates very much in his familiar star character, performing mostly silent slapstick humor and pratfalls, but he is consistently placed opposite bikini-clad young women (most often the actress Bobbi Shaw). This juxtaposition underscores Keaton's visible age and rewrites his performance as a "dirty old man." The

The nefarious elder Minnie (Ruth Gordon) gives the ingénue Rosemary (Mia Farrow) satanic prenatal vitamins in Rosemary's Baby *(1968).*

other earlier stars' performances are similarly rewritten through recontextualization, though Keaton's mostly silent, physically comedic appearances are the closest to what we would now recognize as contemporary elder kitsch, bearing an uncanny resemblance to the many modern advertisements that employ the elder kitsch trope.

Though AIP presented perhaps the most complete collection of these aging-star cameos in youth-oriented pictures, totaling about two dozen films between 1960 and 1966, this trend was not entirely limited to the slapdash AIP youthsploitation pictures. The director Richard Lester, whose work with the comedian Peter Sellers and the Beatles made him hip among baby boomer tastemakers, featured the aged Irish actor Wilfrid Brambell in *A Hard Day's Night* (1964) as Paul McCartney's fictional grandfather, a "clean old man" (as opposed to a "dirty old man") who travels and hangs out with the Beatles, provoking mischief. Lester also cast the older comedians Phil Silvers and Buster Keaton in the musical farce *A Funny Thing Happened on the Way to the Forum* (1966), in which Keaton performs his usual incongruous physical comedy and Silvers sings of the joys of surrounding oneself in advanced age with beautiful young women.

While the focus of this study is on Hollywood film, the elder kitsch trope bloomed simultaneously on television, and there was a close association between the trope and television programming and advertising for decades to come, a relationship that, from the start, reinforced such representations on the cinema screen. On television in the 1960s, the guest-star space, which had been a steady source of employment for older stars throughout the previous decade, began more frequently to reflect a campy context for such appearances. For example, the 1930s sex symbol Mae West made a series of television appearances in the 1960s as "herself," during which the highly sexualized star persona of her younger years was now recontextualized into something laughable and grotesque. And offering a camp aesthetic to a presumably even younger crowd, the television series *Batman* (1966–1968) regularly cast aged guest stars to "ham it up" within its excessive, cartoonish world, including Vincent Price, Francis X. Bushman, Milton Berle, Tallulah Bankhead, Rudy Vallee, Ethel Merman, Edward Everett Horton, Reginald Denny, and Spring Byington. Over the course of the 1960s, through films, television, and advertising, there was a consistent normalization of the trope of using older stars as objects of kitsch in campy products pitched to teen and young adult audiences.

The casting of older stars in roles like those featured in the beach party films and *Batman* demonstrates not only the equalizing effect of camp via a negation of the boundaries erected by generation and stardom, but also the undermining of studio era Hollywood cultural dominance through the irreverent repurposing of discarded stars. Buster Keaton was rewritten as a dirty old man, Tallulah Bankhead as a lascivious old lady, and the age and outmoded personae of a number of other stars became consistent sources of comedy. The aged were repurposed for the amusement of the young.

Yet there was also a flattening effect in these repurposings. Stars like Lorre, Keaton, and Bankhead, performing variations of their previous star personae in these new and later contexts, were oddities to be sure, but these performances were also placed within campy diegetic worlds. When everything—settings, plot contrivances, performances—is amplified and exaggerated to maximize absurdity, things take on a highly artificial quality. Characters cease being representations of people and instead become representations of types, older stars included. In serving the function of "amusingly outmoded star" or "funny old man or lady," these stars began to function as objects, symbols of quaint irrelevancy, their marking of "oldness" serving as shorthand for "funny." The use of older stars in the camp comedic context of the 1960s demonstrated one final way of deflecting anxieties about aging: dehumanizing the aged on screen by transforming them into two-dimensional objects of kitsch to be laughed at.

This tradition continued beyond AIP and the 1960s. *Harold and Maude* (1971) is perhaps the most famous instance of this. We discuss the romantic relationship at the heart of *Harold and Maude* in greater detail in chapter 5, but it is important to examine the film within its youth-centric comedic context as well. In many ways, *Harold and Maude* fits the pattern of the AIP comedies of the 1960s. It is squarely pitched to a youth audience of the period: it features a young protagonist (Harold, played by Bud Cort), original songs by the folk musician Cat Stevens, and strong antiauthority (often antiadult) messages throughout. Within this youth-centric context, Ruth Gordon portrays Maude, an utterly hip and carefree seventy-nine-year-old woman who captures Harold's imagination and romantic interest by being more worldly, fun, and progressive than any of the stuffy adults or square young people that surround him. The majority of Gordon's time on screen is spent comically emphasizing the ways in which Maude behaves like a counterculture youth. She is shown posing in the nude for a bohemian artist friend, stealing and riding a motorcycle, snubbing the authority of police officers and priests, planting trees in acts of guerilla eco-activism, expressing antiwar sentiments, and experimenting with mind-altering substances. All this is surrounded by very broad moments of comedy, most notably Harold's fake suicide performances, as well as the campy characterizations of most other figures in the film, including Harold's snobby mother, military-obsessed uncle, and prearranged air-headed age-appropriate dates.

In the two original trailers for the film, elder kitsch is used as a selling point. In one, a series of scenes from the film are presented over the Cat Stevens song "If You Want to Sing Out, Sing Out." The scenes are almost exclusively of Maude participating in youthful, often rebellious activities. Harold is minimized, and very little sense of plot is given. Clearly, the elder kitsch antics of Maude and the prominent advertisement for Stevens's participation are presented as the major selling points. In a second trailer, much more of the plot is presented, but the focus is still on the outrageousness of Maude's elder kitsch antics, specifically her romantic relationship with Harold. In addition to many of the scenes presented in the first trailer (of Maude dancing, riding a motorcycle, posing nude), there are clips of Maude spouting antiwar and antiestablishment sentiments, as well as a scene of Maude and Harold kissing and groping each other, which is placed prominently in the early portion of the trailer and then shown again at its end. All of this is scored to upbeat marching-band music, emphasizing the film's irreverence. Again, the key selling point of the film appears to be the outrageousness of Maude's youthful behavior and the shock value of the relationship between a young man and a woman of his grandparents' generation.

The most conspicuous image from the second trailer—Maude and

Harold's make-out scene—also happens to be absent in the final cut of the film itself. Though the romantic relationship between the two main characters remains, its physical manifestation is significantly toned down in the film, limited to one scene in which Harold and Maude are shown unclothed in bed, implying a postcoital moment but not explicitly depicting it. This disconnection between the advertisement for the film and its actual content is indicative of the way in which *Harold and Maude* uses the elder kitsch trope to perform a kind of bait and switch. While Maude is sold in the trailers (and presented in the early portions of the film) as a wacky object of elder kitsch, her character is allowed, as the film goes on, to become more than just a joke. She is shown to have multiple and varied talents, and there are glimpses into a personal history appropriate to a woman of her generation, most notably a tattooed number on her forearm, exposed briefly, that suggests she is a Holocaust survivor. In short, the film allows this elder kitsch character to be seen as human. And through the eyes of Harold, who steadily becomes more taken with Maude as the film progresses, she comes to be represented as someone fascinating beyond mere oddity; she is wise and interesting, with valuable talents and thoughts. All camp and kitsch elements are dropped in the film's final sequence, in which it is revealed that Maude has taken control of her own mortality by choosing to commit suicide. Harold initially protests but then chooses to respect her autonomy. The film ends with Harold following Maude's advice as he abandons his death obsession and embraces life, thus validating the wisdom of her years.

ELDER KITSCH AT ITS LIMITS

As we have seen, Hollywood films and television programs by the 1970s had already found success through repurposing older stars in youth-centric situations and within a youth culture increasingly attuned to an irreverent, camp sensibility and its embrace of the detritus of past cultural moments. Two aging stars in the 1970s made something of second (or third) careers for themselves in films that exploited this trope for the youth market: Mae West and George Burns. The latter went on to become the quintessential "funny old man" in a series of family films and television appearances throughout the 1970s and 1980s. Mae West's foray into releasing rock-and-roll albums in the late 1960s and early 1970s, on the other hand, only made sense within the context of culture industries that were clamoring to exploit youth in any way possible.

West also appeared in the notorious counterculture sex comedy *Myra Breckinridge* (1970), playing a has-been former starlet who acts as a mentor to the titular character, played by Raquel Welch. The height of West's elder kitsch moment, however, arrived with her starring role in *Sextette* (1978). In this film, based on a sex farce that West had written for the stage some years earlier, West plays another former movie star, Marlo Manners, who is on her honeymoon at an exclusive hotel with her sixth husband. Marlo and her new husband attempt to consummate their marriage but are perpetually interrupted by a string of men, mostly Marlo's former husbands and suitors, who still wish to have sex with her. The farce continues as Marlo's presence (and sexuality) disrupts a meeting of international political delegates who are staying at the hotel for a conference at which the fate of the world is to be decided. One delegate is so taken with Marlo's sexual allure that he refuses to continue the diplomatic discussions until he has been allowed to have sex with her. The combination of revulsion and derision directed at the notion of the eighty-seven-year-old West still being perceived as an utterly desirable sexual conquest is the centerpiece of the film's comedy and intended shock value. Upon the film's release, the critic Vincent Canby derided it as a "disorienting freak show in which Mae West, now 87 years old, does a frail imitation of the personality that wasn't all that interesting 45 years ago."[12] In an ageist jab expressing displeasure at West's participation in her own elder kitsch exploitation, Canby added, "Granny should have her mouth washed out with soap, along with her teeth."

While West provoked discomfort in audiences by the 1970s, George Burns had more secure success in leveraging the elder kitsch trope in movies such as *Oh, God!* (1977) and *Going in Style* (1979). West's earlier fame as a sexpot limited her elder kitsch value to a single joke, whereas Burns's previous persona lent itself especially well to the new era. The late-career appearances by Burns were very much in line with the hoary, quip-a-minute vaudevillian style he brought to radio, film, and early television. While this style had grown increasingly anachronistic in mainstream comedy, the elder kitsch trope created a niche into which the incongruity of Burns's outmoded style fit perfectly. Additionally, since his longtime performing partner, Gracie Allen, had passed away in 1964, Burns's character had to transition from dry straight-man to dry solo joke-teller. Thereafter, the relaxing restrictions of film and television at the time allowed for his jokes to make frequent "blue" innuendos, further adding to the elder kitsch appeal of his comedic persona.

Burns made something of a respectable comeback in *The Sunshine Boys* (1975), winning an Academy Award for Best Supporting Actor. The film is an adaptation of the Neil Simon play about two senescent former vaudeville comedians, Al and Willy (Burns and Walter Matthau), attempting to reunite on television for one last performance. The majority of the film traffics in senior citizen clichés about cranky old men set in their ways, refusing to acknowledge their own physical limitations, and unwilling to give up grudges of the past. At the climax of the film, Al and Willy perform one of their classic routines on a variety show. The routine, featuring a busty young woman, is laden with dirty-old-man humor. Perhaps because the film is a drama rather than a youth-centric comedy, the characters played by Burns and Matthau are punished for partaking in these antics. Willy suffers a near-fatal heart attack at the height of the performance, and Al comes to the realization that he is a burden on his daughter's family. The film ends with the two retiring together to a nursing home for performers.

Going in Style (1979) takes a more farcical approach. The film features Burns, Art Carney, and Lee Strasberg as three roommates who, growing bored with their retiree lifestyles, decide to rob a bank for the adventure as much as for the money. Ample comedy is made of the slow, hard-of-hearing elders attempting to pull off the heist, but as in *The Sunshine Boys*, there is karmic payback for their disruption of prescribed generational behavior. Willie (Strasberg) suffers first, dying of a heart attack brought on by the stress of the bank heist. Joe (Burns) and Al (Carney) then take the bulk of their bounty to Las Vegas for a wild weekend. After winning big and living it up in Vegas, however, Al passes away. Joe is ultimately arrested for the crime and sent to a penitentiary. In the closing scene of the film, Joe explains that he is content: prison life is not too dissimilar from retired life and is actually an improvement, since there is no need to worry about paying his bills or getting his next meal. It is a bleak note on which to end a film built around the elder kitsch visual of old men robbing a bank and running from the cops.

George Burns's true status as an icon of elder kitsch was secured, however, in the *Oh, God!* films he starred in, beginning in 1977. In *Oh, God!*, Burns plays God as a crusty man in a baseball cap and gym shoes who espouses environmentalism, pacifism, and humanitarianism with wisecracks and sarcasm. He is a deity perfectly aligned with the young, liberal ideals of the Carter era, as well as the shaggy, anything-goes humor of American youth culture of the time, which was epitomized by programming like *The Muppet Show* (which, not coincidentally, featured cameo appearances by Burns). Further underscoring this presentation of God as a 1970s young person's old person is the pairing of Burns with the film's youthful protagonist, the folk singer and environmentalist John Denver, another frequent guest on the *Muppet Show*, who was at the height of his popularity.

God in the film chooses Jerry (Denver), a mild-mannered grocery store manager, to be his prophet, spreading his nondenominational message of general humanitarian spirituality and environmental conservation to an

In Oh, God! Book II *(1980), George Burns plays the eponymous fast-talking, motorcycle-riding deity.*

American people who have lost their way. The problem with American culture, as presented in the film, is that it has fallen victim to the power of capitalism and status quo authority figures. The film depicts, repeatedly, God goading Jerry into undermining conservative figures of authority, such as a bottom-line-obsessed business executive played by William Daniels, a religious blowhard played by Paul Sorvino, and talk-show host Dinah Shore, playing herself. Hope for the world's future, God tells Jerry, lies in the hands of the young. "Young people can't fall from my grace," Burns as God states, "They're my best things."

The film's first sequel, *Oh, God! Book II* (1980), takes this emphasis on young people as the best America has to offer to an extreme, pairing Burns this time with a ten-year-old protagonist played by Louanne Sirota. As in the original film, Burns's God guides his newly chosen prophet to spread his word by undermining figures of authority such as her narcissistic parents, rule-worshipping school administrators, and know-it-all child psychologists. The comedic set piece of the film involves God rescuing his young companion from the grips of clueless authority figures and driving her around on a motorcycle.

The third film in the series *Oh, God! You Devil* (1984), maintains the same

Burns–young protagonist dynamic, this time pairing him with an aspiring musician played by Ted Wass. But it also doubles down on the comedic aspect of aged Burns doing and saying irreverently youthful things by casting him not only as the wisecracking, laid-back God, but also as the wisecracking, devious Satan. In all these films, the humor is centered on the incongruity of the salty words that come out of Burns's mouth and in watching him engage in (or encourage) youthfully rebellious activities. That this idea (and Burns's embodiment of it) was popular enough to inspire two Hollywood sequels speaks to the enduring appeal of the elder kitsch trope.

The comedy of geriatric George Burns acting like a teenager reached its peak of exploitation in *18 Again!* (the last major film that Burns starred in). Cashing in on the body-switch trend popular in comedies of the time, *18 Again!* revolves around a plot in which eighty-one-year-old Jack (Burns) switches bodies with his eighteen-year-old grandson David, played by Charlie Schlatter. While the audience is treated to Burns's characteristic sarcastic wisecracks and the image of Burns as a practiced playboy in a Hugh Hefner–esque silk robe, along with a significantly younger, sexy girlfriend, the majority of the humor is played out conceptually. We do not see Jack himself experience the pleasures of an aged man finding himself in the body of a college freshman again. Instead, we see young David going through the motions, performing an impression of Burns throughout. The lines David speaks are pure Burns, and the physical impersonation is impressively spot-on; however, much of the humor of the film suffers because of this disconnection. There is little novelty in watching a young man run track, score with girls, and party the night away, particularly when the entire selling point of the film is the absurd amusement of watching eighty-one-year-old Burns do so. Elder kitsch needs the visual incongruity of the aging face and body playing against youthful activities and dialogue in order to have full comedic effect.

The drily quipping character that worked so well for Burns was taken up by Estelle Getty's character on the popular 1980s television sitcom *The Golden Girls* (1985–1992), a television series so closely tied to this cinematic trope and time period that it must be mentioned. The series, about four retired female friends sharing a fashionable house together in Florida, was often praised for presenting four women over fifty as strong and interesting protagonists on prime-time television.[13] And yet among these nuanced (by sitcom standards) representations of elder women, the show also includes Estelle Getty as a quintessential elder kitsch type. Although a generation older than the other main characters, Getty's Sophia behaves in a much younger, fearless fashion, and speaks her mind with far less reserve, often resulting in sarcastic, blunt Burns-esque comments that serve as frequent punch lines within scenes. Getty's character on *The Golden Girls* was so popular that the actress, who wore a wig and thick glasses to appear much older than her actual age, played similarly aged, sarcastic characters in film comedies such as *Mannequin* (1987) and *Stop! Or My Mom Will Shoot* (1992). The hit film *Cocoon* (1985, discussed in chapter 6) similarly employed elder kitsch within mainstream, middlebrow entertainment to serve as comedic dressing to bland protagonists. The young hero, Steve Guttenberg, gets the main plotline and romantic interest, but the sideshow antics of Don Ameche, Wilford Brimley, and Hume Cronyn as partying, sexed-up, newly rejuvenated retirees, steal the screen.

More recently, one of Getty's costars from *The Golden Girls*, Betty White, has been popularized as an icon of elder kitsch, making frequent appearances on popular, youth-friendly television programming such as *The Daily Show with Jon Stewart*, *Saturday Night Live*, and *Community*, as well as playing a starring role on the sitcom *Hot in Cleveland* (2010–2015) and the senior citizen prank show *Betty White's Off Their Rockers* (2012–2014). White's star persona in this latest incarnation is notably not that of the shrewd and scheming character she originally became famous for playing on *The Mary Tyler Moore Show* in the 1970s. Instead, it is an elder kitsched-up version of the sweet but dim character she played on *The Golden Girls*, with whom a much younger generation is familiar, whether through original airings or reruns. White's recent elder kitsch roles repeat a pattern originally played out in the first generation of elder kitsch stars in film and television. Just as stars like Buster Keaton, Peter Lorre, and Bette Davis were repurposed for the youth of the fifties or sixties, so too were Mae West, George Burns, and Betty White for the youth of their late-career eras. Elder kitsch has become established as a space in which older stars can perform a version of their previous personae to public delight. Whether this delight is invoked by feelings of nostalgia, laughter-producing incongruity, or some combination of the two, it has become an utterly normalized and ubiquitous trope in our culture.

The trope continued to be a presence in film comedies throughout the 1980s, 1990s, and 2000s, including the notable examples *Grumpy Old Men* (1993) and *Grumpier Old Men* (1995; both discussed in chapter 5). These films rely on the earlier star personae of Jack Lemmon and Walter Matthau and on the pairing that they made popular twenty-five years earlier in *The Odd Couple* (1968), playing their same cantankerous rapport for laughs in the new context of older age.

While the *Grumpy Old Men* films were pitched to a general audience, broad, farcical comedies clearly aimed at youth audiences continued to employ older stars for comedic purpose. The comedian Adam Sandler's massively popular comedies of the 1990s were perhaps the most notable instance of this. Sandler's comedies regularly exploited the trope of the funny elder man or lady partaking in incongruously youthful activities, including the silver-haired *The Price Is Right* host Bob Barker fistfighting with Sandler on a golf course in *Happy Gilmore* (1996), and the recurring "rappin' granny" character played by Ellen Albertini Dow in *The Wedding Singer* (1998). In both these films, the use of elder characters was clearly played for easy humor. The audience was not meant to identify with these elder figures in any fashion. Rather, the audience was positioned to point and laugh at these figures' absurdity. Such representations continued in youth-centric comedies such as *Road Trip* (2000), *Bubble Boy* (2001), *Old School* (2003), and *Wedding Crashers* (2005).

More recently, the comedy-action picture *RED* (2010) and its sequel, *RED 2* (2013), combined this comedic trope with the newer trend of the aging action star. Playing the idea of extremely capable, violent, and devious elders for comedy (the classification "RED" for the former CIA agents in the film is an acronym for "Retired Extremely Dangerous"), the *RED* films feature a large ensemble cast of aging stars, including Helen Mirren, Morgan Freeman, John Malkovich, Bruce Willis, Richard Dreyfus, Ernest Borgnine, and Anthony Hopkins. In the tradition of the AIP comedies, these stars play variations on the earlier star personae that made them famous (Mirren as a dangerous femme fatale, Malkovich as a creepy, sexually ambiguous oddball, and so on), which become a source of incongruous comedy within the context of their senescence. The *RED* films' popularity, along with the recent spate of action pictures that revisit former stars of the genre like Willis, Clint Eastwood, Sylvester Stallone, and Arnold Schwarzenegger (covered in chapter 4), perhaps reflects the wish of the vast baby boomer audience to see itself represented on screen as it always has been, regardless of age. That the *RED* films employ a touch of elder kitsch for laughs, however, demonstrates how accepted and ingrained the trope has become in our culture over the last forty years.

This grotesque comedic representation reaches an odd extreme when young stars begin donning "gray face" in order to perform elder kitsch. One of the more popular advertising mascots on television for the past decade has been Mr. Six, a frenetically dancing old man whose lust for life and hip hop moves lure young people to the Six Flags amusement parks every summer. Mr. Six, like many elder kitsch figures in television advertisements, is actually a young actor in age makeup. This style of role-playing, while less common in cinema, has some precedent. Two recent examples worth considering in depth are Tyler Perry's character Madea and Johnny Knoxville's "Bad Grandpa."

Perry's introduction of his enduring Madea character in the early 2000s

Tyler Perry wears old-age makeup and dresses in drag to play the irrepressible elder kitsch figure Madea in many films, here in Madea's Witness Protection *(2012).*

turned elder kitsch in a decidedly different direction.[14] Starting in 2002 with a series of filmed plays that were released on video, the thirty-three-year-old Perry wrote and directed productions in which he cross-dressed as Madea, a physically large and emotionally unhinged grandmother who—as in many depictions of grandparents with extensive offspring—tries to maintain some level of family unity and pride, although she extols Christian beliefs and orthodox wisdom through often bizarre behavior. After four video releases, Madea made her way to feature films with a supporting role in *Diary of a Mad Black Woman* (2005). As its title made clear for those unfamiliar with Perry's previous productions, his agenda included an examination of African American familial, gender, and class conditions through its plot of Madea endeavoring to help her granddaughter cope with an abusive, philandering husband.

According to many critics, Madea broke the boundaries of previously questionable kitsch by becoming outright ludicrous, as Roger Ebert expressed: "Grandma Madea, who is built along the lines of a linebacker, is a tall, lantern-jawed, smooth-skinned, balloon-breasted gargoyle with a bad wig, who likes to wave a loaded gun and shoot test rounds into the ceiling. This person is not remotely plausible; her dialogue is so offensively vulgar that it's impossible to believe."[15] The character's incongruity, however, was apparently what gave her such an ironic charge for audiences, and Perry was motivated to adapt another play into a film with the wild grandma at its center, *Madea's Family Reunion* (2006). This and nine more Madea movies (to 2015)—covering such otherwise solemn issues as funerals, incarceration, domestic violence, health crises, racism, and Christmas—feature more unlikely scenarios as the pistol-packing matriarch tries to teach her progeny important lessons through her antics.

As with other extreme depictions of elders, the question must be raised about how far the audiences for these films are able to suspend disbelief. Ebert was not alone in his initial shock, though nearly a decade later, Madea has yet to generate any substantial controversy for her treatment of aging, because comedy has allowed her imprudence to not be taken seriously. The past conventions of doting elders passing off platitudes with reverent charm are exploded in Madea, making her continuing efforts to support her children and grandchildren simultaneously familiar and humorous. Rather, the racial context in which these films operate has far more often been the target of critics who feel that Madea and her kin represent African American stereotypes, despite their farcical intentions. And Perry's recurring approach has drawn ire beyond age and race: his "strategy as a dramatist," Wesley Morris writes in his review of *Madea's Big Happy Family* (2011), "is to create excessively wretched and lowly characters, then use tragedy, comeuppance, or the biblical rod that keeps a child spoil-free, to make them behave. It's rarely fair."[16] The divide between the audiences that continue enjoying Madea movies and the critics that find them reprehensible may reveal more about tensions among the monitors of tolerance and taste in America than about the public perceptions of age, race, and class. After all, Hollywood has conditioned the culture to laugh at these delicate dynamics rather than scrutinize them, and that conditioning in itself exposes the extent to which elder kitsch can still be exploited to devalue legitimate concerns for the aging population.

Jackass Presents: Bad Grandpa (2013) exploits elder kitsch perhaps more blatantly than any prior film example. In this hidden-camera comedy, forty-two-year-old shock comedian Johnny Knoxville plays the title character, a

Jackass Presents: Bad Grandpa *(2013) features Johnny Knoxville in old-age makeup as the title character. Here, Billy (Jackson Nicoll) copes with his grandfather's drunken, troublemaking antics.*

foul-mouthed, oversexed, politically incorrect grandfather, in extremely convincing old-age makeup.[17] Using concealed cameras and elaborate special-effects technology, the film captures the reaction of unsuspecting Americans as Grandpa engages in a variety of sexual, violent, scatological, or just plain distasteful activities. While unsuspecting citizens watch, Grandpa celebrates when informed of the death of his "frigid bitch" wife, tosses his dead wife's body from her casket in front of a volunteer church choir, gets drunk and talks loudly about Asian whorehouses at a bingo tournament, shoplifts groceries by shoving them down his pants in front of store workers, hits on women and pulls down his pants at a male strip club, dresses his seven-year-old grandson in women's lingerie and enters him in a child beauty pageant for little girls, and gets his penis caught in a vending machine, among many other incidents.

The pranks that Knoxville chooses to undertake while playing his elder character are interesting for what they reveal about American culture and what kind of behavior we presumably consider "shocking" when associated with the visibly aged. Again and again, Knoxville uses vulgar language, expresses vile opinions, engages in deviant behavior, and reminds all passersby, sometimes quite explicitly, of his active libido and sexual potency. Most of the unsuspecting people Knoxville encounters appear to provide the properly appalled or derisive responses, resulting, presumably, in the film's intended humor. What is perhaps more troubling, however, is how the filmmakers chose to play on the sympathies of these gullible marks. While many of these people laugh at Bad Grandpa's antics or look to others around them for confirmation that what they are seeing is absurd, a surprising number of people take sympathy on this elder figure and attempt to help him out of his predicaments or save him from further embarrassment. *Bad Grandpa* reveals a fascinating picture of a culture's mixed feelings of derision, discomfort, fear, and pity toward the senescent, particularly those who do not adhere to prescribed social roles.

Knoxville and the other actors in on the joke exploit this discomfort and pity, using the sympathy and offers of assistance to prolong the individual comedic vignettes. As with many hidden-camera comedies of recent vintage, the source of humor often transfers from the over-the-top character to the unplanned responses of bystanders. Unlike hidden-camera comedies such as *Borat* (2006) or *Bruno* (2009), however, the bystanders in *Bad Grandpa* do not always become a source of comedy by responding with shocking behavior or by expressing outrageous thoughts; rather, they often behave in ways that are unfailingly decent, attempting to assist an old man despite the continued and escalating revulsion he elicits. The fact that many of these bystanders appear to be lower- or working-class Middle Americans and people of color in Rust Belt and southern towns adds a further level of questionability to this comedic exercise.

Perhaps the final masterstroke of discomfort is the filmmakers' choice to deny the viewer the moment of revelation. In a hidden-camera television series such as the aforementioned *Betty White's Off Their Rockers*, part of the presumed pleasure for the viewer is the "reveal" at the end of the prank, in which the bystander is let in on the joke. Such a revelation theoretically provides a moment of release for the viewers, who have just experienced the comedic discomfort of the prank—once all parties on screen are laughing, a satisfying equilibrium is achieved. In *Bad Grandpa*, the reveals are never witnessed on screen. As a particularly problematic example of elder kitsch, *Bad Grandpa* is unsettling, to say the least.

This history reveals the development of the elder kitsch trope during a period when the isolation of the aging (from the nuclear family, from the community at large) became increasingly normalized in American culture The aging and aged moved further from the center of family life and mainstream society during this time, moving from the family home to rest homes or to retirement communities set apart from external, broader communities. At the same time, there was in Hollywood, and in other media industries to varying extents, movement away from creating products with an all-encompassing mainstream audience in mind, and a move instead toward focusing heavily on the youth market and segmenting the remaining audience into separate niches and demographics. This could be seen in the psycho biddy horror cycle, in the beach party films, in the late careers of stars such as George Burns and Betty White, and in the niche-focused broad comedy of Tyler Perry and Johnny Knoxville.

As aging faces and bodies become less visible in many people's daily lives, and as the aged become separated increasingly as something other, one can easily view the repeated embrace of this trope as a kind of cultural self-medication, temporarily numbing the troubling things that older age had come to represent. Elder kitsch offers a simple and entertaining vision of older age, one unburdened from such fears and featuring older people who are less threateningly "other" and more like the youthful audiences they are employed to entertain. And yet the elder kitsch trope still involves a problematic dehumanization of the aging population. These figures may behave as if old age is no reason to stop acting "young," but the flatness of so many of these roles—presenting older characters as two-dimensional walking gags—emphasizes the sense of otherness, ultimately reaffirming generational separation and difference.

CHAPTER FOUR

The Emergence of the Elder Odyssey

You have no fuckin' idea who I am. I built a billion-dollar business out of nothing. Presidents seek my advice, I've dined with goddamn royalty, and you want to make out like this one trip was supposed to mean something to me. Like it was gonna change me.

EDWARD (JACK NICHOLSON) TO CARTER (MORGAN FREEMAN) IN *THE BUCKET LIST* (2007)

THE POSTWAR REVOLUTIONS THAT GREATLY EXPANDED the availability of automobiles and television sets are crucial factors in the etiology of that strange genre known as the "road movie"—tales of adventure in which one or more characters take a long journey, often to an unknown place, and learn much about themselves along the way. The influence of the automobile on the genre is clear: as more Americans became able to afford and purchase cars, more of them began to travel not only between work and their new homes in the suburbs, but also to recreational destinations that had previously been out of their reach. Trips that had once been long and lonely on buses and trains—or prohibitively expensive on airlines—became attainable in cars, providing a new generation of Americans with a sense of freedom and exploration that they had never known before.

Postwar prosperity further provided the most geographically expansive public works project in the nation's history, the interstate highway system. The need for longer, uninterrupted roads that would allow for travel outside towns and cities was evident by the 1950s, leading President Eisenhower to sign the Federal-Aid Highway Act of 1956, which earmarked over $33 billion to build or refurbish 41,000 miles of limited-access highways over the next thirteen years.[1] By the end of the 1960s, much of the nation was interlaced with high-speed freeways. The most significant aspect of this development was the spirit of exploratory independence that the roads afforded. Americans embraced that spirit as part of a new mythology based on visiting places only read about or seen in photographs, and for older citizens, such visits often included trips to see relatives who had moved away, or to return to places that they had left in their younger years.

The influence of television on the road movie genre was in many ways subtler. As discussed in chapter 2, the expanding allure of television encouraged American consumers to stay at home rather than go out to movies (or anywhere else), thereby sending Hollywood scrambling for means to retain its audience. After all, this new medium provided a primarily live and quite often sweeping view of the country, and even the world. A great deal of television broadcasting in the late 1940s was produced locally in small markets, but by the 1950s more shows were gaining national audiences through the expansion of major networks. Most Americans were soon familiar with the popular culture circulating around shows that aired nationally from coast to coast, giving the populace a form of immediate visual communication unavailable at the movies, one having a more pervasive influence than radio had enjoyed in previous decades. In the process, national television broadcasts showed Americans their country as they had never seen it before, its sights right before their eyes, instilling its newly mobile citizens with a further longing to be connected with other people and places that they could now reach in person.

The road movie can be traced back to the earliest days of cinema, at least to 1904, when Hale's Tours began projecting films inside faux railway cars to simulate the view of looking through a moving train window, thereby immersing the spectator in the travel experience.[2] Throughout the silent era, American movie audiences enjoyed travelogues on larger theater screens, featuring places they had only read about or seen in scant photographs (most newspapers and magazines were not heavily illustrated with photographs until the expansion of photojournalism in the 1930s), and fictional tales set in foreign lands were quite popular, even if they were rarely filmed in the places they were about. Until the rise of national news reporting on television in the 1950s, newsreels remained popular as short subjects before features in movie theaters, again exposing Americans to real events in the country and around the world, and filling them with a curiosity for travel.

In keeping with this expanding vision of travel, which was further fostered by the overseas experiences of returning World War II veterans, many postwar movies followed characters on adventurous journeys. For older characters, however, these journeys were often presented as a culmination of their ambitions, or as an opportunity for fulfillment or redemption before their ultimate journey to death. The tradition can be traced back to works as ancient as Homer's *Odyssey* and medieval tales of men returning from long crusades to enjoy their waning days with families they had left behind. Whereas characters in a romance sought the attainment of true love before living happily ever after, journey narratives were built on reaching a destination with an objective, sometimes returning from that place to where one had started, and at the end reflecting upon what had been gained and learned. Consider the literary antecedents of this genre, dating to the numerous tales of sacrificial journeys in biblical texts and continuing through the common quests of heroes in every culture, which were studied by Joseph Campbell in the postwar years.[3] In something of the reverse of the bildungsroman tradition, in which young people come of age through knowledge gained from new experiences, the elder odyssey focuses more on resolution through rediscovery of what was already known, or on serenity through acceptance of what had been denied.

The appeal of a penultimate quest before dying is understandable within elder narratives, and cinema is the ideal medium to render such stories with captivating images shot on location in diverse surroundings.[4] The elder odyssey is an opportunity for long-delayed enjoyment and escape, perhaps to return to a meaningful place from youth or see an important person after many years (particularly old friends and relatives), and for setting aside the responsibilities of younger life in order to at last indulge in a personally momentous voyage of self-awareness. Such narratives may be necessarily sentimental, but they are not always maudlin. The tales can be comic and tragic, romantic and even arousing, and are always significant for the travelers. At their most dramatic, penultimate quests are completed with just enough time for the protagonist to finish the trip and absorb its significance before dying, usually in a quietly peaceful manner that can cause the audience to pause and reflect, and that can provide some level of reassuring gratification to an uncertain life.

This chapter takes up its primary examples beginning in the 1970s, by which point American cinema had formulated a subgenre of the elder odyssey movie (which in some cases could be called the "geriatric journey"), with three primary agendas to motivate protagonists. The "family trip" became highly visible, in which an elder either joins family members in a departure from the comforts of home or seeks out family members alone in a search for reconnection. Older men especially have been featured in "one last job" stories, in which a retiring professional (or criminal) seeks a final opportunity to win glory, liberation, or enough money to die with. And emerging in recent decades with striking popularity has been the "pursuit plot," in which an aged protagonist (again usually male and often criminal) is chased by the authorities or tries to solve some kind of mystery. There are exceptions and variations to these three approaches, yet all have as their central narrative device the journey that brings an elder from apparent discontent to determination, and almost all of them celebrate the process of traveling or searching as a redemptive experience for their older heroes and heroines.

THE ROAD TO A SUBGENRE OF PENULTIMATE QUESTS

As automobiles began to proliferate in the United States in the 1930s, the road movie genre began in earnest. It was most clearly inaugurated with the first of seven popular movies featuring Bob Hope and Bing Crosby in comic misadventures to foreign lands, *The Road to Singapore* (1940)—even if the primary means of travel in these films was not by car. While Hope and Crosby made road movies until 1962, they did not play elder characters (except in *The Road to Utopia* [1946], in whose frame story they appear as aged men recalling their adventures searching for gold in Alaska). But another 1940 film, *The Grapes of Wrath*, featured elder characters in an archetypal journey of hope against demise. Jane Darwell won an Oscar as the matriarch of an Oklahoma family heading west to escape the devastating Dust Bowl, with nine relatives packed into a jalopy for the trip, and two grandparents dying along the way.

Other movies about elder characters taking fateful trips in their waning years were sparse until the 1970s, and they tended to focus on men inspiring younger characters to free themselves from misfortune, as in the seafaring adventure tale *Down to the Sea in Ships* (1949), which showcases Lionel Barrymore as a ship captain teaching his grandson life lessons during his final voyage. A more popular sea journey starred Spencer Tracy as the title character in Ernest Hemingway's *The Old Man and the Sea* (1958): an aging fisherman fights valiantly to land the catch of a lifetime, showing a boy the unfailing power of the human spirit. And perseverance may have been the only virtue of John Wayne's rogue character Rooster Cogburn in *True Grit* (1969), the story of a crotchety marshal hired by a girl to track down her father's murderer, a mission that takes them hundreds of miles across forbidding territory. Wayne returned as the same character in a 1975 sequel titled *Rooster Cogburn*, joined by Katherine Hepburn (both age sixty-eight) as another character out to avenge her father's murder. The films' celebration of the fading yet dogged Western adventurer—recalling Wayne as the traveling hero of perhaps the greatest Western ever made, *The Searchers* (1956)—was brought forth in Cogburn's closing line from the first film: "Come see a fat old man sometime!"

Indeed, the "old man" on a journey for justice or a quest for completion developed into a much more common trope in films about elders over the later twentieth century, although women slowly became the figures of these late-life excursions as well. The two most popular examples from the 1970s maintained a humorous emphasis, a trend that dramatically changed in the next decade; as usual, comedy offered an easy way for audiences to accept what could otherwise be sappy or doleful subject matter. Such was the case in the promising yet panned *Bunny O'Hare* (1971), in which Bette Davis stars as the title character, a sexagenarian widow whose home is taken by her bank. By chance, she meets a wanted thief played by Ernest Borgnine, and together they take to robbing banks in the Southwest, traveling on a motorcycle and disguised as rebellious hippies. The characters' exploitation of youth counterculture comments on their desperate radicalism as they elude the law in search of a new life, and as Bunny realizes the exploitation she has endured from her greedy children.[5] *Travels with My Aunt* (1972), another story of elder expedition, is told from the perspective of a middle-aged nephew who embarks on a European train adventure with the wily and salacious title character. The seventy-three-year-old George Cukor directed the thirty-eight-year-old Maggie Smith as the long-lived aunt, which allowed for flashback scenes that amplify her colorful tales of younger days as a vibrant courtesan. The trajectory of discovery, though, is essentially dislocated from her to her milquetoast nephew.

The emphasis on male experience remained prominent in these films throughout the decade, while the subgenre itself was still in an embryonic phase. Older actors from Hollywood's heyday found roles in relatively forgettable fare such as *The Cheyenne Social Club* (1970), wherein retiring 1880s cowboy Jimmy Stewart travels from Texas to Wyoming with his good friend Henry Fonda to claim an inheritance that he shortly learns is a whorehouse. Fonda returned to this aging cowboy mode in *The Great Smokey Roadblock* (1977), playing a trucker who makes "one last run" in his rig before an encroaching illness kills him, gaining media attention by hauling prostitutes as cargo, and capitalizing on the popular trucking mythos of the time. The open road was also the lure for the aged hobo played by Jack Albertson in *Pickup on 101* (1972), in which he joins two young hitchhikers on a southwestern journey, only to die along the way, asking in his dying wish to be buried on his old farm. Journeys of deliverance for older characters became increasingly prevalent in American cinema of the time, with the road opening to auspicious, if ambiguous, destinations.

To be fair, most 1970s films featuring aging stars such as Davis and Fonda were given marginal releases and thus gained little exposure, but two stories of older men on penultimate quests rose to a higher level of prestige. Jack Lemmon directed *Kotch* (1971), which features his real-life friend Walter Matthau as an opinionated but kindly retiree living with a son whose wife

Harry and Tonto *(1974) features Art Carney and his tabby cat as the title characters in a cross-country road trip that became a seminal elder odyssey for the era.*

wants the codger out of their house. Rather than face the ignominious fate of being relegated to a retirement community, Kotch sets out by car to go his own way, yet becomes concerned for a pregnant and homeless teenage girl, and finds an unexpected paternal role in helping her deliver and raise her baby. Again, destination is far less important than departure for the elder character, and *Kotch* introduces a theme that became increasingly relevant to movies and American culture over subsequent decades: how younger family members fail to handle the broadening needs of their older relatives.

Harry and Tonto (1974) became a groundbreaking paradigm of an elder's penultimate quest while further exploring the topic of family tension in tending to the needs of an aging parent. The fifty-four-year-old Art Carney plays Harry (age seventy-two), a retired teacher; like Matthau in *Kotch*, he was nearly two decades younger than his character in real life, but the director, Paul Mazursky, found that more age-appropriate Hollywood stars—such as James Cagney (seventy-five), Cary Grant (seventy), and Lawrence Olivier (sixty-seven)—did not want to play someone clearly characterized as over-the-hill.[6] Curiously, an evident ageism, and perhaps pride, prevailed among older actors of the time. Lighter roles for aging actors in the 1970s may have remained appealing, such as those played by Fonda, Stewart, and Wayne, but older actors tended to avoid playing characters that might belittle the vigorous images they had developed in their younger years. At the same time, Carney and Matthau earned some of the best reviews of their careers for these senescent depictions while still in their fifties, and both were nominated for Best Actor Oscars (Carney won).

Mazursky opens the film with numerous shots of authentic aged people on the streets of Manhattan going about their day, signaling that the film will actually explore the lives of older characters rather than employing them as props. Harry emerges as one of these elders, walking his tabby cat Tonto down the street as he quotes Shakespeare's *King Lear* aloud, foregrounding the impending loss of his humble apartment and consequent search to live with one of his three children. After he is evicted from his building, Harry takes up with his eldest son in the suburbs, who has trouble managing his own two grown sons, one of whom, Norman (Joshua Mostel), has taken an oath of silence. Harry soon realizes that he does not fit in with this son's family, and sets off to visit his daughter Shirley (Ellen Burstyn) in Chicago, launching what becomes a classic elder odyssey. As Roger Ebert pointed out, "The road becomes a strange and wonderful place for Harry, mostly because of his own resilient personality."[7] Because he can't take Tonto on an airplane, Harry starts out on a bus, although this choice offers no freedom to walk his cat, so he soon buys a cheap car to continue his journey. Harry's resilience persists as he later picks up a teenage runaway, Ginger (Melanie Mayron), and when they reach Chicago, he is surprised to find Norman already there visiting Shirley.

The film and Carney's performance are distinguished by their acknowledgment of aging stereotypes that are nonetheless understated, such as Harry's slow pace, mild stammer, and bad hearing. He is justifiably angry about being thrown out of his home, yet he is not bitter at the world. He is not disappointed in his son for his family troubles, and he quietly agrees with Shirley that the two of them are too disagreeable for him to live with her. There is some subtle sexual tension between Ginger and Harry, although he certainly knows better than to act on it. In fact, Ginger displaces this tension by convincing Harry to visit Jessie (Geraldine Fitzgerald), a long-lost love now suffering from senility in a nursing home, and in one of the most touching scenes in the film, the aged couple dance together one last time.

Harry next plans to visit his younger son, Eddie (Larry Hagman), in Los Angeles, and Ginger and Norman accompany him to Arizona, where he gives them his car so that they can run off together. As Harry continues west by hitchhiking with Tonto, he meets an unexpected siren, a hooker from Las Vegas, who agrees to drive him to the city of sin and happily services him along the way. After a short time in jail for urinating outside a casino, Harry finally reaches LA and is impressed with Eddie's superficial status until his son confesses that he is broke and desperate. Harry has nothing to offer Eddie other than a little money and a lot of encouragement, and he realizes he needs to live on his own, especially after Tonto suddenly collapses and dies. Then, in a vaguely optimistic ending, Harry meets an older woman who is looking for a roommate and who also happens to love her many cats.

Unlike odysseys in many other stories, Harry's does not return him to the home he once knew, nor does he come "full circle" in the ways of so many long-lived characters, but he does make it from one US coast to the other: the film closes on him at the shore of the Pacific Ocean. He is more akin to Alexander than Odysseus or Lear, having no more of America to conquer. Harry has been through the city and across the country, over snow and sand, and his heirs offer him little security for his future. His one reliable companion, Tonto, has even left him, although he is in no way downtrodden or defeated. In the closing shots, Harry finds a tabby cat on the beach that resembles Tonto, bolstering the continuity between his old life and the new life he will be living in the west. His penultimate quest thus brings him not closure or resolution, but rejuvenation, and he will end his days in a world of sunshine and open spaces much more liberating than the confines of his previous home, a liberation that few other films provide to elder characters outside death itself.

The later 1970s were an idle era for the elder odyssey film, as they were for the elder romance. During the rise of that era's youth-centric blockbusters (*Jaws* [1975], *Star Wars* [1977], *Superman* [1978]), the industry promoted largely lunatic stories about the aged, including *The Sunshine Boys* (1975), *Marathon Man* (1976), and *Oh, God!* (1977), not to mention the exuberant coaching curmudgeon played to Oscar-nominated perfection by Burgess Meredith in the huge boxing franchise that started with *Rocky* (1976).

The next relevant journey film, which appeared in the following decade features a humble immigrant couple traversing America: *Tell Me a Riddle* (1980) focuses on Eva (Lila Kedrova), who survived the aftermath of the Russian Revolution as a teenage activist, when she met her husband David (Melvyn Douglas).[8] Many decades later, they live alone after their children have left home, and David learns that Eva has terminal cancer, although in keeping with paternalistic custom, neither he nor her doctors tell her. As in so many journey narratives, they travel west with hope, first to a daughter in Nebraska and then to a grown granddaughter in San Francisco, yet David knows that their lives are essentially ending as they go. The director, Lee Grant, celebrates Eva's pioneering spirit and feminist ambitions, particularly through her anger at David for selling their house while they are away, and her journey exposes the incredible literal distance she has taken in seeking relief. In contrast to most elder journeys in this mode, however, Eva does not

In The Trip to Bountiful *(1985), Thelma (Rebecca De Mornay) provides some company to Mama Watts (Geraldine Page), who momentarily returns to the forsaken hometown of her younger years.*

reach a comfortable completion, passing away in the end after reflecting on the unfulfilled goals of her energetic youth. A woman of such potential and capacity, in the context of 1980s second-wave feminism which augmented gender revolution, remains unable to find her place in a man's world.

A less sweeping though more confident depiction of a woman's penultimate quest arrived in 1985 with *The Trip to Bountiful*, a drama that debuted as a teleplay in 1953 and ran successfully on Broadway afterward. In the film, another exemplar of the subgenre, Geraldine Page plays Mama Watts, the weathered mother of an underachieving middle-aged son named Ludie (John Heard), who is badgered by his demanding wife, Jessie Mae (Carlin Glynn). The trio have lived together in a tiny Houston apartment for the fifteen years leading up to 1947, and during all that time, Mama has had the dream of returning to her tiny Texas hometown of Bountiful, just to see it one last time before she dies, an ambition that her son refuses to honor. Her dream is not delusional regarding the distance to be traveled—the town is only a few hours away by car—yet she has held on to a vision of her past that she has not accepted as being extinct, even when she tries to get to Bountiful by bus and no dispatcher has heard of the town. Along the way to the closest town that Mama recalls, she meets Thelma (Rebecca De Mornay), a kindly young woman whose love of her husband is starkly different from what Mama felt about her own before he died. As Mama explains, she always loved another man, whom her father forbade her to see, revealing the patriarchal chain that she is now breaking by evading her son's confinement.

Mama has only one friend remaining in Bountiful, so unlike most other elder travelers, she is not seeking any reconnection with family; her longing to simply be in the place of her past, to see and touch the location where she spent most of her life, is made even more immediate when she learns that her friend has just recently died. Page brings to her Oscar-winning performance an array of emotions, especially after Mama's bus brings her within twelve miles of Bountiful and she becomes nearly hysterical when a local sheriff detains her. Ludie and Jessie Mae have managed to get word to the police to apprehend her, but as she points out, she has the freedom to continue as she pleases, a protest that raises germane questions about elder rights beyond her original recognition of the gender oppression that has compromised her life.

The sheriff soon relents, with unexpected understanding, and drives Mama to the handful of abandoned buildings that once constituted Bountiful. She is dismayed at their decaying state, and when she arrives at the empty homestead she had known for so long, her reaction articulates the film's central themes. Mama anticipates but cannot feel the presence of her parents or children, and while her mind may be filled with memories, the material that remains is all but arbitrary. When Ludie at last arrives to take her back to Houston, she points out the same to him: they will soon be gone, leaving behind nothing but the land, which will be filled by people who will come and go knowing nothing of their experience.

This mild epiphany is truly bounteous to Mama, as she soon tells the disagreeable Jessie Mae, for all she wanted was this moment of presence in her past in order to say good-bye before she died. "Having lived for years with her increasingly idealized memories of Bountiful," Vincent Canby observed, "she doesn't hesitate—when her jig is up—to reconcile fantasy with reality."[9] After this reconciliation, the story quietly closes with Mama having achieved a humble and humbling closure to her life, if only for a few minutes at a barren house in an isolated field, a far greater dignity than she can expect in her eventual death.

The increasing popularity of elder odyssey stories in the later 1980s presaged the ubiquity of the trope across genres in the 1990s and thereafter. The nostalgic gangster-comedy cycle of that decade—*Little Miss Marker* (1980), *Dead Men Don't Wear Plaid* (1982), *Johnny Dangerously* (1984), *Wise Guys* (1986)—employed the road trip device in *Things Change* (1988), in which Don Ameche plays an unassuming Italian shoemaker hired by a Chicago mafia gang to take the rap for one of their bosses. In his last few days before going to court, his handler decides to show him a good time in Lake Tahoe, leading to a series of delightful mishaps that the senescent man would have never enjoyed in his regular life. After barely escaping jail and murder, his return to dull older life leaves him with a bemused gratitude for his short escapade.

In the male fantasy *Field of Dreams* (1989), the trip taken by a reclusive author from Boston to Iowa occupies only the second act of the movie, yet still elevates the power of travel conveyed in other films about elder journeys. Terence Mann (James Earl Jones) accompanies the ostensibly irrational protagonist, who thinks that the ghosts of deceased baseball players reside in his cornfield, on a drive across the county in search of a particular old legend who abandoned his efforts to play pro ball so that he could become a doctor. After they discover the player along the road—who is not the aged doctor he should be, but rather his youthful 1920s self seeking to join a team—they reach Iowa and their confrontations with lost ambitions. For Terence, that means passing away into the mystical realm of players that he too wanted to join in his youth, and for the doctor, that means forsaking baseball glory to save the protagonist's daughter from choking, both compromises that the story suggests men must make in their lives even as they hold on to their dreams.

Another 1989 film handled the journey theme in less portentous terms, presenting traveling as a parallel to codependence. *Driving Miss Daisy* (1989) was unusual for depicting so many differences between its characters—class, religion, race, age, gender—that become erased through the years-long process of the somewhat younger Hoke (Morgan Freeman) driving his elder charge Daisy (Jessica Tandy) throughout their Georgia town for a quarter century after World War II. Daisy's initial resistance to Hoke's assistance is not based in mere prejudice but in damaged pride over her declining ability to handle a car, so her recognition of his value comes with humility, and very slowly builds throughout their many travails. With the exception of one trip to Alabama to visit her ninety-year-old brother, Daisy never takes the long journey many elders pursue for resolution, because her path is internal: coming to terms with the fact that she and Hoke have relied on each other for support more than anyone else in their lives.

Less known than the Oscar-winning *Driving Miss Daisy* yet more demonstrative of journey themes for elder characters, *Crossroads* (1986) tells the story of the teenage guitar virtuoso Eugene (Ralph Macchio), who is fascinated by early American blues music. After learning that the aging icon Willie "Blind Dog" Fulton (Joe Seneca) is toiling away in a Harlem hospital, Eugene makes a deal with the nearly-eighty bluesman: he will take him back to his hometown in Mississippi in exchange for a lost song Willie knows. Thus they set out by bus to Memphis, where Eugene is disgruntled to learn that Willie does

Willie "Blind Dog" Fulton (Joe Seneca) does his best to guide the guileless teenager Eugene (Ralph Macchio) on a trip through Mississippi blues country in Crossroads *(1986), trying to exorcize some demons of his own youth along the way.*

not have the money to take them on to their destination, Yazoo City, a problem that the elder tells his protégé is really their opportunity to "hobo" their way down toward the Mississippi Delta, just as former bluesmen always did. Thus, the true exploration of blues culture begins for Eugene. Willie, meanwhile, is secretly preparing to confront a literal demon from his past, whom he met at the titular crossroads in his youth to sell his soul for his musical talent.

Eugene hopes the missing song that Willie knows will be his ticket to contemporary blues fame, yet the youngster is continually cavalier about the wise man's knowledge of life, gained from decades of experience as a black man in the segregated South, and moreover as a musician whose skills were sinfully purchased, not learned and practiced like Eugene's. The plot makes little of the moral repercussions for Willie's Faustian bargain until the end, filling its middle with a distracting subplot for teen heartthrob Macchio in which Eugene acquires and quickly loses a temporary girlfriend. By the time Willie and Eugene finally land in Yazoo City, after foiling lawmen and nefarious locals along the way, Willie has confessed that there is no missing song for him to teach Eugene, and he reveals that his primary objective is to return to the crossroads to seek the return of his soul. Upon reaching the desolate intersection, they encounter the devil in human form, who will reconsider Willie's contract only if Eugene agrees to a guitar duel with another player whose soul he has purchased.

Setting aside the occult aspects of the story, and the inevitable showdown that develops, in which Eugene soundly defeats the devil's disciple, the redemption and deliverance that Willie seeks through reaching his destination accord with other elder journey narratives. Willie has been carrying the guilt of his evil compact his entire adult life, and before he dies, he seeks to be released from its dominion. In the process, he passes on his lifetime of insights to the younger man so that his genuine talents may flourish without the burden of doubt and fear that Willie endured. Even after cheating the devil himself, Willie does not die in the end, but rather continues on the road with Eugene; the duo plan to head north to join the Chicago blues scene. The elder traveler achieves vindication through his alliance with youth, and is presented with rejuvenation in return. In contrast with the context of most elder journeys, family is an insignificant topic here—the script is scant on details about Willie's many ex-wives and Eugene's estranged parents—which allows the film to emphasize how opposing sides of the age (and race) scale find fulfillment in each other. To that end, *Crossroads* is one of the rare teen-elder pairings in American cinema without a family connection.[10]

THE ELDER ODYSSEY IN EXPANSION

The number of elder odyssey films in the 1990s was roughly double the figure from the previous decade, with a further widening of generic applications. The Western epic *Unforgiven* (1992) modified the *Searchers* narrative: Clint Eastwood plays an aging cowboy who comes out of "retirement" from his previously despicable ways to seek a reward and eventually revenge before enjoying a placid upright life in his later years.[11] *The Shawshank Redemption* (1994) concluded its prison escape mystery with a belated journey for its career convict (Morgan Freeman), who had given up hope for release, only to be freed; he finds a former inmate friend, who offers him a complete escape for the rest of his life. In that same year, an unassuming Canadian production sought to capitalize on the journey theme with the penultimate appearance of Jessica Tandy on screen, as the title character of *Camilla* (1994), an octogenarian who absconds with a young woman on an excursion to Toronto, during which she recounts her acclaim as a violinist.[12] And Spike Lee's *Get on the Bus* (1996), a political tribute to the historic Million Man March of 1995 to promote African American unity, was a group road movie featuring black men on a cross-country trip. The men represent a number of racial concerns; a recovering alcoholic sagely played by Ossie Davis hopes the march will absolve him of his regretful detachment from the civil rights protests of his younger days.

Hollywood by this point had recognized the worth of elder journeys, as most abundantly demonstrated by the highest-grossing film of the century, *Titanic* (1997). The story of the famous ship's sinking was built within the memories of a centenarian survivor of the tragedy played by Gloria Stuart (eighty-seven at the time), who is brought to a ship near the crash site to recall her memories of the experience. Her journey back to the sea takes her a considerable distance from her home, yet within the narrative, her primary travel is back through eight decades of accumulated memories and wisdom. Hers is not the personally enjoyable resolution that so many elders achieve in their journeys—although her discarding of a period necklace at the end reveals some level of release from her past—and certainly the story is invested in her onboard teenage love affair and the ship's historical tragedy much more than her aging experience. Because her type of character arc had become relatively common in the 1990s, *Titanic* could simply use her frame story as a device with little narrative effort, a development that indicated the extent to which the elder odyssey was achieving generic status.

That development was evident in other films of the later 1990s as Hollywood exploited the successful formula, especially by showing established actors traveling in familiar parts of the country. *A Family Thing* (1996) cast Robert Duvall as a white southerner who learns late in life that his birth mother was black, and then travels to Chicago to warily engage with the family members he never knew. His actual trip is a short detail of the film, although the "fish out of water" dynamic that runs through many of these stories—in this case, an aging rube has to adjust to the bustling city, and to being a white man in black culture—enlivens the aspect of elder rediscovery that permeates all of these films.

The contrasting tensions in another 1996 film, *My Fellow Americans*, were more comically political. Jack Lemmon and James Garner play former presidents from opposing parties who use just about every conceivable means of transportation to elude hired assassins, lampooning some of the inanities of contemporary government while questioning the capabilities of older leaders, a tactic likely not lost on audiences when the film was released one month after the failed presidential election bid of the seventy-three-year-old senator Bob Dole.

Almost every critic at the time—including Roger Ebert, apologetically—referred to *My Fellow Americans* as "Grumpy Old Presidents," cynically commenting on Hollywood's ambition to exploit the success of *Grumpy Old*

Men (1993) and *Grumpier Old Men* (1995) and to continue abusing the 1990s phenomenon of putting established elder actors in cantankerous roles. But whereas *Grumpier Old Men* had grossed nearly $70 million at the box office the year before, *My Fellow Americans* earned less than a third of that amount, an omen that did not deter yet another teaming of Jack Lemmon and Walter Matthau, in what the studio must have thought was a more reliable moneymaker, a notably tardy sequel to their tale of middle-aged divorce malaise, *The Odd Couple* (1968). The original film (and the television series that followed) thrived within the confines of their small New York City apartment, but *The Odd Couple II* (1998) took the bickering buddies Felix (Lemmon) and Oscar (Matthau) on the road for their children's wedding in California.

The story picks up thirty years from when they first moved in together after failed marriages. The sardonic Oscar lives in Florida and enjoys the company of fellow retirees. Felix, still fastidious and fragile, meets him in Los Angeles to rent a car for a leisurely drive to the wedding, and the duo soon find themselves lost and far off course. This sequel, written by the untiring originator, Neil Simon, attempts to recapture the charm of these codgers by pointing out their differences—Felix is a neat freak with medical needs, Oscar cares little for his appearance or health—yet the setup misses its opportunity for the old friends to learn about each other as new in-laws during their trip. Simon understandably maintained the antagonism between the two, but now their tensions are built more on the inability of elders to accept change than on their contrasting personal styles. Along their unexpectedly extended journey, they accidentally destroy their rental car, become wrongly accused of many crimes, and take a ride with an even older man who dies while he is driving them to the wedding—slapstick events that do little to encourage them to connect with each other. By the time they arrive at the wedding, Felix has fallen in love with yet another woman who is wrong for him, and Oscar is called upon to illogically convince his son that he should go through with his marriage.

The Odd Couple II reveals some of the liabilities within the cultural typing of older men as disagreeable, which was becoming less humorous by the late 1990s, but even more importantly, it provided evidence that audiences were losing interest in elder stereotypes (the film grossed less than $19 million). In looking back at related strategies, Edvins Beitiks explained the tired film's central fault: "'Odd Couple II' follows the same dusty pattern of 'Oh God,' 'Sunshine Boys' and all those Lemmon-Matthau movies that wallow in old men waggling their chins, falling into paint pots and doing the donkey dance with hot mamas."[13] By the end of the 1990s, cloying products like *Odd Couple II* had become anachronistic, and within the frame of the elder odyssey, the characters could not achieve any lasting satisfaction through the completion of their journey, particularly since the film predictably ends with Felix asking Oscar to move in with him again. Similarly manipulative efforts that followed were doomed, such as the "comeback" of Kirk Douglas from a serious stroke to star in *Diamonds* (1999), a family road trip movie with ample father-son bonding that critics panned and audiences ignored.

Three other 1999 films are relevant to the subgenre, although *The Last Great Ride* did not reach for a level of meaningful accomplishment typical of most elder odysseys by that time, if only because it was made as a family movie for kids. The tale of a former chauffeur (Ernest Borgnine), who carries a concealed fortune in his antique car from his supposed gangster days, portends an exciting adventure as he drives two children around their small town and regales them with stories, yet the film is content to conclude with no greater revelation than the anticipated stash of cash. Another Ernest Borgnine vehicle that year, *Shadows of the Past*, which was more in line with the pilgrimage saga of the subgenre, borrowed its concept from a true story made into a more popular film that same year, *The Straight Story*. In *Shadows*, the fictional protagonist travels over a hundred miles on a riding mower to visit his estranged, ailing brother, meeting a local sheriff to whom he reveals his repressed pain.

The Straight Story was based on the adventure of Alvin Straight, who rode his mower over two hundred miles in six weeks during 1994 to visit his brother, who had suffered a stroke. Straight died in 1996 at the age of seventy-six, and soon thereafter the Disney studio bought the rights to his story, to be directed by an unlikely choice, the avant-garde auteur David Lynch. As Alvin, Richard Farnsworth conveys a stoic fortitude rarely seen in elder roles to that time, a learned patience and wisdom that informs his conversations with the many people he meets along his route, plodding forth at a speed slightly faster than walking. Lynch does not use the dawdling pace to imply geriatric fatigue; rather, Alvin overcomes his ambulatory disability and musters the energy to confidently make the trip alone, leaving behind his mentally challenged daughter, who had been his primary caretaker. The tractor and its shabby trailer of supplies carry Alvin to his brother in a caravan celebrating the strength of the supposedly infirm and the social value of a supposed geezer, who in fact has much to offer everyone around him, resulting in one of the most redemptive portraits of an elder character ever filmed.

The story begins with the seventy-three-year-old Alvin being taken to a doctor by his daughter, Rose (Sissy Spacek), after he falls on his kitchen floor. Alvin ignores the doctor's diagnoses and recommendations, refusing all operations and tests, and continuing to smoke cigars. Yet he is not so averse to change when he receives the news that his brother Lyle (Harry Dean Stanton) has barely survived a stroke. In one of his many powerful moments through-

The Straight Story *(1999) is one of the most direct iterations of the classic odyssey fable. Alvin (Richard Farnsworth) treks hundreds of miles on his riding mower to see his estranged brother, meeting many profound figures and overcoming expected obstacles on his road to redemption.*

out the film, Farnsworth quietly conveys the anguish and regret he has felt regarding Lyle, the result of a feud from a decade earlier. Any journey from Alvin's hometown in Iowa to Lyle's home in Wisconsin would be arduous for him, as Rose points out, and his strange idea to make the trip on his riding mower—because he can't drive a car and no buses cover the route—makes her even more worried. Alvin reassures her the evening before his departure, telling her to look up at the stars, a theme of space and scale that permeates the story. He is but one light in the firmament, as Martha Nochimson elaborates: "Alvin's perspective is pure American frontier individualism, oblivious to the collaborative response, composed of the love that dare not reach out and intervene in personal business, in all its pristine nobility, loneliness, and disregard of the obligations of intimacy."[14] The liabilities of this perspective are exactly what have hindered him up to this point, and from what he seeks to be liberated in his quest.

Lynch populates the film with many other elder compatriots for Alvin, starting with a few nagging friends in his hometown, who warn him against his foolhardy expedition, which requires him to buy a new mower (he blasts the old tractor with a shotgun, as if putting a horse out of its misery). Once on his way, Alvin has the first of four encounters on the journey, with a teenage runaway who is five months pregnant. She assumes that her family will never accept her condition, to which Alvin, a widower with seven children, responds with a revealing parable: someone can easily break a stick, but not a stick in a bundle, and family is such a bundle. The next morning, the girl has gone, leaving a bundle of sticks behind in grateful recognition. This explicit message connects with later revelations about his relationship with Rose (her children were tragically taken away) and his rift with Lyle (caused by a combination of anger and alcohol). He also offers an unsubtle message to some young bicyclists at another stop: "The worst part of being old is remembering when you was young."[15]

His third sojourn is the lengthiest. Five weeks into the trip, his tractor breaks down, and he is befriended by a middle-aged man who offers to drive him the rest of the way. Yet Alvin remains steadfast in his stubborn ambition: "I want to finish this one my own way." As Sally Chivers points out, Alvin's ongoing denials of assistance are all but illogical to those who pity him, because "he defies underlying assumptions about what it means to be old."[16] Such assumptions are challenged in Lynch's revision of the traditional war story. Held up for a couple of days while his tractor is being fixed, Alvin goes out with a World War II veteran like himself, and they each ruefully recall their darkest hours—in Alvin's case, he accidentally shot one of his own men. Unlike the vets in so many movies, whose combat confessions cause them to lose their composure and rage at their repression, these two senescent soldiers have expended their frustrations and simply want to be heard, to share their guilt with another man who can relate. Reflecting again on his state of aging, Alvin bemoans that after all these years, he has grown old but the faces of his comrades remain young in his mind, a somber acknowledgment of random survival that denies any heroic bravado or dramatic anguish in his past.

In Alvin's last night before his arrival, he chats with a priest at the edge of a cemetery, implicitly seeking forgiveness for his quarrel with Lyle, adding that his goal is to simply look up at the stars with him as they did when they were kids. He makes his way onward the next day, stopping to have a beer—a gesture that effectively breaks his presumed sobriety even as he takes pride in his willpower. The bartender, another aged man with whom Alvin shares a temporary kinship in their appreciation of his lengthy trek, says with understated jocularity, "You must be thirsty." The moment sets up the greater appreciation that Alvin shares with Lyle when he finally reaches his shack deep in the woods. After Alvin calls out his name, Lyle emerges with the aid of a walker, aching and wizened, and they sit on the porch together. When Lyle sees Alvin's riding mower and asks whether that was how he made his way, he softly wells up in recognition of his brother's dedication and love. The two men look up in silence, anticipating the stars they will at last see together again, and their simple shared presence is utterly stunning, two wounded men hanging on to life and their love for each other. Alvin does not need any further expression of completion for his journey.

Pamela Gravagne sees profound promise in the film, suggesting that Alvin's mission rejects "the narrative of aging as a series of increasingly devastating losses," portraying Alvin instead as "reworking the meaning of his 'losses' and the inevitability of his supposed enfeebled power and agency."[17] *The Straight Story* thus became a new paradigm for the elder odyssey as it entered the next century: its protagonist is enabled by very modest means and emboldened by an unwavering determination to reach his destination for elusive salvation.

After earning an Oscar nomination for his performance at the age of seventy-eight, Farnsworth unexpectedly killed himself in 2000 following many distraught years of living with cancer.[18] The sad contrast between his suicide and his final film role (after sixty years in the business) is exceptional among older actors, many of whom continued to enjoy affirming roles in further journey films, such as Paul Newman (age seventy-five) as a thief out for one last heist in *Where the Money Is* (2000).

Perhaps the longest trip (in distance) ever offered to elder characters was in *Space Cowboys* (2000), in which four aging test pilots who never made it into space are brought out of retirement by NASA to fix a damaged nuclear satellite in orbit. Stories of men just starting retirement or brought back to work after retirement became increasingly common in films of the 2000s, in parallel with the age status of many bankable male stars, further indicating cultural tensions around an aging population not ready to quit working for a living. Almost all these men find their return to work quite adventurous or at least gratifying, and retirement is revealed as a less appealing alternative than previously thought. The attitudes and job experiences of these men, however—usually adventurous by definition—are contrary to those of most of their real-life counterparts. Men generally do no want to remain cogs in corporate machines, and corporations indeed want them to retire so that they can be replaced by younger, cheaper labor.

Because *Space Cowboys* has four character arcs to follow, the story cannot offer a coherent quest for any one protagonist, although the journey is indeed a penultimate endeavor for three of them: a last chance at a singular adventure that will demonstrate the enduring worth of elder expertise, and for the group's leader (Clint Eastwood, who also directed), a chance for redemption from the denunciation of his early career. The film maintains its focus on the intrigue of their undertaking rather than on the characters' fulfillment; the youngest of them (Tommy Lee Jones) sacrifices his life—because he already has terminal cancer—to drive the lethal satellite away from Earth. In an ironic conclusion, his body lands on the moon, having achieved in death a lifelong goal, albeit through a sacrifice that is justified only because he is diseased and dying. Thus, the worth of elder life is suspiciously compromised in what becomes, ultimately, his final journey.

INVESTIGATING AND EVADING

The box-office income of *Space Cowboys* (over $90 million domestic) heralded audiences' healthy enjoyment of elder roles, despite being accustomed to Hollywood's typical casting of much younger actors in such genre films. Aging stars could increasingly be found in action films as the decade continued.[19] While most movies in the journey subgenre in the 2000s did not reach comparable financial success, many achieved surprising recognition—and curiously, continued a theme of self-sacrifice on some level.

Elder action had already found a familiar face in the aging badass role that Charles Bronson made famous in his later years after making *Death Wish* (1974) at the age of fifty-three; he followed its unexpected success with four sequels through 1994. (Clint Eastwood was meanwhile promoting a similarly angry older man with his brute cop Harry Callahan after *Dirty Harry* [1971], although he retired the character before the age of sixty in *The Dead Pool* [1988].) In all five *Death Wish* films, Bronson plays an architect drawn into vigilantism, seeking out and killing urban hoods with violent prejudice as he moves between New York and Los Angeles from film to film. His urban fights are not intentional journeys, nor are his excursions entirely altruistic, yet traces of his aggressive attitude certainly lingered in other roles featuring elder investigators resolving personal crises, as three films in the early 2000s indicate.

In *The Pledge* (2001), Jack Nicholson's detective suspends his retirement by pursuing a murder case, honoring a righteous promise even as it leads him to morally dubious actions in his search for the killer. The search plot was likewise used in *Spy Game* (2001), in which Robert Redford, a CIA officer about to retire, tries to stop the execution of his protégé in China, strategically played by Brad Pitt for youth appeal. While the agent's pursuit rapidly moves forward, the film presents a survey of his past, resulting in travel through time and around the globe as he questions his beliefs in a career filled with massive deceptions.

Yet another investigator has his retirement disrupted in *Blood Work* (2002), directed by and starring Clint Eastwood in an apparent final homage to his

Dirty Harry days: an FBI agent continues his hunt for a serial killer after receiving a heart transplant from one of the victims. His condition thus intimately connects him with the criminal and all but comically renders him weak as he traverses predictable routes of clues to solve the case. These films do not reveal any distinct public interest in aging detective characters so much as they demonstrate that venerable actors, those who handled forceful action roles three decades earlier, could maintain heroic credibility in elder odyssey plots.

Jack Nicholson became perhaps the foremost representative of the elder odyssey subgenre in two more films of the 2000s, both of which achieved iconic status without the macho trappings endemic to action movies. *About Schmidt* (2002) further revises his trademark role as an arrogant rogue and casts him as a modest insurance actuary—starting on his first day of retirement—who is glumly confused at the prospect of living without a profession, having "paid out a lifetime of workdays calculating precisely when a man is likely to die but never letting himself feel the painful astonishment of what it's like to live," as Lisa Schwarzbaum adroitly noted.[20] Warren sadly learns that he was not very valuable to his company: on a return visit to the office, he finds his old files in the garbage. And he is not enthusiastic about the idea of traveling the country in a motorhome with his wife, whom he obligingly loves but finds mildly oppressive and boring. In a pathetic attempt to find new meaning, he "adopts" a Tanzanian child named Ndugu through a charity service, to whom he begins writing rather candid letters about his life, revealing that he is concerned about his daughter's impending marriage to an underachieving salesman.

At the age of sixty-six, Warren's new chapter in life and imminent journey are set in motion when his wife suddenly dies. His daughter, Jeannie (Hope Davis), and her fiancé arrive for the funeral; Warren becomes only more distraught as he tries to convince her to not go through with her wedding. His torment is further elevated after he discovers that his best friend had an affair with his wife many years earlier. Now soured by the deceit of romance, Warren packs up his motorhome and sets off from Omaha to Denver to visit Jeannie in an effort to steer her away from a doomed marriage, although she dissuades him from arriving early, compelling him to take a leisurely pace.

As in other elder odysseys, he explores aspects of his past from which he has grown disconnected (the site of his childhood home, which is now a tire store; his college, where he is a relic). He catches up with his present life when he meets two kindred spirits at a trailer campsite. The vivacious couple sympathize with Warren's difficulties until he makes a fumbling and unrequited play for the woman, leaving him once again alone with his thoughts. Throughout the journey, Warren writes letters to Ndugu, essentially lying about his experiences to this imagined, disembodied spirit, a practice that allows him to indulge in positive illusions about his life. In fact, Warren's air of contentment, belied by abundant evidence to the contrary, exposes the functioning contradictions of his passive existence.

Warren at last arrives in Denver, where he has a series of comically strange meetings with his looming in-laws, events that induce him to further deter Jeannie from the marriage, even as he faces his inability to influence her. (In ostensibly the film's most famous scene, the somewhat corpulent fifty-four-year-old Kathy Bates, playing Jeannie's future mother-in-law, strips naked to join Warren in a hot tub, showing off a sexual confidence that he clearly lacks, and marking one of the rare fully nude scenes for any actor over the age of fifty in any studio movie). Considerable family strife arises, Warren's back goes out after he sleeps on a waterbed, and he subsequently gets high on painkillers, yet the wedding goes off well, and he gives a respectably restrained toast to his daughter and son-in-law at the reception.

On his trip home, Warren stops at a museum and marvels at the courageous journeys that pioneers made going west, prompting him to ponder what he has accomplished in the direction of his life. He woefully relates to Ndugu that his recent trip to Denver was trivial compared to those made by so many before him, and that his only child's life will go on without his presence. With poignant reflection, Warren sighs: "Relatively soon, I will die. Maybe in 20 years, maybe tomorrow. It doesn't matter. Once I am dead and everyone who knew me dies too, it will be as though I never even existed. What difference has my life made to anyone? None that I can think of. None at all."

In the stack of mail waiting in his messy house, he finds a letter written by a nun at Ndugu's orphanage; she explains that Warren's letters have made Ndugu quite happy, and even though he cannot yet write, she has enclosed a picture that he painted for Warren, of a smiling adult and child holding hands. Having returned from his penultimate quest, Warren at last finds a tangible symbol of the meaning he has in life, far beyond those who know him. At the same time, Nicholson's heartbreaking emotional reaction betrays its duality: he has joy in this breakthrough *and* anguish over his distance from those otherwise closest to him, just as his delusions of happiness break down under this realization of his marginal importance. Many elder odyssey films end on similar notes, raising the question of what the protagonist can do next with what is left of life: is there still time enough for rejuvenating change, or has the character reached a saturation of significance and thus must now fade away, as Warren does here?

These questions were rephrased in more selfish terms five years later in *The Bucket List* (2007), the title of which became part of the American ver-

In The Bucket List *(2007), Jack Nicholson and Morgan Freeman play Edward and Carter, whose determination to fulfill some lifelong goals before dying brings them to unlikely places and emotions, as in this moment before skydiving.*

nacular for many older people, signifying goals to achieve before the end of life, before "kicking the bucket."[21] The film was a financial success, perhaps owing to its relatively facile conflicts about the impending deaths of two men pushing seventy: Carter (Morgan Freeman), a lifelong auto mechanic with an intelligence he uses mainly for playing trivia games, and Edward (Jack Nicholson), an arrogant, very wealthy businessman who owns many hospitals. The men find themselves sharing the same room in one of those hospitals when they learn their terminal cancer diagnoses. As they strike up a friendship over a few weeks, Carter reveals his devotion to his wife and family, while Edward has long scorned his four ex-wives and seems to have only his paid assistant for any companionship. One day Carter begins his "bucket list," explaining to Edward that the idea started as a college course project he never finished. He begins the list with "Witness something truly majestic" and "Help a complete stranger for the good," concepts that Edward tells him are too vague. Since they know they have less than a year to live, and Carter suddenly feels that he needs some time for himself, Edward suggests they plan some truly audacious escapades, like skydiving.

The second act of the film thus becomes their carefree journey away from the hospital and their slow demise. They begin with skydiving and racing cars and move on to a worldwide trip conveniently funded by Edward's millions, all the while showing no realistic pain or limitation due to their diseases. "The parade of visual effects–generated scenes in which these two visit wonders of the world," Todd McCarthy argues, "proves as realistic as a Hope-Crosby 'Road' picture and about as profound, if not as funny."[22] The lack of humor and profundity becomes more frustrating as the constant companions share a few short conversations about their lives and beyond—Carter has the faith to believe in God, Edward is resigned to "resist all beliefs"—the one deeper revelation being Edward's alienation from his only child, whom he once saved from an abusive marriage by having her husband sent away.

While the two ridiculously revived men traipse through African savannas and Himalayan mountain passes, they reveal precious little more about themselves or their lives, even during a final stop in Hong Kong, where Carter is almost seduced by a smart prostitute Edward hires. This incredibly long, lighthearted adventure then ends most acrimoniously when Carter brings Edward to visit his estranged daughter, an attempt at reconciliation that Edward furiously rejects. Carter had temporarily separated from his wife in a justified getaway from her, whereas Edward's reunion with his sole family member threatens to burden him with the guilty obligation that Carter briefly rejected.

With their friendship broken, Edward quickly returns to his unsatisfying life as a rich bachelor, and Carter returns to the warmth of his large family until he suddenly collapses again. Edward's cancer has meanwhile gone into remission, and he rushes to find Carter at the hospital, where the two men share a hearty laugh about Edward's favorite coffee, and Carter gives him a letter, asking him to "find the joy in your life." As Carter dies in the operating room, Edward goes to visit his daughter, and we hear nothing of the dialogue that plays out between them, knowing no more of the emotional response the man has for the greatest regret of his life, and barely glimpsing his joy as he meets the granddaughter he never knew he had. Edward then eulogizes Carter at his funeral, appreciating how much life he gave him in just a few months and crossing another line off their tattered bucket list, "Help a complete stranger for the good," although clearly Carter by far helped Edward the most. In the closing scene, Carter narrates as we witness Edward's assistant placing a second can of crematory ashes at the summit of a mountain some time later, joining the men's remains, and their bucket list, in a sadly cold and remote memorial to two men who hardly knew each other.

That lack of knowledge remains within the film itself, which comes up short by failing to convey many of the simple delights that the two elders feel in their fast yet vast excursion, or any legacies the men may have bequeathed before passing away. When the assistant crosses off the list "Witness something truly majestic," this last goal casts into doubt whether either man ever achieved these wishes: in the majestic, desolate resting place that neither man can witness, there is no suggestion that the assistant or anyone else has appreciated what they did. Audiences may well have enjoyed the humorous contrast between Freeman's ascetic style and Nicholson's brash demeanor, yet Carter and Edward remain banal caricatures of elders who—despite great knowledge and experience—have discovered little, and thus have little to impart. Worse yet, they are figments of a Hollywood fantasy in which dying coots can casually cast aside their entrenched resentments and physical maladies to chase some thrills, erasing decades of dissatisfaction in life with a few fleeting moments of frivolity.

Many other elder odyssey films were made in the late 2000s, yet none achieved the recognition of these Jack Nicholson vehicles. *The Thing About My Folks* (2005) detours into the realm of lowbrow comedy as it sentimentalizes the days an aging father and son spend driving an old car. *Little Miss Sunshine* (2006) was more conspicuous, providing an Oscar-winning role for Alan Arkin as a grandfather who joins his son and four other family members on an overwrought road trip, yet his coincidental journey offers little insight into the character before his unexpected death less than halfway through the story.

Joining other aging actors who found success with investigatory roles, Tommy Lee Jones played two characters on personal expeditions at this time, the latter of which, *In the Valley of Elah* (2007), tells the story of a father searching for reasons behind the murder of his son, a journey that is brief compared to his character's quest in *The Three Burials of Melquiades Estrada* (2005). Jones (who also directed) plays Pete, a Texas rancher whose eponymous friend (Julio Cedilo), whom he treated like a son, is shot and then subjected to cruel handling in two local burials. Pete embarks on his own pursuit to find his friend's killer because the racist local police dismiss the deaths of illegal immigrants, although his aim is not revenge but rather to honor his promise to bury Melquiades in his Mexican hometown. After much hunting, Pete abducts the responsible (though accidental) shooter, a young and risibly inept Border Patrol officer, and brutally forces him to exhume the body of Melquiades so that they can take him south for proper reinterment.

As Pete and the battered patrolman travel many miles by horseback with the rotting corpse, they encounter an almost expected series of strange circumstances, including a senescent blind man who gives them succor yet thereafter asks Pete to kill him out of mercy, which Pete is too principled to do. His unrelenting dedication to his commitment is even more evident after he helps the patrolman overcome a lethal snakebite and calmly abandons the romance he had back home. Pete operates on the kind of elemental justice so often seen in Westerns, the man on a mission of honor, and in the elder tradition, he achieves a refined grace by following through on his goal, under his sole direction.

When Pete and the patrolman finally reach the rubble that Melquiades once called home, they make some decorative arrangements before Pete forces the wounded cop to bury his friend, whereupon he releases him. Having reached the end of the road, Pete pauses where he is, alone and absolute, disregarding what he left behind and not yet sure of where he will go: a man who has traveled so far late in life while commemorating the end of life. The journey across borders has verified his paternal affection for a friend who was otherwise disregarded in a culture that relegated him to cheap labor, and whose proper burial liberated—perhaps fated—Pete to reconsider his own direction.

Other elder odyssey films in the late 2000s were less substantive, including two more Morgan Freeman films. At least *10 Items or Less* (2006) gained fleeting attention for Freeman playing an older actor, very much like himself, who meets a feisty grocery cashier while doing research for a role; the two set out on a spontaneous day trip beyond their comfort zones, during which he coaches her for a job interview, resulting in some cute yet strained culture clashes. *Thick as Thieves* (2009), a story about an aging thief (Freeman) "out for one more big score," was so flawed that it went straight to DVD as *The Code*, a ruinous release that could have deterred the industry from investing in further elder-led thrillers, although two films in the following year began a budding trend of elder action films with a wider range of older stars.[23]

Meanwhile, the lack of substance in *Everybody's Fine* (2009) was more emotional than narrative. Robert De Niro plays Frank, who has tended to his empty home since his wife's death in the past year; he invites his four grown children to visit for a weekend, and all of them cancel their plans at the last minute. Despite his pulmonary condition, he sets off on a cross-country trip to visit each of them, in a journey that has every reason to be poignant, reflective, and illuminating. Instead, Frank determines that all four kids have been lying about their lives and were afraid to tell him, and he ultimately has little insight into why his parenting would make his children so reticent. Worse yet, after he learns that one of them tragically died before he could visit, he slides into self-deception, delivering the dreadfully anticipated title of the film as a message to his deceased wife at her gravesite. In contrast to the subtly perceptive *Harry and Tonto*, this graceless story returns to where it began, with more lost than gained. The sheer defiance of understanding by the protagonist, and the suspension of any consequential resolution, after so many previous films featuring satisfying elder odysseys for meaning, confirmed that Hollywood was still struggling at the end of the 2000s to bring coherence and consistency to this otherwise proven and still popular subgenre.

Action elders were revivified in the next decade in two films that deviated considerably from other odysseys. *The Expendables* and *RED* (which appeared

A force to be reckoned with even in her previous roles, Helen Mirren became stylishly lethal in the two RED *films (2010, 2013) as a "retired" sexagenarian spy.*

two months apart in 2010) grossed over $90 million each and were built on stories of over-sixty stars embarking on expeditions: the former features the actor-writer-director Sylvester Stallone (along with roles for fifty-something Bruce Willis, Mickey Rourke, and Dolph Lundgren), and the latter includes Morgan Freeman and Helen Mirren (along with the fifty-something John Malkovich and the headliner, Willis). Both belong to a tradition of gathering diverse action experts for an assignment; Stallone leads a brute band of mercenaries to assassinate a South American dictator, and Willis mobilizes "retired and extremely dangerous" covert spy operatives. *The Expendables* is relevant here primarily because in it Stallone continued to exhibit remarkable physical prowess for a so-called senior citizen at the age of sixty-four, both on screen and behind the camera, as he did in the two sequels, the third of which, *Expendables 3*, carried him to age sixty-eight in 2014.[24]

RED is somewhat more applicable as an example of an elder odyssey: Willis, a retired CIA agent, travels all over the country to assemble information and help from former colleagues as he uncovers a conspiracy. Yet despite the auspicious casting of Helen Mirren as an irrepressible sexagenarian assassin, *RED* and its 2013 sequel largely focus on the same kinds of kinetic thrills seen in the *Expendables* films. The missions are invested with vengeance, frenzy, and fury, but the characters offer scant reflection on their journeys or their lives even as they provide heartening demonstrations of elder authority.

THE ROAD FROM HERE

In the current decade, elder odyssey films are proliferating as a subgenre, though some examples remained little seen, such as the problematic *Montana Amazon* (2011), in which Olympia Dukakis takes her criminal grandchildren on the run. Evasion of the law as a motivation for penultimate quests has stayed common in recent years, providing the plot for thrillers such as *Come Morning* (2012), in which a hunter and his grandson accidentally shoot a man and then set out to hide the body deep in the wilderness, and *The Company You Keep* (2012), a much more visible film directed by the seventy-six-year-old Robert Redford. His age as the director of an action film that traverses the entire country would be astonishing enough, yet Redford is so well preserved that he convincingly portrays a former college activist from the Vietnam War era who has become a middle-aged lawyer with an eleven-year-old daughter. The protagonist makes his way from Albany to the Upper Peninsula of Michigan by way of Chicago as he dodges FBI agents who want him in connection with a bank robbery, and along the way a young reporter unearths secrets from his past. Even though the fugitive is ultimately cleared, his flight is distinctly uninspiring because of his dull detachment from his radical past, quite clearly in contrast with the stance taken by his former lover—played by Julie Christie, quite sprightly at seventy-one—whose youthful anger at government corruption burns remarkably bright.

The fascination with career criminals chasing last hurrahs remains a dominant stimulus for elder odyssey narratives, providing further opportunities to cast older actors in lively roles. While not a journey story per se, *Robot & Frank* (2012) features the title characters—the latter a dementia patient played by Frank Langella—pulling off an improbable heist. That same year, *Stand Up Guys* brought together Al Pacino, Christopher Walken, and Alan Arkin as a trio of aging gangsters who have one last night of mayhem and sexual hijinks while roaming across a generic city. Arkin's character dies of natural causes, and Pacino and Walken go down in a preposterous blaze of glory as they make their way to a mob boss and shoot up his hideout.

Those sorts of grossly undignified fates are avoided in the subsequent elder reunion *Last Vegas* (2013), in which the wealthy Billy (Michael Douglas) invites his childhood friends—played by Kevin Kline, Morgan Freeman, and Robert De Niro—to his Las Vegas wedding, which turns into a party weekend for the men, all about seventy. The process of their arrival is less compelling than their sheer survival of the drinking, carousing, and fornicating that they quickly discover to be the activities of a younger generation. At least and at last, Billy gets some comeuppance when he realizes he should not marry his fiancée—who is nearly forty years younger—and finds a nice lady closer to his age, even though their upcoming wedding seems to be only another excuse to get the crusty cronies back together. For aging male actors in particular, the "buddy reunion" plot will almost certainly remain a staple, as could be seen when Hollywood brought together familiar stars to boost projects such as *Escape Plan*, *The Big Wedding*, and *Grudge Match* (all 2013).

A few other recent elder odyssey stories work quite differently from these aging ensembles, most exceptionally in the case of *All Is Lost* (2013), in which Robert Redford plays an unnamed man adrift at sea on a damaged sailboat with a depleting amount of supplies and time. As the only character in a film with virtually no dialogue, Redford withstands the entire grueling expedition to nowhere in particular until he is saved by unseen rescuers at the end. His lack of background and destination unfortunately vitiates the importance of his endurance.

Nebraska (2013) upholds the more archetypal elder odyssey with its story of the septuagenarian Woody (Bruce Dern), a retired and almost senile mechanic who believes he has won a million dollars in a national magazine sweepstakes. To collect the prize, the wobbly Woody sets out from his home in Montana to the sweepstakes office in Lincoln, Nebraska—on foot. His son David (Will Forte) collects him and tries to convince Woody that the contest is bogus, but after a series of arguments with his cynical brother and malcontent mother, Kate (June Squibb), David relents and agrees to drive Woody to Lincoln himself. A. O. Scott describes Woody well: "He is an inarticulate, alcoholic lump of humanity—too passive to be a monster, too distracted to be charming. . . . He is far from heroic, or even noble, but Woody's stubbornness, and the waves of unacknowledged feeling that emanate from his grizzled, shapeless face and unsteady, bulky frame, make him worth caring about. Not that it's easy for anyone."[25]

Nebraska reverses the trajectory of the earlier *About Schmidt*, also directed by Alexander Payne, since this failed working man, whom his son does not

Nebraska *(2013) features Bruce Dern as Woody, whose son takes him on a bittersweet trip across the state to inevitably discover that he has not won a million-dollar sweepstakes. (Autographed image, author's collection.)*

even know was wounded in the Korean War and who ran his own garage before giving it up because of alcoholism, heads east with more serious delusions than Payne's previous protagonist. Whereas Schmidt wanted happiness for his daughter and some sense of validation for his life's labor, Woody wants the money for initially less sophisticated reasons: to buy a pickup truck and a new air compressor. David takes on the long drive to Lincoln, as he later admits, because he just wanted to spend time with his dad, for whom he clearly has more compassion than his brother and mother. Their trip is rendered in muted black-and-white cinematography and covered with an acoustic score more languorous than the one accompanying the slower *Straight Story*. Woody, who is unimpressed by the terrain, has only complaints when they stop by Mount Rushmore, and gets drunk during their one night in a motel. That incident leaves Woody with a gash in his forehead, and needing to rest, so David makes the decision to stop in Woody's small hometown of Hawthorne, Nebraska, to visit relatives.

Woody's return to the past geography of his life is fraught with unexpired resentments, and the decaying town epitomizes the lonely Middle American lives that produced curmudgeons like him. He has nothing to say to his brother or his family, he laments the loss of his business, and he runs into the phony old friend whom he still blames for stealing his air compressor when he lived there. When Kate shows up by bus to scold her husband and son for their misadventure, she unleashes a further series of contemptible criticisms of their deceased family and friends. She finds herself defending Woody against the suddenly greedy relatives, who do not believe he has *not* won the money, and after just a couple of days of being in town, Woody is eager to leave. In a poignant moment, the family drives out to his abandoned childhood house, where his burning silence expresses the desperation he has always known. Unlike Mama Watts in *The Trip to Bountiful*, Woody has such little connection with the place he once called home that he has no need for closure.

Worn down and questioning his own belief in the prize, Woody tells David that in addition to the truck and compressor, he really wanted the money to leave something for his sons. The moment illustrates the sort of desperate longing that film fathers so often articulate toward the end of their lives, and David resigns himself to transporting Woody to the site of his anticipated fulfillment. They arrive in Lincoln at the nondescript office of the sweepstakes and, after a moment of dull suspense, learn that Woody is not a winner. Woody reacts with compliant disappointment, prompting David to make a further assertive decision as they head back to Montana: he trades in his car for a pickup truck and buys his father a new air compressor. When they again reach Hawthorne, David invites Woody to drive the truck through town, and the father tells his son to hide so he can be seen in momentary triumph by those he is once again leaving behind. These sudden seconds of lucidity reveal, as David Edelstein points out, that Woody's dementia "must be partly willed, the long-for stupor of a man who doesn't want to reckon with a half-lived life."[26] His reckoning here embodies the simple revision of his life that Woody had hoped the entire trip would offer him, a chance to show some pride in himself, to find some salvation in a random redemption of his misspent years.

An even more unconventional journey for family that gained less attention in 2013 was *Redwood Highway*, in which Marie (Shirley Knight) decides to set out on foot from her retirement community to attend her granddaughter's wedding, some eighty miles away on the Oregon coast. In keeping with the Western mythology common to other journey narratives, Marie is clearly an independent and confident spirit, and she is among the most remarkably intrepid elders ever put on screen, managing to carry a backpack, build fires, and sleep in the woods while also overcoming injuries and warding off thieves. (She does not need the comfort of motels or even a riding mower.)

Her longing to reach the wedding on her own two feet is connected with her own lost love from nearly fifty years earlier, and in true odyssey fashion, she meets a number of influential figures along her path, including a kindly shop owner who stirs the romantic potential that Marie has repressed for decades. Undistracted and undeterred, despite being chased by a search operation launched by her well-meaning son, Marie finds her way to the ocean and up the beach to her granddaughter's ceremony, bringing to a climax a voyage that reunites the family and signifies Marie's closure of youthful torments that she had left to linger inside far too long. While not without some clichés—such as Marie's occasional hallucinations—the film is notable for featuring a most capable older woman who overcomes the doubtful assumptions of family and community to stomp out the cancerous distress of her past and find her way to an emancipated present.

More recently, Hollywood banked on a different kind of adventure, this one for a grandmother *with* her granddaughter, in the inconsistent comedy *Tammy* (2014). The title character, played by Melissa McCarthy, leaves her boring burg to get away from a dead-end job and cheating husband, and consents to bring along her impetuous grandma Pearl (Susan Sarandon), because she has money and a car. Pearl, who is escaping from torpor and her daughter's plans to put her in a retirement home, takes this opportunity not only to regale Tammy with tales of her wild younger days but also to embark on a drugging-and-drinking bender with giddy insensitivity.

The story makes some attempt to explain that Tammy felt abandoned by Pearl as a child, and the frisky elder shows off her intact carnality with a man they meet on the road, a lecherous streak that goes back to her attempt to seduce Tammy's father—her own son-in-law—years earlier. This discomfiting attempt at humor, punctuated by Pearl's offensive public meltdown at a lesbian celebration, followed by a mawkish hoax that threatens to kill her off in the end, pushes the boundaries of elder kitsch to the point of indecency, which audiences did not find endearing (perhaps because they also noticed the mere twenty-four-year age difference between the actresses playing characters two generations apart). The duo's journey predictably takes them back where they started, in a compromising conclusion that finds Pearl relieved to be removed to the retirement home. Her travels have granted her little insight, and a tacked-on last trip with Tammy to Niagara Falls merely reveals the film's lack of certainty about the value of Pearl's journey. To paraphrase the World War II slogan made popular before the road movie became a genre, this is a trip that was not necessary.

Other penultimate quests for elders will remain perennial cinematic odysseys as the aged continually attempt to find purpose in their lives before dying or to discover a new direction toward resolution with family, friends, and their pasts.[27] They will achieve lifelong goals or experience climactic triumphs, they will elude pursuit and finish their own pursuits, and they will find unexpected knowledge. In some cases, the destinations themselves will be unexpected, as with the retired brothers-in-law of *Land Ho!* (2014), whose impulsive jaunt across Iceland evokes the whimsy of a college road trip as they recall old times, party with young people, and enjoy the clash of their conflicting personalities. As this book goes to press in 2015, at least four more elder odyssey films are being released: *Don Quixote*, *Grandma*, *A Walk in the Woods*, and *Woman in Gold*. Thus, whether elder odysseys continue as further attempts by Hollywood to capitalize on aging stars (such as *Tammy*) or as modestly ebullient indie productions (like *Land Ho!*), the subgenre will undoubtedly flourish through further permutations as the search for significance continues in American movies and in the population of older citizens who ever long to understand more about themselves. The open road holds such promise.

CHAPTER FIVE

The Repression and Release of Old Romance

Age has some convenience, you find: one can profess love, and feel it, too, without that attendant apprehension which young people have.

GEORGE CRABBE, *THE ROMANCE OF AN ELDERLY POET* (1913)

THAT OLDER PEOPLE LONG FOR LOVE JUST AS THE YOUNG do comes as little surprise, although Hollywood has so infrequently featured elder romance that an objective cultural observer might think its occurrence is rather rare. Until recent decades, fervent love was all but exclusively the domain of young adult characters, most often before marriage; few movies allowed even a sentimental suggestion that amorous affections continued for a couple into their elder years, such as the aging grandparents in the exceptional *Make Way for Tomorrow* (1937).

While heavily discussed studies by Kinsey (1948, 1953) and Masters and Johnson (1966) indicated that older people maintained active sex lives—and later research by Breecher (1984) revealed that over half of those over seventy were engaging in intercourse at least once a week—any depiction of this condition was consistently avoided in American movies of those eras.[1] The film industry and the culture at large were deeply invested in the repression of any notion that the aged—supposedly delicate, revered, and reserved—had any remote experience of carnal, or even romantic, desire. As Masters and Johnson argued in 1985: "In America, sex is generally regarded as something for the young, healthy, and attractive. Thinking of an elderly couple engaging in sexual relations usually provokes discomfort. The idea of sexual partners in a nursing home seems shocking and immoral to most people. Despite these cultural myths, the psychological need for intimacy, excitement, and pleasure does not disappear in old age, and there is nothing in the biology of aging that automatically shuts down sexual function."[2]

Yet this ongoing discomfort with elder intimacy has radicalized the topic for a very long time. The puritanical ethos of American culture imposes a moral innocence on sexual practice among the aging, not entirely unlike the cultural assumption that children are somehow naturally asexual as well (a myth that studies since the early twentieth century have revealed to be a fallacy).[3] The perception of romance among the aged as an unorthodox and ultimately aberrant phenomenon has been reflected in movies that treat these otherwise healthy relationships with apprehension, suspicion, and irony. Fortunately, with the increasing population of senior citizens and the further erosion of regressive moral codes in the culture, Hollywood in recent years has depicted more elder relationships as romantic without the trappings of taboo, and has promoted more aging performers as passionate and even sexy, well past the threshold at which previous standards would have ruled them too old to be so appealing.

Honest depictions of romantic feelings among the aged were faintly evident in movies of the 1980s and became more completely realized in the 1990s. Much earlier in the twentieth century, many films before the Great Depression and the enforcement of the Production Code in the 1930s tended to sensationalize the moral complications of romance between older and younger characters, and themes of transgression have continued in love stories about elders to this day. One of the more melodramatic cases in the silent era was *Through Darkness to Light* (1908), in which a young woman from an upper-class family resists her father's insistence that she marry a wealthy yet much older merchant. The heroine runs away to marry her true love, who is much closer to her age, and through tragic yet redemptive turns, the family is reunited.

Romantic transgressions also led to greater immoral activity, as in *Her Temptation* (1917), the story of a woman hypnotized by a young suitor to murder her aged husband for his money, only to learn that he willed most of his estate to her sister. Such tales were plentiful in the 1910s and early 1920s, such as *The Avalanche* (1915), *Ashes of Embers* (1916), *Arizona* (1918), *In Honor's Web* (1919), *Gay and Devilish* (1922), *Lucretia Lombard* (1923), and at least a half dozen from 1917: *Broadway Jones*, *Money Magic*, *The Natural Law*, *Panthea*, *The Price She Paid*, and *A Soul for Sale*.[4] Many of these stories implicitly ridiculed elders for being both susceptible to the feigned affections of youth and gullible about threats to their wealth, if not undeserving of it. They also castigated greedy young Americans who exploited the aged as an easy way out of making a more decent and hard-working living. At the same time, virtually all the romantic affairs of elders, male or female, were with considerably younger partners. Romance *between* elders was all but unknown, indicating the anxiety of the industry and the culture regarding the concept.

While Hollywood moved toward a more sensitive depiction of troubled souls in the grim 1930s, romance for older characters became more endearing, though still sensually subdued, particularly in films starring one of the most popular actresses of the time, Marie Dressler.[5] Even though she was heavy-set and in her sixties when the decade began, her emotional appeal made her films hugely profitable, especially when Greta Garbo gave Dressler her first speaking performance in *Anna Christie* (1930), in which Dressler played the alcoholic mistress of Garbo's estranged father.

A more notable performance for Dressler in that same year was her Oscar-winning turn in *Min and Bill*; her title character runs a dockside inn that houses not only her (assumed) lover, a slightly younger fisherman named Bill (Wallace Beery), but also her adoptive teenaged daughter. Min's devotion to the orphaned child is the focus of the story, and she goes to arduous lengths to keep the girl's drunken birth mother from taking her away to a life of servitude. In keeping with the financial fantasies of the time, which Hollywood promoted so well, Min sends the girl to finishing school and eventually murders the birth mother to ensure the daughter will marry a wealthy boy, revealing that her maternal impulses are a mightier force than her tempestuous love for Bill. Their relationship is comically lacking in affectionate displays: one famous scene has Min fighting Bill in an exaggerated burst of furious jealousy, demonstrating that Hollywood studios were more at ease with applauding absurdly warped ardor among older couples than anything resembling conventional canoodling.

Dressler won accolades and wider audiences in subsequent years with movies such as *Reducing* (1931) and *Emma* (1932), and then revived many of the romantic sentiments she had previously conveyed with Beery in *Tugboat Annie* (1933). As the redoubtable title character, she again faces a troublesome family situation in a marine setting. Beery is her alcoholic husband, who jeopardizes her tugboat business and nearly kills himself until his unlikely redemption saves the boat and their son's marriage. Despite the husband's inexcusable dipsomania, his wife endures and even admires him. The film paints their habitually abusive relationship as comical and, given their ages, excusable, suggesting that even the dysfunction of this romance is preferable to the alternative of being old and alone.

Dressler died in 1934, so her potential success beyond her mid-sixties will never be known, but no other actresses of her age and size have enjoyed such a celebrated following. At least some part of her legacy can be found in Hollywood's further promotion of older stars in romantic roles, even if they continued to be minor elements in a story, as with the affection that a small-town mayor harbors for a local grandmother in *My Old Kentucky Home* (1938). Other times, elder romances were compromised by the attention paid to younger adults' conflicts, as in *Make Way for Tomorrow*, which was arguably Hollywood's first ardent love story about two people of truly senescent age.

In the prior year, *Dodsworth* (1936) was lauded for its story of a wealthy retired executive grown distraught by the vainly fashionable demands of his wife. Their impending divorce was made justifiable to moral guardians of the time through the wife's flirtations with other men (affairs that were permitted by the puritanical Production Code Administration because they were primarily articulated through innuendo). The unhappy title character, played by Walter Huston, overcomes the regrets of his failed marriage and soon discovers renewed romance with a much younger woman who is clearly more compatible with him, an outcome presumably bestowed by his class standing and gender. The influence of patriarchal privilege persisted in many films about elder romance, providing older men with more opportunities to find love later in life, and often chastising older women for their resistance to accepting destinies as "old maids" or lonely widows.

By the 1940s, elder romance was most often being relegated to two styles—the already-familiar relationships with younger characters and "wistful memories" of earlier days in love—thereby continuing the resistance to explorations of romance between elders themselves. Hollywood dutifully maintained some emphasis on youth for these older characters, averting any demotion of supposedly saintly elders to commonly desirous lovers, and further problematizing the possibility of additional love after the death of spouses. This emphasis allowed studios to cast newer actors alongside established stars, a symbiotic promotion of youth and experience by a business dependent on audience members from a wide range of ages.

Plots based on the nostalgia for younger love often followed a literary tradition by using a framing device: an elder in the present, provoked by an incident, sets up the narrative to recount his or her past in lengthy flashbacks. With the amorous activities of the characters removed to their youthful years, the elder characters could recall and enjoy the memories of romantic desire, which might still run through them, filtered through years of sagacious experience. In their postsexual state, they feel sensual pleasure only through loss, implying that such a state is the inevitable and natural destination of younger love.

In keeping with many of the tropes of melodrama, which came to cinematic fruition during the years of the Great Depression in movies such as *Imitation of Life* (1934) and *Stella Dallas* (1937), the memory plot tended to center on female protagonists, using their pain and supposedly jubilant suffering, often the result of self-sacrifice, to bolster the story. In *Maytime* (1937), a former opera star inspires a young woman with her story of love and loss, and in *Remember the Day* (1941), a schoolteacher recalls her troubled romance before World War I.

The early years of World War II brought forth two further tales of sentimental romance.[6] *Cheers for Miss Bishop* (1941) followed the popular British import *Goodbye, Mr. Chips* (1939), both stories about teachers who devote much of their lives to their pupils rather than themselves, although in the earlier story, the title character was at least able to enjoy a brief marriage before his wife died in childbirth. His devotion to pupils is quite plainly meant to replace his devotion to family, as he realizes in his old age. Yet widowhood was not an option for Miss Bishop (Martha Scott), who spends the film in a pensive pause as she recalls both the boyfriend she lost to her cousin and another love, who was already married, while rather inexplicably dismissing the affections of a third man. As if such self-denials did not meet her quota of feminine sacrifice, she raised the daughter of her cousin—who also died in childbirth—and later raised her niece's daughter as well; her students, of course, further provided her with maternal meaning, which they individually honor when they return around the time of her retirement. The theme of displacement, which is so traditional to elder women's lives, from serenity through romance to validation through caregiving, is especially prominent here, and it continued to permeate the great majority of such stories for another half century.

Another 1941 tale of recollected love was the Merle Oberon vehicle *Lydia*, in which she plays the wealthy title spinster, who has reached her later years without marrying, much to the consternation of her three former boyfriends, who come to visit her; each recalls their roles in four decades of thwarted courtship with her. Despite her early assertion that philanthropic work is more important to her than marriage—and women would soon be expected to join charity and labor causes in World War II—all along she has carried a desire for a fourth man, who abandoned her. At last, in a culmination of her melodramatic anguish, that one true love returns in the end, only to reveal that he does not remember her. She realizes that repression has denied her numerous possibilities for romantic fulfillment.

Remembrance and denial remained the prevailing forces in the few films about elder romance in the decade thereafter. *Mrs. Parkington* (1944), for instance, uses flashbacks to follow a wise and wealthy widow through her youthful ascent to high society via marriage. She eventually—yet temporarily—descends to destitution after the death of her son, only to be reunited with her husband, a story that inspires her great-granddaughter. This uplift could be found after the war years in *Love Nest* (1951), with its mildly progressive story of two characters who fall in love and marry late in life; the man is revealed to have been a womanizing cheat, but he reforms for his new bride. At the same time, Hollywood continued to be captivated by older women's experiences of lost love. In *The Blue Veil* (1951), a widowed nanny diverts a possibility of remarriage into decades of caring for her charges, sustaining the theme of female romantic sacrifice into the postwar years.

THE MAY-DECEMBER ROMANCE AS A GENRE DEVICE

The second dominant plot approach, in which an elder finds love with a much younger partner, is worthy of further exploration. The term "May-December romance" arises from the notion of the younger person being in the springtime of life and the older being in the slowly darkening winter's end of life. This is of course not a phenomenon new to the twentieth century. Pairings of older men with much younger women for the sake of (often aristocratic) procreation had been common for centuries: younger women generally had a higher capacity than older ones to become pregnant and carry children to term, and men well into old age could impregnate younger women. Partly because of this tradition, the social perception of older men loving younger women has been generally more accepted than its inverse, raising relevant debates about the gendering of beauty standards and the privileging perversity of patriarchy.

A famous example from literature is the 1847 novel *Jane Eyre* by Charlotte Brontë. The story of the eponymous teenage governess falling in love with her employer, who is roughly twice her age, became a paradigm of the May-December phenomenon in cinema. The first silent film adaptation of the story was made in 1910, followed by three others before the sound era. Granted, the relatively young age of Jane's beau does not qualify the story for our study, yet its heroine's disastrous longing ends in bitter disappointment, initiating a theme of feminine naiveté and consequential penance that would characterize most subsequent women's romances with older men. Most film versions—of which there had been at least nine by 2011—adhere to the ending of the original Brontë story: Jane is reunited with her beloved after his wife dies and he is seriously wounded, thereby ultimately extending the torment of their initial transgression to both lovers. A price must always be paid for breaking age boundaries.

May-December romances became quite prominent after World War II, coinciding with social trepidations about women's independence and with the growing public visibility of "senior citizens," whose lives were becoming longer than ever before thanks to developments in healthcare.[7] Tensions over shifting dynamics in gender roles were evident in May-December affairs with middle-aged characters as much as with the older aged. In *Mildred Pierce* (1945), the daughter of a successful business owner lures her playboy stepfather away from her mother, inevitably leading to his murder and her imprisonment. A similar fate befalls the lovers in *Sunset Blvd.* (1950), although in this case the aging actress who falls into a psychotic obsession with a younger screenwriter is so heavily engrossed in self-preservation that she "plays" older than she really is. Some softening of the outcomes of these relationships could be seen in *All That Heaven Allows* (1955), in which a well-off widow overcomes the prejudices of her social and familial circles to romance a hunky young outdoorsman; in this case he is only wounded in an accident as a penalty for his deviance.

More extreme May-December romances became typical in the postwar era as well. A perhaps infinite age difference separates the title characters in *The Ghost and Mrs. Muir* (1947), as a young widow falls in love with the spirit of an already dead man and lingers until her old age, waiting to be reunited with him in the afterlife. Over thirty years separate the lovers' ages in *Song of Surrender* (1949), about a woman whose much older husband resents her love for a man closer to her age; she is finally freed by her husband's timely passing.

A similar age chasm exists between the quailing couple in *Limelight* (1952). In arguably the last great film Charlie Chaplin directed, he plays a drunken vaudeville comic who valiantly holds on to his pitiable final years as he inspires a dejected young ballerina to overcome psychological paralysis. After she at last achieves success, he dramatically succumbs to a heart attack from the strain of a performance intended to be his triumphant comeback. The elder once again gives way to death, having steered his adoring darling toward the affections of a young composer so that she could have a brighter future. Perhaps because Chaplin essentially controlled the entire film, he was able to challenge the gendered rite of female martyrdom that the studios continued to so heavily promote, yet he still retained the theme of sacrifice inherent in depictions of parental elders.

The emotional gravity of the May-December tradition, and of elder romance in general, was somewhat eased in the 1950s as studios progressed with a renewed attention to comedies after the country had moved beyond the difficult war years. Romance among older characters took a different turn in 1950 with the release of *Louisa*, which featured the sixty-four-year-old Spring Byington as a widowed grandmother who juggles *two* suitors, one dubious but doting, the other prosperous but pompous, and both unusually close to her age. This lighthearted comedy inaugurated other elder love stories, including two 1954 films indicative of Hollywood's slowly growing comfort with older stars playing romantic leads: *Sabrina* cast Humphrey Bogart (age fifty-five) in a charming competition with his younger brother over an even younger woman, and *Three Coins in the Fountain* featured Clifton Webb (sixty-five) as a supercilious author who becomes engaged to an adoring secretary at least thirty years his junior. Perhaps the apex of absurd elder romance arrived at the end of the decade with *The Remarkable Mr. Pennypacker* (1959), in which Webb plays a bigamist who maintains two families, leading to anticipated comic mayhem that is eventually resolved because one of his two wives has long since passed away.

The studios' exploitation of elder romance in the 1950s was symptomatic of their expansion into other generic conventions, particularly in an effort to combat the threat of television taking away Hollywood's theatrical audience. Thus, film noir thrills were combined with female melodrama in *Autumn Leaves* (1956), about a lonely spinster marrying a much younger man, who happens to be a dangerous schizophrenic traumatized by his venal first wife's ongoing affair with his father. Such psychodrama became more prevalent in films of the time. It marked the relationship in *Middle of the Night* (1959), which focuses on a widowed businessman who falls into tormented love with a boldly sexual woman over thirty years younger, forcing both to come to long-winded terms about their mutual lack of contentment with life. Hollywood then refashioned the 1950s Broadway musical *Fanny* in 1961 (which originated as a French film trilogy in the 1930s) by replacing its singing with a surfeit of flamboyant acting, yet retained its story: a teenage girl becomes pregnant by her boyfriend and then marries a man at least three times her age in order to cover up her illicit condition. The narrative varieties of the May-December romance by this point had been cultivated by an abundance of malleable scenarios suitable for any genre.

As 1960s cinema became more radical in style and themes, Hollywood slowly evolved toward more unorthodox romantic roles for elder characters, moving beyond the May-December dyad. *A Majority of One* (1961) was a downright odd mélange of postwar concerns about older romance, cross-cultural unity, and racial tensions. An aging Jewish American woman and an older Japanese diplomat (played by the white Alec Guinness) fall in love despite their tragic losses from the war and the lingering bigotry of those around them. Racial tensions were also at a high pitch in *Guess Who's Coming to Dinner* (1967), in which a white liberal couple in their sixties have their views tested by their daughter when she introduces her black fiancé to them. And testing perhaps the most revolutionary "old age" taboo of the decade, *Never Too Late* (1965) daringly joked about the complications of a woman over fifty—with a husband over sixty—becoming unexpectedly pregnant.[8] Since the question of abortion was too controversial to consider at the time, which

One of the most unusual love stories in American cinema, Harold and Maude *(1971) follows the title characters, played by Bud Cort and Ruth Gordon, into a sincere romance that flouts their extreme age difference and celebrates their lively eccentricities.*

thereby made the couple's very late parenthood inevitable, the story mined its humor from the tacit sexual capability that the elders' situation reveals, as well as from the efforts of their daughter to become pregnant, resulting in a child and grandchild who would be the same age. Remaining a comedy, however, the film closes before the reality of either baby disrupts its cloying levity.

In advancing the most exhilarating representation of elder romance to date, the 1971 feature *Harold and Maude* became a landmark in cinema history, featuring what is likely the most extreme age difference of any May-December romance. The title characters, played respectively by Bud Cort and Ruth Gordon, are a disenchanted twenty-year-old with an overbearing mother and a penchant for fake suicides, and a free-spirited and energetic seventy-nine-year-old woman who befriends him at a fortuitous funeral and soon comes to love him. Maude later takes Harold to her home, an old train car stuffed with an incredible array of unusual artwork, musical instruments, and vivacious décor, and we recognize the clear contrast between these two souls: Harold lives in an enormous house that is dreary and uninviting, whereas Maude fills her home with objects of creativity and celebration, and even then has a bigger presence than the place itself.

As previously discussed, the film develops the burgeoning romantic and sexual tension between Harold and Maude without elaborate pronouncements explaining why they are attracted to each other, and minimizes their physical exchanges to avoid exaggerating the generational violation posed by their passion. (The consummation of their relationship, while suggested from some scenes, is never shown.) Harold may indeed have virginal *and* Oedipal angst, as various counselors tell him, but his unusual affections are sincere, and not driven by his adolescent rebellion against the conformity expected from his mother. Maude, on the other hand, routinely and candidly commits minor crimes such as stealing cars and replanting public trees, creating a pattern of increasing acceptance for her proud deviance that further allays any worry about her union with such a young man. Their reciprocal alliance of idiosyncrasies transcends their age difference.

Harold's discovery that Maude is a Holocaust survivor, while quick and unspoken, expresses volumes about the delighting in life that Maude promotes: she is happy, determined, and assured. Furthermore, her intense appreciation of life after a time of such terror further explains her final and very shocking decision, which is to kill herself on her eightieth birthday, *that same night*. She has already intimated to Harold that eighty is the right time to go, for she does not want to face the ravages that may arise in the years thereafter. He pleads with her to not die, reminding her that he loves her, to which she replies, "Go and love some more." Maude's death becomes a sacrifice for the younger character, and since she is so much older and has lived a generally fulfilling life, we are given the message that not only has Harold learned how to live and love from her, but also because of Maude, his life will now really begin.

The 1970s were otherwise a fallow decade for elder romance, despite producing other important films about older characters in other genres. *A Walk in the Spring Rain* (1970) was curious for featuring a woman in her late fifties who rather openly falls for the charms of a new neighbor her age, despite her stable marriage, and *Ash Wednesday* (1973) offered a provocative plot in which a woman of her forties gets plastic surgery to look younger for a husband in his sixties, but neither film was remarkable. More progressive for the time was the depiction of a grandmother cohabitating with an elder boyfriend in *Black Girl* (1972), since their unmarried state is noted, although both roles were secondary to the main plot.

CALMLY INCREASING HONESTY

Just as the elder odyssey did not come to fruition until the 1970s, romance between elder characters began in earnest only in the 1980s. In fact, many people may think of the first great elder romance as *On Golden Pond* (1981) because it gained such wide recognition, but the fact that the few elder romances of the preceding eight decades had gone essentially unappreciated reveals how little American audiences previously noticed the storyline. Further, the fact that an independent company shot the film on location a world away from Hollywood, with two legendary actors over the age of seventy who had each received their first Oscar nominations over forty years earlier, suggests some of the particular differences between the film and existing customs.

To be sure, *On Golden Pond* did not exactly open the floodgates for elder love stories, because the only other notable example in the 1980s actually appeared the year before with *Atlantic City*, in which an aging gangster temporarily renews his criminal confidence through a fling with a younger woman before returning to his beleaguered yet caring relationship with an aging moll. Later, the most successful network sitcom to ever focus on older characters, *The Golden Girls*, debuted in 1985 and maintained high ratings until it ended in 1992.[9] The show revolved around four women over fifty, and while not exclusively focused on their love lives, the episodes often depicted them dating elder men and lampooning their sexual pursuits, both past and present. The image of sensual older women and men in popular culture was well received then—perhaps because the concept was readily applied to comedy—yet it found only sporadic reception in Hollywood productions over the next two decades.

On Golden Pond nonetheless remains a milestone as a romance fully invested in two elder characters who, while distracted by mild family tensions, spend the film often doting on each other. There is essentially no extraneous action or drama to derail the story into the typical genre trappings that had become endemic to Hollywood movies by the 1980s, particularly after the rise of multimillion-dollar blockbusters in the late 1970s. In fact, *Raiders of the Lost Ark* was the highest-grossing movie of 1981, with $212 million at the domestic box office, and still *On Golden Pond* managed to place second, with

Oscar winners Henry Fonda and Katharine Hepburn play Norman and Ethel in On Golden Pond *(1981), an endearing portrait of an aging couple still learning how to navigate familial tensions.*

slightly over half that amount, although roughly 40 percent of its gross was not earned until its extended run after the Oscars in March 1982.[10] This impressive profitability unfortunately did not spur the studios to roll out further films in similar molds.

The story begins and ends at the New England cottage of Ethel (Katharine Hepburn) and Norman (Henry Fonda), who return to the dulcet sounds of loons singing on the titular lake and the smell of musty covered furniture in their summer home. Their comfortable banter betrays the somewhat failing memory of Norman, who was a respected college professor and remains too proud to admit any geriatric limitations on his part, even though he does express a certain preoccupation with the topic of dying now that he is about to turn eighty.

The cinematography and ambient music convey a languor that Fonda and Hepburn accentuate in their performances, although the movie contains a handful of disquietingly tense moments, the first of which arrives when Norman goes for a walk and loses his way. Increasingly frightened by his disorientation, he soon panics, panting and sweating as he stumbles through the woods trying to find his way back to the main road. After he returns to the cottage, Norman waits for a guest to leave before mentioning the incident to

Ethel, who reassures him with one of the most indelible expressions of love between two older people in cinema history: "Listen to me, mister. You're my knight in shining armor. Don't you forget it. You're going to get back on that horse, and I'm going to be right behind you, holding on tight. And away we're going to go, go, go!"

On Golden Pond does not further develop the theme of Norman's encroaching senility, a topic that was perhaps still too sensitive for audiences adjusting to the stoic survivors of World War II entering their twilight years. The sublimation of this concern into a more familiar conflict about Norman's repressed love for his daughter was also indicative of Hollywood's ongoing denial of realistic depictions of senility, which were derailed by so many of the horrific stereotypes promoted in films of the past generation and would continue to be elided in American movies until the next decade.

Audiences would have also been sensitive to the casting of Fonda's daughter, Jane, as his character's daughter, Chelsea. Jane Fonda had spent much of the 1970s as an imposing left-wing political rebel, but as Chelsea she portrays an emotionally feeble self-absorbed woman seeking some level of approbation from her distant father, especially regarding her new relationship with a dentist. Chelsea's recurring appeals to her mother are cumbersome: after she laments her dad's conspicuous criticisms of her, she asks the couple to look after her paramour's arrogant teenage son while she goes to Europe for a month with his father.

While Chelsea is away, Norman surprisingly bonds with the boy during fishing trips, and the older man's typically cantankerous moods slowly diminish into a genial demeanor. In an unsettling event, they have a boating accident that results in them saving each other from drowning, and more famously, Ethel comes to save them, diving into the water in a stunt that the seventy-four-year-old Katherine Hepburn actually performed. Surviving this ordeal seals a connection between Norman and his stand-in grandson, especially when they catch a legendary large trout at the same time that Chelsea returns to once again regale her mother with frustrations over her father. Ethel's own frustrations boil over when she slaps Chelsea, in her most emotional outburst of the story, revealing her limits of tolerance as she defends Norman: "That old son of a bitch happens to be my husband." The gulf between these elders and their offspring appears abysmal compared to the differences between the two of them, since Ethel's cheery optimism harmoniously boosts Norman's defeatist tendencies. Chelsea is the villain here, disrupting the functional facade of stability that her parents have cultivated so well, and again transcribing a generational turmoil for post–World War II children of prewar parents.

In a film of such relatively subtle spectacle, the denouement arrives with little aplomb, after Chelsea endeavors to do a backflip off a dock in symbolic demonstration of the capability that her father doubts she has She is at least passably successful, and Norman is at least passably enthused, yet she is most relieved by her father's startling support of her happiness, which comes to him with less effort than it seems either one of them expected. This effect, and its recurrence in many other films about the aged, reveals the older character's deeper humanity, buried under years of deferred joy, suggesting that senescence has dissolved his inability to simply be a pleasant person, or more profoundly in this case, a caring father.

Norman and Ethel's idyll is at last restored after the younger people leave, yet they are given strikingly little time to enjoy it. Soon enough they are packing up the cottage to conclude another season and return to even less entertaining lives, which Hollywood would continue to generally ignore. But before that closure, Norman collapses while lifting a heavy box. The story threatens to end with his death, and Ethel compassionately cries with that fear, until he just as suddenly seems to recover after taking a nitroglycerin pill. Their lives and their love endure, without any further calamity to make their fragile hold on each other more pronounced. They are content to simply watch the loons once again float away on the lake, to stand in the golden glow of the sun on the water, to embrace as the credits roll and provide American culture with a reassuring image of stalwart elders relying only on each other's love rather than on the devotion of their children or community.

This kind of ideological illusion was also at work under the dominant American political influence of the 1980s, Ronald Reagan, who was two weeks shy of seventy when he became president in 1981. After rising to fame as a movie star of adequate talent in the 1940s, Reagan gained political traction in the 1970s as the governor of California, recuperating conservative ideals that had been tainted under the disgraced Nixon presidency earlier that decade. Married to the former Hollywood actress Nancy Davis, Reagan brought a "tall, dark, and handsome" aura to his office that was lacking in predecessors going back to Kennedy. His difference from the young Kennedy, who fathered toddlers in the White House, was part of Reagan's appeal; he was America's first divorced president, with grown children from his previous marriage who had made him a grandfather. He often spoke of his reliance on Nancy and recalled his modest midwestern youth, qualities that aligned him with average citizens.

Reagan dealt with his status as the country's oldest president through a determined effort to emphasize his capability and deny any infirmity, especially after being shot in an assassination attempt during his third month in office. This strategy was most strikingly displayed in his 1984 reelection campaign, when, during his second televised debate with Walter Mondale, he delivered one of the most famous lines of his two terms: "I will not make age an issue of this campaign. I am not going to exploit, for political purposes, my opponent's youth and inexperience." More infamously, yet far less often cited, Reagan lost track of his thoughts in his closing statement (about writing a letter for a time capsule) and, after rambling for some time, had to be cut off by the moderator. Few commentators mentioned Reagan's observable wavering, and most proclaimed him the superior speaker for his strong support of military defense, upholding the mythology of the fighting cowboy, which he strenuously espoused.

At the same time, during the eight years that Reagan was the nation's most famous senior citizen, the population age sixty-five and older increased by 16 percent, and those relegated to nursing homes increased by 35 percent.[11] Not only were the geriatric living longer, but their numbers and needs were also expanding accordingly. Meanwhile, speculation about Reagan's encroaching senility was considered impolite in media circles of the time, and concerns about the encroaching crisis in elder healthcare were largely dodged by the healthy, happy Reagan screen.

The stifling of concerns about aging during the Reagan years may also explain Hollywood's parallel detachment from the older population during this decade. After *On Golden Pond*, the industry produced a mere handful of films focused on elder characters during the rest of the Reagan era, of which the only box-office hit was *Cocoon* (1985), a tale that addressed some aspects of romance but was more occupied with its mystical promises of immortality (discussed in the following chapter).

One film at the end of the decade, *An Unremarkable Life* (1989), was radical for its depiction of a budding interracial romance between an elder woman and a mechanic, yet went virtually unseen despite employing the *Golden Pond* approach of casting two Oscar winners, Patricia Neal and Shelley Winters, as sisters. Two more Oscar laureates, Paul Newman and Joanne Woodward, were cast the following year as the title characters of the British coproduction *Mr. and Mrs. Bridge*, a story that maintained the romantic restraint of most elder depictions to that time.

The narrative proceeds through episodes in the lives of the Bridges and their grown children in Kansas City during the 1930s and 1940s. He is a well-off lawyer who shows few effects from the onset of the Great Depression, and she is a content housewife whose most pressing concern is a mentally unstable friend. In fact, this unruffled upper-middle-class contentment becomes the ultimate theme of the story, for Mr. Bridge will not allow his legal practice or his children's needs to interfere with his industriously poised home life. Taking on little conviction of her own, Mrs. Bridge can only muster occasional pleas for her husband to show her more affection, since his cold composure does not yield to passion. Theirs is supposedly a secure love that lasts over four decades, although the corollary of such longevity is apparent tedium, for the characters and the audience. Despite its star casting and its pedigree as a Merchant-Ivory production, the film garnered little more attention than *An Unremarkable Life*, which was particularly revealing after the box-office and Oscar success of *Driving Miss Daisy* the year before. Audiences were still more comfortable with that film's idea of an isolated grandam with no possibility of romance, and given the lack of significant action between the Bridge characters, watching Jessica Tandy being driven around the Jim Crow South was a far grander adventure.

Four years later, Paul Newman showcased his astonishing physical preservation in *Nobody's Fool* (1994) at the age of sixty-nine. His character, Sully, is a grizzled small-town construction worker resisting retirement; his younger looks and spirit betray the crusty manner he upholds. The film is only marginally a romance, focusing more on Sully's relationships with quirky locals, including Jessica Tandy as his landlady (in her last role). Sully has spent years filtering the abuse he suffered from his father into a decided detachment from his son, leaving him with some regrets now that he sees his son's own son carrying the family line of discontent.

This bitter background explains his ongoing lack of enduring connection with any women, including his boss's young wife, with whom he maintains a playful flirtation until she offers him two tickets to Hawai'i to escape from their shared frigid doldrums. Sully is excited, but only momentarily, explaining to her that his newfound obligation to his son and grandson are more important than his selfish erotic fantasies. His decision to stay is not a denial of any potential love he has been seeking, since she is not offering him such love, only the forgoing of an indulgent opportunity. This late in life, the codger recognizes his ability to atone for at least some of the patriarchal damage done to him, which he has inflicted on his own son, and which he can perhaps avoid in his grandson, a recognition of the value of paternal love over romantic mythology.

The most visible 1990s film addressing elder romance, *Grumpy Old Men* (1993), was not only a sleeper hit at the box office, but also the first to believably honor a level of explicit lustful desire between older characters. Once again the industry banked on recognizable older stars, in this case Jack Lemmon and Walter Matthau, yet shifted the accent from romantic bonding to sexual competition between the title characters. The title alone projected the attitude of the story, in which John (Lemmon) and Max (Matthau) are widowed neighbors in a small Minnesota town, typical lonely curmudgeons who comically bicker with each other and hold onto a mutual resentment going back over fifty years. Because that resentment originated in their youth, and

By deliberately exploiting the kitschy aspects of elder representation, Grumpy Old Men *(1993) mines convincing comedy from a romantic competition between John (Jack Lemmon) and Max (Walter Matthau).*

their squabbling takes on such childish tones, Lemmon and Matthau embody the "make cute" phenomenon that Hollywood had begun to practice with elder characters by the 1990s.

The film mines their perpetual feud for easy laughs, such as when one leaves a dead fish in the other's car, and they exchange acerbic but harmless bons mots to ridicule each other. This approach, along with a narrative built around the duo's apparent competition over ice fishing, may have been enough to sustain a popular comedy in a previous generation, but by introducing a romantic triangle leading to an unusually randy result for one of them, *Grumpy Old Men* gave the emergent rom-com genre of the 1980s an earnest maturity.

The tip of the triangle is Ariel (Ann-Margret), a slightly younger widow who moves in across the street from John and Max just as winter is setting in. She is curvy, beautiful, and adventurous enough to ride a snowmobile on the local streets at night, and the two pensioners immediately take to spying on her. Their immediate longings for Ariel are not expressed in crassly salacious terms; rather, their interests seem to be rooted in boosting their egos by winning her affection and, consequently, triumphing in a contest with each other. Another salty fisherman friend, Chuck (Ossie Davis), interrupts one of their many arguments by pointing out that they are not particularly attractive to women: John and Max are both breaking seventy, with the former balding and the latter heavily wrinkled.

Both men are also preoccupied with nagging each other so much that this new object of attention threatens their choleric balance, as demonstrated when Chuck pays a visit to Ariel one evening and thereafter tells the rivals that he did not have sex with her, but enjoyed a more spiritual awakening. This kind of vague mysticism would be mawkish if the men had not already expressed sexual desire for Ariel, and Chuck's report of their time together makes John and Max only more licentious in their pursuit of her, bordering on a perversity that had for so long marked older male desire as particularly profane and appalling.

The level of sexual innuendo and discomfort rises when Max invites Ariel into his ice-fishing shack—which is surrounded by many others on a lake, including John's—and they happen to catch a legendarily enormous fish (echoes of *On Golden Pond*). While struggling to bring in the fish, they create a sweet ruckus of physical labor that the men around them interpret as robust intercourse, yet the climax that Max reaches in landing the fish shrivels when Ariel releases it back to the water. Ariel's lack of understanding for this truly meaningful achievement for Max, and the feigned recognition he gets from his peers for his prowess with her rather than as a fisherman, are tacit indicators of their incompatibility as a couple.

John, on the other hand, is more appealing to Ariel for reasons not explicitly explained. He is arguably better looking and less irritable, and he intrigues Ariel by telling her how he and Max became enemies: fighting over another woman much earlier in life. Taking the advice of his ninety-four-year-old father (played by Burgess Meredith), John makes his move by planting a deep kiss on Ariel, and she is receptive. Then, in a scene both tactful and sensual, Ariel invites John to bed, an act that is lightened by his declaration of the exact last date he had sex, some fifteen years earlier, and her intimation that they do not need to worry about venereal disease. These jokes infuse the potentially taboo moment with a cuteness meant to specifically contrast with the concerns of younger sexual couples, although John's dancing around the house alone the next morning is in keeping with a traditional male sense of sexual success. After *Harold and Maude*, where the lovemaking was nebulous and only one partner is older, this was Hollywood's most candid depiction of sexual congress between older characters up to that time.

The situation energizes Max to amplify his contempt for John, and John tries to give up Ariel to Max, because he married the woman whom Max loved many years earlier. This sacrificial solution makes no one happy, and under the ongoing pressure, John succumbs to a heart attack. As in so many movies about elder characters, a life-threatening event brings the story to closure; while John is in the hospital, Max helps him out of his debt to the IRS, and Ariel forgives him for forsaking her. The threat of John's death lingers for a few moments when people begin to gather at a church for what appears to be a funeral, although this is revealed to be his wedding to Ariel, complete with his father giving her away. With this ending, John has once again stolen love away from Max, which is justified by his compatibility with Ariel and, perhaps more so, by his nobility and durability.

The pairing of Lemmon and Matthau was the most profitable casting coup for elder actors in the 1990s. Two years after the original, the duo starred in the sequel *Grumpier Old Men* (1995) and then modified these characters only slightly for *Out to Sea* (1997). To expand the story and add appeal, *Grumpier Old Men* added the legendary Italian siren Sophia Loren to the cast, who, at the age of sixty-one, was certainly a fair rival in beauty to fifty-six-year-old Ann-Margret, returning as John's wife. With most of the bickering between them eased, John and Max do not fight each other as much as they fight Loren's character, Maria, who plans to open a restaurant on the location of Chuck's former bait shop. Another major change is that Max slowly falls in love with Maria, allowing this sequel in many ways to work as a romantic corrective to the first film. (And in an exasperating subplot, John's nonagenarian father pursues Maria's mother, only to dismissively pass away in the process.)

The courting that then proceeds between Max and Maria is in many ways more endearing than John and Ariel's, which was addled by the men's competition. Without the need to one-up a rival, Max is better able to be himself with Maria, whom he does not even want to like at first because she poses a threat to his fishing locale. When he tries to convince her of the thrill in digging for worms, his boyish enthusiasm and delicacy compel her to begin making love to him in the wet grass where they are searching. Maria shelters a secret though, which is that she has had five failed marriages, bringing a temporary pause to her further pursuit of Max and further adding vulnerability to her character, in contrast with Ariel's steadfast confidence. Thus, both this film and its original give their elder female protagonists a depth well beyond that seen in the remorseful widows of so many previous films, and moreover show them revivified by the possibilities of love, with the end of life nowhere in sight.

In equipoise with the first film, *Grumpier Old Men* concludes with Max and Maria getting married—but only after he and John reel in that elusive, coveted fish out on the lake and then return it to the water themselves. Having together achieved such an important goal, which puts a final finish on their lifelong contest of superiority, both men are now able to move on with fulfilling relationships, both romantic and fraternal, quite late in life.

Out to Sea was the last pairing of Lemmon and Matthau in a romantic comedy (they did reprise their *Odd Couple* roles in a road movie the following year). Perhaps its weak gross, which was less than half that of *Grumpier Old Men*, was the biggest factor in ending the industry's interest in these two actors as amorous leads, but the fact that they were well into their seventies certainly could have been a contributing deterrent. Herb (Lemmon) and Charlie (Matthau) are not as grumpy as they had been, even though they still uphold other elder markers: Charlie is an incorrigible gambler, and Herb continues to mourn his wife in order to keep himself insulated from the world.

When Charlie signs them up as dance hosts on a cruise ship as a ploy to evade his bookie, Herb is especially skeptical: the implied prostitution of their roles—providing single older ladies with partners at parties—sexually commodifies these older men, a most unusual scenario among elder roles. Then as they each fall in love with older women on the cruise, they become embroiled in deeper deceptions. The resulting farce of secrets and lies leads everyone, including the ladies, to reveal their scams and settle on their true loves. The level of treachery in the story justifies the lack of weddings at its ending, and for six years this tentative romantic attainment was the last popular depiction of elder love by Hollywood.

The 1990s showed measured progress in depictions of older romance outside dominant hits, and very slowly introduced audiences to the reality of elders with queer identities as well as sex lives after sixty. One of the first American features about an elder homosexual, *An Empty Bed* (1990), was quite low-budget and essentially limited to the festival circuit, offering a modestly pioneering depiction of a gay man reflecting on his lost loves, as the title suggests. John Wylie plays the lonely protagonist, who reflects on a lifetime of repression that yielded only sporadic happiness, although there is little critique of his sexual identity; even his one failed relationship with a woman is recalled with sensitivity to his cultural context, which was far from tolerant of anyone who was not heterosexual.

When a studio star vehicle first broached the topic, it was so greatly compromised that it rendered the queer aspect all but irrelevant. In *Prelude to a Kiss* (1992), the newlywed Alec Baldwin is more than perplexed when a paranormal force turns his new bride, Meg Ryan, into a geriatric man, played by the relatively unknown actor Sydney Walker. The resulting gender switch leads to mild schizophrenia as the new husband wrestles with whether he can still love his wife as a humble geezer who is purportedly still his wife—and in a male body failing from lung cancer, no less. Via this transformation, the film thus displaces the evident tensions surrounding homosexual desire onto the loss of longevity, a tactic that troublingly expands morbidity *and* homophobia in an "allegory of relationships in the AIDS era, when a lover can start deteriorating overnight," as Peter Travers saw it.[12] The story does deliver on its title, though, as Baldwin and Walker kiss in a convoluted scheme to resurrect the real Ryan, resulting in the usual preservation of youth over age, as well as the restoration of heteronormative love.

A handful of other 1990s films depicted lesser levels of elder romance, including *Don Juan DeMarco* (1994), in which Marlon Brando, playing a retiring psychologist, is inspired to restore some sensuality to his marriage by treating the title character, who has passionate delusions of being the world's greatest lover. *The Last Good Time*, which appeared that same year, features a septuagenarian widower who becomes a temporary deliverance for, and lover of, a beautiful but abused woman in her twenties. Despite performances by esteemed elder actors such as Armin Mueller-Stahl, Maureen Stapleton, and Lionel Stander, this May-December romance was anachronistic by the 1990s, holding little appeal for contemporary audiences and leaving critics such as Mick LaSalle embittered; he called the film "a rueful meditation on what an old guy has to go through to get some action these days."[13] *The Annihilation of Fish* (1999), by the acclaimed director Charles Burnett, was even more promising, with a cast featuring James Earl Jones and Lynn Redgrave in an interracial late-life romance replete with senescent hallucinations. Despite great reviews and a few minor festival awards, the film has remained commercially unavailable.

These diverse films of the 1990s signposted the direction that elder romance was taking at the end of the century: the films were becoming more mature in their handling of characters as everyday people with developed histories. Characters began to reveal both amorous and erotic longings, and encountered intriguing circumstances in their pursuits of love, within plots that depicted this richness without lapsing into absurd circumstances. In the next decade and thereafter, elder romance in movies continued to grow from these developments, and most significantly, it became increasingly plentiful.

ELDER ROMANCE MATURES

The first decade of the new millennium started at roughly the same pace as its predecessor in its rate of releasing elder romances, averaging one notable example each year until 2008, when *The Curious Case of Benjamin Button* radically altered the concept of romantic love across ages. On the way to that feat, elder romances continued to diversify in their topics and genres, and in one unpredictably imperfect case, even nationality. The veteran actor Robert Duvall wrote and directed *Assassination Tango* (2002) and played its aging Brooklyn hit man, who takes an assignment to kill a corrupt figure in

In The Notebook *(2004), Gena Rowlands plays Allie, whose husband valiantly attempts to bring back her lost memories of their passionate youthful affair. (Autographed image, author's collection.)*

Buenos Aires, leaving behind a somewhat younger yet doting girlfriend and her daughter. When his assignment is extended, he takes to frequenting local tango halls, quickly falling under the spell of a beautiful young dancer. His seduction by the dancer and the dance is all on the surface though, for Duvall and his new love do not consummate their relationship, and few consequences arise from his problematic profession, leaving the story fleetingly fragmentary.

Greater fulfillment for elder characters was found two years later in *The Notebook* (2004), the wildly popular adaptation of a Nicholas Sparks novel that alternates between young and old characters, past and present. The story structure thus allows for dual ensembles with screen time proportionate to the audiences the studio sought; thus, the respected elder actors are prominent in the film, but the younger actors fill up most of the duration (and further occupied virtually all of the film's advertising). Such a formula for broad age appeal to audiences was by this point so often successful—in romances and across other genres such as comedies (*Anger Management*, 2003) and dramas (*Runaway Jury*, 2003)—that movie studios by the mid-2000s were making few films about older characters without younger stars to support their stories and their marketing campaigns. Speaking specifically about the performances in *The Notebook* yet more broadly about its intended exploitations, Stephen Holden commented, "In Hollywood, old age is even more difficult to depict with real honesty than young love."[14]

The Notebook uses a classic framing device in which Duke (James Garner), a venerable man in a nursing home, narrates the film as he reads the story in a notebook to another resident at the home, Allie (Gena Rowlands). The film is quite deliberate in not initially revealing that the story he is telling is their own, about how they fell in love in South Carolina before World War II and ran afoul of her overbearing mother because his working-class status was unacceptable to her. Allie went on to college and became a nurse, through which she met a rich war hero; Duke—Noah in her past—returned to their hometown and set about restoring a big old house, taking on a war widow as a lover. These conflicting fates threaten to leave them separated forever until Allie's mother relents with her own confession of regretfully denied romance, and the two true loves reunite. Their relationship may be rife with portents of postwar class revision and failed southern proprieties, yet in the present, Allie's evaporated memories of the entire experience, as well as her inability to recognize Duke as this same single beloved of her life, question the durability of love, which the story ultimately seeks to uphold.

Such questioning elevates the couple's romance to metaphysical heights, for Allie's currently irreversible dementia, while occasionally making her frustrated and confused, nonetheless does not destroy the core connection she has with the Noah of her past and the Duke of her present. Allie still attends to her appearance and dress with diligence, and can still play the piano as she did as a young woman. Despite her failing facial recognition, she enjoys Duke's presence and affections, which culminate in him cooking her a nice dinner. During this brief scene, Allie's memories of Duke as Noah, and of their enduring love, which overcame her mother's perfidious efforts to keep them apart, return for just a few evanescent minutes. Duke is elated, not so much with validation for his efforts to help her remember, but rather with the emotional realization that she still shares his love.

As the framing narrative closes, the notebook is revealed to have been Allie's preemptive means of preserving their love story should she ever forget, and so that Noah could read it to her in her old age. While the notebook is thus a rather practical device for the preservation of Allie's memory, it also represents a modest means of restraining any sense of excessive grandeur that might creep into their story. Their children have since grown up well and borne them grandchildren, and their accomplishments in the culture at large were not extravagant. As Duke says at the start of the story: "I am a common man. . . . But in one respect, I've succeeded as gloriously as anyone who ever lived. I've loved another with all my heart and soul, and for me that has always been enough." For him, the most special aspect of their love is that it has indeed been *enough*, his success being the sheer survival of his love for Allie through the challenges of class, distance, disease, and time. In the end, their love even cheats death, since they pass away together in bed with the notebook—and so much of its meaning—between them.

The romantic gravity of *The Notebook* remained relatively rare in elder romances, even with its apparent appeal. The far more typical approach to the subject in the mid-2000s was the ensemble comedy, captured quite effectively in *Something's Gotta Give* (2003) with the star casting of Jack Nicholson and Diane Keaton, who have more screen time than their youthful counterparts, Amanda Peet and Keanu Reeves. Nicholson had won a Best Actor Oscar for the lighthearted *As Good as It Gets* (1997) at the edge of sixty, wherein he played a neurotic, sexist author who gauchely woos a single mother over twenty years younger, so this slightly similar vehicle must have seemed a safe bet for the studio. Here his perennial bachelor, Harry, has a record of dating much younger women, including Marin (Peet), who happens to be the daughter of accomplished single author Erica (Keaton). The story moves quickly to align the elder characters after Harry suffers some heart trouble in anticipation of his commingling with Marin, and the erectile enhancement medication he took only enhances his embarrassment.[15] Erica shows greater concern for Harry than her daughter does, and he shows genuine appreciation of Erica, especially after he sees her completely naked for a second, a scene that Keaton pulls off with kinetic panache.[16] Erica entertains the obvious interest that Harry's young doctor (Reeves) shows toward her, yet she remains cautiously captivated by the older man's passions.

After Harry and Erica first make love, both of them cry in strikingly sincere relief: for her, that she is "not closed up for business" after years alone, and for him, that their fine frolic has been safe for his (literal and symbolic) heart.[17] The tentative couple nonetheless has a falling-out, and even though during that time Erica does fall for the young doctor, Harry goes on an implausible trek to expiate his past dalliances with former lovers, bringing closure to his classically masculine evasions of affection. When Harry and Erica are finally reunited in the end, this closure becomes an antidote to the May-December trajectories of their other relationships (particularly in contrast with *As Good as It Gets*, where the couple's final union is all but provisional), offering a corrective to so many similar elder romances proposed by Hollywood in past decades. What finally "gives" in this film is the perception that two older people can be happy together in a sensual, sensitive romance.[18]

Other ensemble depictions respecting the comedy of romance thrived at mid-decade, and there was an increasing presence of elder characters in supporting roles. Such was the case in *Must Love Dogs* (2005), which focuses on the awkward dating life of a divorcée who dreadfully discovers that her widowed septuagenarian father took to Internet dating before her. *Rumor Has It . . .* (2005) attempts to update the classic May-December farce *The Graduate* (1967), with a middle-aged man moving his way down the generational scale from a woman to her granddaughter over the course of three decades. Despite some corny aspects, *Boynton Beach Club* (2005) offers some surprisingly straightforward commentary on a community of older singles who revive their love lives and sexual appetites after the loss of their spouses. *Feast of Love* (2007) pushes the ensemble envelope further: its tales of characters revolve around a coffee shop frequented by the protagonist, a sage Morgan Freeman, who reluctantly advises his younger associates on their romantic entanglements while still learning from his own mistakes. And the writer-director of *Something's Gotta Give*, Nancy Meyers, tried to revive its success in 2009 with *It's Complicated*, in which sixty-year-old Meryl Streep gets caught in a splendid bind between her rejuvenated ex-husband and an appealing new man.

As films like these continued the gradual expansion of elder romance in American cinema, they were met with little attention at the box office, which left in doubt whether this generic growth could be nurtured without further audience support. The same applied to the more daring approach of *Steam* (2007), which follows three generations of women who are each rediscovering romance, with the irrepressible Ruby Dee powerfully conveying the delicate doubts of a widow who has found new love. Frank Langella also gave an outstanding performance that year in *Starting Out in the Evening*, about an aging writer becoming attracted to a student, but it went relatively unseen, while his work in *Frost/Nixon* (2008) garnered him an Oscar nomination for a role that was emphatically unromantic.

More profound casting questions arose in a film that surveyed multiple perceptions of elder romance, *The Curious Case of Benjamin Button* (2008). The premise was not a contemporary Hollywood creation, but rather originated with an F. Scott Fitzgerald story from 1922 in which the title character is born an old man and then over time regresses toward infancy. But the use of a single middle-aged actor to accomplish the ruse was primarily the result of twenty-first-century digital technology. That heartthrob Brad Pitt was chosen for the role was especially significant, since his handsome visage could be altered to fit the anatomically accurate features of a geriatric figure who, by deigning to appear like Brad Pitt, even decades older, would remain handsome by association. Further, the studio exploited the 2005 hurricane tragedy in New Orleans to give the film relevance for contemporary viewers.

The story opens just as Hurricane Katrina is moving in, with the imminent death of Daisy (Cate Blanchett), a withered patient in a New Orleans hospital. Her daughter provides the background to this frame story by read-

The Curious Case of Benjamin Button *(2008) presents a chronological conundrum: the title character ages backward. Here, Queenie (Taraji P. Henson) encourages Benjamin (Brad Pitt) to dance as he uses his juvenile impulses to liberate his geriatric body.*

ing a journal, rather unlike the one in *The Notebook*. We learn from Benjamin Button's own words how he was born under tragic circumstances in 1918: diagnoses of multiple old-age diseases indicated he did not have long to live. His environment was extraordinary, however; from childhood he lived in a retirement home filled with aging tenants, who welcomed the strange boy as a kindred spirit. Thus, his development offers an immediate contrast with the decaying denizens around him as he gradually overcomes his physical ailments and gains knowledge while their abilities further decrease. Fitzgerald certainly must have intended to make some comment on the similarities between infancy and senility, since in both stages of life we are frail; yet of course by virtue of his peculiar condition, Benjamin has a lifetime of becoming physically younger ahead of him.

Benjamin first encounters Daisy as a little girl at a party for one of the residents, and while he is instantly smitten, his appearance as a fading octogenarian is incongruous with childhood puppy love. They pursue harmless juvenile rituals such as telling stories until Daisy's grandmother begins to suspect that Benjamin may have carnal interests, which she recognizes in this older "peer." A few years later, after Benjamin has become a few years younger in appearance, he is coerced into visiting a prostitute to lose his virginity, bearing out the grandmother's suspicions, since he is otherwise entering the mental adolescence of his life, with its attendant sexual changes. The film labors to some extent in efforts at noting Benjamin's chronological age, which is about five years more than Daisy's, yet of course he still seems septuagenarian when she is an adolescent. And he has spent his childhood watching his closest friends die from old age, making him all the more eager to leave home as a "middle-aged" man, which he does in his late teens, promptly starting an affair with a sophisticated British woman that does not last long. This first great romance remains Benjamin's entrée to the world of adult love, and it provides him with the appreciation he needs to respect Daisy's slowly reviving interest in him after World War II, when they are both in their twenties.

Daisy grows into an accomplished dancer, and while they have a few short and uneasy meetings, the two do not spend much time together until after her dancing career is ended by a car accident. By then, Benjamin has achieved the mature good looks we associate with Brad Pitt the actor, and again the distinct contrast in their characters is evident: Daisy is at the end of her youthful growth, and Benjamin is handsomely entering his prime. For some years in their forties the couple are at least closely aligned in their ages, even as they know this balance will not last long; their days are filled with a 1960s bohemianism that denies any graver concerns until she becomes pregnant. Benjamin knows that at the same time he is having a child, he will be moving toward childhood himself, and after their daughter's birth, he leaves the family. In a touching scene, his daughter discovers his many letters to her over the years thereafter, during which he became younger. When he at last meets his daughter, she is twelve and he is aging backward toward his twenties.

Similar examples of the incredible dual performances of Pitt and Blanchett aging throughout the film are scarce in the history of American cinema, and their love story has one of the most affecting endings ever achieved in elder romance. Daisy goes to see Benjamin when he is in his teens but afflicted with dementia and unable to recognize her; for more than a decade thereafter, she cares for him as he descends into childhood and continues toward death. The scenes of Daisy growing stooped and wrinkly as Benjamin becomes a baby and dies in her arms are harrowing, for whether geriatric or infantile, they are cruelly unable to reverse the time given to them. Few other movies capture the intimacy and devotion of lifelong love through so many vivid scenes, or grant characters such complete identities that they persist throughout the corporeal changes of eighty years.

Because of the film's comprehensive sweep, it does not linger on any particular period in their lives, moving swiftly over its nearly three-hour running time in mere moments that signify the rapidly, often randomly captured memories of life. *The Curious Case of Benjamin Button* not only made a powerful case for the durability and longevity of love, but also gave elder romance a new repute in American movies with the accolades and box-office income it earned, even if it remained entirely predicated on problematizing the very notion of aging. Nearly a dozen films in the next few years featured elder romance as a topic—an influential increase, although none of them achieved a similar level of success, perhaps owing to their lack of younger stars.

This was the case with three other 2008 movies. *Lovely, Still* had perhaps scant chance of making a splash despite starring two Oscar winners, Martin Landau and Ellen Burstyn, given its modest budget and sad subject matter: what appears to be a blossoming relationship between two aging neighbors is revealed to be a woman's last-ditch attempt to bring her senile husband back to the romantic and familial fold. Their children join in trying to help restore the faded memory of their father so that their mother can enjoy one last Christmas with him. It is a mildly captivating though unrealistic mystery, analogous to *The Notebook*, with the genders of the dementia sufferers switched. *Last Chance Harvey* continued the trend of featuring two Oscar winners as aging lovers, although Dustin Hoffman's title character becomes too quickly smitten with Emma Thompson's middle-aged spinster, and their tentative union is unconvincing. An even greater age difference marks the story of an arrogant professor and his adoring grad student in *Elegy*, in which Ben Kingsley and Penelope Cruz—again two Oscar winners—essay a love affair that neither seems to much desire or deserve.[19]

As the decade moved to a close, the studio tendency to cast highly visible Oscar-caliber actors in elder romances continued without abating, and Hollywood's new comfort with depicting elders in explicitly sexual relationships became more noticeable. The approach did not prove popular with audiences, as was first made evident by the indifference shown to the farcical *Play the Game* (2009), although its story featuring octogenarian Andy Griffith—who receives fellatio and a lot of other attention from the ladies at his retirement home—was perhaps a bit lecherous for some tastes. *Solitary Man* (2009) was also generally dismissed. Michael Douglas plays a rascally older businessman so morally bankrupt that he sleeps with his middle-aged lover's teenage daughter. Rather than resulting in the ludicrous escapades of *Play the Game*, the consequences of these actions hasten the demise of the protagonist's deceptive lifestyle, because his lack of respect for the women in his life dooms him to age in sexist oblivion. Woody Allen may have intended to mine similar pathos from *You Will Meet a Tall Dark Stranger* (2010): Anthony Hopkins leaves his wife after forty years and quickly takes up with a wildly incompatible, much younger woman. The character receives his comeuppance when he realizes that his new bride has become pregnant by another man, and that his first wife will not take him back because she has now taken to following psychic revelations. As is common in elder romances, he cannot restore his youthful libido despite his best efforts (which include Viagra as well as fur coats), leaving him peevish, foolish, and alone.

In an overlooked yet somewhat intriguing development, two films about male gigolos for older ladies appeared toward the end of the 2000s, both gaining little attention: *The Walker* (2007), about a middle-aged gay dandy who is drawn into a dull murder mystery, and *The Extra Man* (2010), a droll comedy wherein the escort, played by Kevin Kline, is an older man himself. Movies about male prostitutes for women originated in the silent period at least as early as *Gigolo* (1926), in which the title character and his ilk are euphemistically identified as paid dancers for lonely women seeking company while out on the town. Further examples were plentiful in the prewar period, including *Ladies' Man* (1931) and *Mad Youth* (1940), and the type appeared again in *The Roman Spring of Mrs. Stone* (1961), *Midnight Cowboy* (1969), and, perhaps most famously, *American Gigolo* (1980).

Gigolos are almost always assumed to be younger men servicing older ladies, usually of wealth, the implication being that these women can no longer find lovers devoted enough to pursue them out of passion—a compromising position to be sure. In many of these stories, gigolos are exposed as degenerate cads who care far less about their clients than about their money. *Out to Sea* elevated the plot to more comical status in 1997, without sexual propositions, but the few mildly popular comedies that continued to exploit the theme did so with primarily middle-aged characters, and any woman pursuing a younger man had come to be known as a "cougar" by the late 2000s. *The Extra Man* at least handles its grandes dames with a modicum of respect, largely evading pertinent questions about older sexuality for the sake of celebrating the macho delusions of its sexist protagonist.

While dominant American cinema essentially continued to avoid queer elder roles, an independent production offered a corrective perspective of aging women reflecting on their lives as lesbians. *Hannah Free* (2009) cast Sharon Gless in the title role as a hardened woman living out her final days in a nursing home but kept away from her lifelong partner, Rachel (Maureen Gallagher), because of supposed family objections. After a college student named Greta (Jacqui Jackson) shows up to interview Hannah for a project on elder histories, they develop a sympathetic friendship, through which Greta reveals that she is actually Rachel's great-granddaughter.[20] Together they struggle to secure Hannah's access to visit Rachel, who is in a terminal coma in the same facility, and by the end Greta is able to convince Hannah that she could assist in Rachel's death.

Thus, besides addressing the political topic of visitation rights for same-sex partners, the film takes on the controversy of euthanasia, which is here handled in compassionate and, ultimately, approving terms by the remaining family dissenter. Along the way, *Hannah Free* offers unusual glimpses into the lives of two women in love, both of whom made considerable sacrifices for their relationship, going back to the 1940s, and were not even public until their twilight years. Yet because one of the protagonists is diminished by a coma, the tale of their flourishing romance at the end of life is weakened. American cinema thus still waits for a lesbian love story akin to the joyful Canadian *Cloudburst* (2011), in which an aging woman rescues her partner from a nursing home and together they embark on a liberating journey. As in *Hannah Free*, one woman succumbs to a terminal illness, although the story is able to honor their many years together while they relish their remaining time in a last hurrah of compassionate and even comical adventure.

Elder male homosexuality is a theme in *Beginners* (2010), although a somewhat secondary one to its tale of a man preparing for the death of his father, whom he helps through hospice care. Oliver (Ewan McGregor) surprisingly learns, after the death of his mother, that his seventy-five-year-old father, Hal (Christopher Plummer), is gay. His mother knew of her husband's preference throughout the marriage but kept it a secret, because they lived in a codependent state of denial: hers about being Jewish, his about being gay.[21]

The story thus hits notes of postwar social suppression similar to those found in *An Empty Bed* and *Hannah Free*. Yet in this case, Hal is liberated in his waning years of life to openly explore his local gay community for the first time, where he finds empathetic brethren as well as a younger lover. Hal affirms with radical confidence that "a person may at any age continue to desire sexual intimacy despite living under the shadow of a life-threatening condition," as Pamela Gravagne argues.[22] Because we know from the start that Hal has just a few years to live and love anew, his death is removed from heavy tragedy, although Oliver is pained by his own emotional distance from the women he has loved, thinly implying that he has yet to accept his own true romantic or sexual identity. If only for the final chapter of life, Hal was able to embrace his own truth without reservation, the wisdom of age arriving with enough time for it to be appreciated.[23]

More recently, *Love Is Strange* (2014) offered a self-consciously normalized depiction of *two* elder gay men. John Lithgow plays Ben, a seventy-one-year-old retiree who marries his partner of twenty-eight years, George (Alfred Molina). George is then immediately fired from his position as a music teacher at a Catholic school that will not abide public confirmation of an employee's homosexuality. For all the film's evidently good intentions in praising the persevering union of these two esteemed characters as they endure the indignities of losing their apartment and living apart with other family members—shades of *Make Way for Tomorrow*—the story is distracted by subplots and the contrived sudden decline of Ben's health. The latter results in yet another elided elder death (a topic discussed in the next chapter), revealing a weakening of the film's otherwise notable ambition to depict gay lovers aging together. It is unfortunate that such a story was still considered innovative in 2014, suggesting how much progress the film industry needs to make in understanding same-sex romance among elders. One evident step in that progress will occur when both lovers are still alive at the end of the movie.

THE LIFE LEFT IN LOVE

The state of elder romance has in recent years remained vibrant and fully capacious enough for considerable growth. Three films featuring distinctive love stories involving older characters appeared in 2012, maintaining familiar pathways. *Hitchcock* is ostensibly a biopic about two years in the life of the famous movie director (played by Anthony Hopkins), and his occasionally tempestuous but entirely needy relationship with his long-suffering wife becomes the emotional core of the story. Fearing publicly that by turning sixty he might lose his touch for the thrilling and macabre, he sets off to make *Psycho* in order to demonstrate the length to which his almost manic tactics can reach. Along the way, he tries to dismiss the loathing felt for him by much younger starlets and to accept his marriage as the domestic salvation to his professional turmoil.

While less acclaimed, *The Magic of Belle Isle* is more meaningful as a portrait of budding May-December romance between a crotchety black writer (Morgan Freeman) and a white middle-aged mother (Virginia Madsen). He harbors bitter resentment over the drunk driver who shattered his legs and his baseball career when he was a young man, and over the fairly recent death of his wife. The attractive mother is overcoming a bitter divorce and trying to find some level of autonomy with her three daughters. The couple's consummation cannot occur in the traditional sense, because he is wheelchair-bound, nor can it come through his fantasy of dancing with her in the moonlight. But the lingering kiss she gives him when he prepares to leave at the end is enough to bring him back, to her and to his romantic vision of life, affording an unexpected level of passionate sensual contact between two people of such disparate ages.

The most visible and directly confrontational elder romance of 2012 arrived with *Hope Springs*, an actor's showcase for Meryl Streep and Tommy Lee Jones, who play Kay and Arnold, a midwestern couple whose marriage has become lifeless after thirty-one years of routine. Their children have grown up and moved on, and the duo long ago adopted the practice of sleeping in different rooms; despite Kay's efforts to encourage him, Arnold shows no physical affection toward her anymore. Arnold seems content with their workaday lifestyle: Kay cooks him breakfast every morning before he goes to his job in an accounting firm, and she has a menial job in a clothing boutique. As in so many portraits of aging characters, Kay and Arnold have begun to ossify from the bland permanence of their lives, but unlike Arnold, Kay has grown distraught from their lack of desire.

In an assertive move, Kay pays for a one-week couples' therapy vacation to see the renowned Dr. Feld (Steve Carell) in the title town on the Maine shoreline. Arnold is adamantly opposed at first, yet after Kay begins to leave without him, he relents. The film thereafter contains some of the most blunt dialogue between two older lovers ever rendered in a Hollywood film. When Dr. Feld asks them about their marriage, Arnold persists with his claim that it is "adequate," expressing a level of satisfaction far below Kay's tolerance—in effect, challenging the contentment quota achieved by the husband in *The Notebook* some eight years earlier. Arnold clearly does not know how to respond to Kay's claims that he no longer touches her and that they do not talk about anything meaningful, claims that he knows are true but cause him to recoil in shame. Arnold can't seem to say that he does not know why their marriage has lost its intimacy, and he transfers his frustration with that lack of understanding into complaints about how much the therapy costs.

In their next session, Dr. Feld amiably but firmly continues pushing them to discuss their sex lives; as it turns out, only Kay remembers the last time she and Arnold had sex, over four years earlier. Arnold, who seems to have little appreciation of their sexual experiences together, is visibly flustered by the level of candor this topic requires, although he passively volunteers to go along with their assignment for the evening, which requires them to lie together and hold each other. The initial discomfort this brings to Arnold may be intended to help the audience relate to his unease, as Joe Morgenstern deftly considered:

> The most unexpected aspect of the film is its emphasis on sex and physical intimacy. Kids don't want to think about their parents having sex, and the movie business, ever more focused on youth, usually shrinks from the subject of sex in later life, or falls back on discrete editing as if to say yes, these quaint oldsters want to do it too, but we'll spare you the details. This film, obviously made for an older audience, embraces the subject explicitly, and sometimes hilariously, or quite clumsily, with equal emphasis on feelings, and on helping

> its repressed, inarticulate couple find the words to express what they feel.[24]

The emotion expressed in embracing, which would be expected in a happy marriage, is quite awkward for Arnold; by contrast, Kay awakens the next morning all but jubilant when she finds her husband in bed next to her for the first time in many years, his arm around her. The two are happy about this bit of progress, although Dr. Feld continues with his questions about their sex lives. Both of them admit to a rather vanilla range of experience, and neither one expresses much pleasure in the sex they did have, but to the film's credit, the explanation for this is not tritely stated: neither one reveals a dramatic trauma from the past or a repressed moral crisis. This therapy is not based on resolution of their past conflicts; it is aimed at recognizing the true affection that they still have for each other in the present. Sex is such a sensitive topic for Arnold because it gets at the deepest level of their closeness, a level that he has stopped striving for.

As they move through more tongue-tied sessions with Dr. Feld, Arnold recalls one of their most passionate sexual moments from many years earlier when Kay was pregnant, an afternoon liaison on the kitchen floor, which Kay also recalls with tearful joy. In the process, Arnold taps into the lust he felt for her back then, although they both immediately lament the loss of that desire in the years that followed. In a bold endeavor to reignite some sexual excitement between them, Kay and Arnold go to a local movie theater, where she tries to perform fellatio on him within the darkened seats: he is initially thrilled, but she is thwarted by being unable to see and runs out in embarrassment. Arnold's reassurance of Kay afterward reveals his growing gratitude for her efforts, and he takes on his most motivated plan yet, booking them a night at a romantic inn. The strategy is effective at first as they giddily reminisce about their earlier years over dinner and retire to a room with provocative accoutrements—strawberries, champagne, soul music—that encourage their lovemaking. But at an ominous moment, Kay looks up at Arnold looking down at her and senses in his expression that he is no longer attracted to her.

The surface tension in the film concerns whether Kay and Arnold should stay together in a dull marriage, but the latent conflict is whether love can be revivified in a couple after so long. Such domestic anxieties fill the domains of many millions of lasting marriages all over the world, yet Hollywood movies have until recently been very reluctant to explore any details of romantic dissolution for older couples, who have been left by the culture to "age out" of their long love lives. Given enough time, many older couples fade into a quotidian monotony, and a film like *Hope Springs* deliberately disrupts that mundane veneer, as is so jarringly shown when Kay stares at Arnold's blank face during sex. She has been seeking not merely rekindled romance but also appreciation, and up to this point the film has done well to elaborate on the importance of her efforts to achieve both goals.

Alas, in the final scenes of the film, so much of the previous exploration of their emotions is compromised by a traditionally happy Hollywood ending. Kay and Arnold leave Hope Springs with evident doubts about the future of their marriage. They return to their routine lives and spend many scenes in reflective silence, suggesting that Kay's goals have gone unfulfilled. She even begins packing a bag with the intention of leaving Arnold, but then he comes to her room, apologizes for being boorish, and makes love to her in the traditional missionary style he enjoys. This gesture is meant as reconciliation, of course, yet it also demonstrates the compromise they each must continue to endure: their ardor may only ever be adequate.

While the apprehensive honesty of this moment rings true, a subsequent scene hastily expands the possibility of further desire between them as Arnold pauses to intensely kiss Kay on his way to work. A closing shot of the freshly flirtatious couple chatting with a neighbor, whom Arnold had fantasized about inviting into a threesome, brings a facile merriment to the many years of lingering tensions they may yet face. Then, in a ploy to further reassure the audience during the end credits, Kay and Arnold are shown renewing their vows on the beach with their kids in attendance and Dr. Feld officiating. This tacked-on closure—clearly shot in cheap haste to look like a home movie—should not be a surprise, coming as it does from an industry that works to satisfy its customers, yet it promotes such a fleeting and artificial solution to the complex concerns of their lives. Their vows are themselves rather petty agreements, such as changing television and travel habits, and their deeper needs—or at least Kay's—are left silently effaced by this ephemeral ritual, with no consideration of how the next ten or twenty years of their marriage may actually evolve.

American cinema itself needs further maturity in dealing with elder romance, which is still in relatively small supply on screen compared to its presence in real life. In 2012, nearly 60 percent of Americans age sixty-five and older were married and living with a spouse.[25] That same year, out of eighteen American films featuring elder characters, only four depicted any kind of romance: those listed above, and the parents played by Robert De Niro and Jacki Weaver in *Silver Linings Playbook*, which otherwise focused on younger characters.

The next year, of twenty-three examples, only *one* addressed the topic of elder romance in any considerable terms, the clumsy family comedy *The Big Wedding* (2013), in which Diane Keaton and Robert De Niro play di-

Don (Robert De Niro) goes down on one knee to propose to his girlfriend, Bebe (Susan Sarandon), while a priest (Robin Williams) attempts to officiate other nuptials—all part of the family farce in The Big Wedding *(2013).*

vorced parents who pretend to be married for the sake of their adopted son who is marrying into a conservative Catholic family. Hijinks between the older couple lead to them passionately making love at one point, entangling them in further deceptions between lovers and friends, and there is generally bawdy behavior by all involved. Regrettably, their erotic reunion does not rekindle their love for each other, and the patriarch realizes that he truly wants to marry his longtime girlfriend, played by Susan Sarandon (the same age as Keaton, sixty-seven). To its credit, the film does show its older lovers to be just as affectionate and confused as its younger characters, and like many other recent elder romances, it promotes generational balance.

The cultural visibility of *The Big Wedding* was nonetheless negligible despite its stars. Things improved a bit in 2014, when at least four of the nineteen elder movies released that year featured romances, including the strangely dark May-December folly *The Humbling*, which cast Al Pacino as a possibly psychotic actor besotted with a lesbian half his age.

Along with the aforementioned *Love Is Strange*, two other films in 2014 depicted passion between elders. *And So It Goes* is a rather conventional comedy about an embittered widower who refuses to retire from work and resists giving in to a new romance with his widowed neighbor. The leads, Michael Douglas and Diane Keaton, display a spry and almost innocent rediscovery of love late in life, which is uneasily evident after they first have sex and wonder about their performances.

In a somewhat similar setup, *Elsa & Fred* follows its eponymous leads (Shirley MacLaine and Christopher Plummer) into a shaky octogenarian affair as the quietly dying Elsa slowly convinces her new neighbor, Fred, to liberate himself from denial, and he in turn evolves into the mythical gentleman she has longed to love. Her penchant for fantasy calls into question her motives, even her sanity. They eventually arrive in Rome to faithfully duplicate the Trevi Fountain scene from *La Dolce Vita* (1960), resulting in an inimitable homage to both cinema history and the rejuvenating capacity of love even at the end of life. This theme of rejuvenation continued in 2015 with the refreshing *I'll See You in My Dreams*, with widow Blythe Danner gracefully discovering new love, then confronting tragedy when her adorable suitor suddenly dies.

It is heartening that Hollywood has been increasing the quantity of elder romances, but the quality of those romantic depictions deserves further scrutiny by the elder audience. Without more sincere and sensible attention to the love lives and sexual experiences of elders, even aspirational depictions like *I'll See You in My Dreams* will remain scarce if Hollywood continues to disregard these elements that are so vital to most older people.

CHAPTER SIX

Deceptions and Delusions of Elder Death

Dad's dying. He's been doing it for about twenty years so I don't miss anything.

BESSIE (DIANE KEATON) IN *MARVIN'S ROOM* (1996)

THE FINAL FOCUS OF OUR STUDY MAY SEEM INEVITABLE, for death is anticipated far more often among the old than the young, and perhaps next to criminals, elder characters likely have the highest rate of mortality in movies. Stories about the end of life are understandably quite often depressing, but in true Hollywood fashion, the elders in many films facing death either avoid the dreaded end before the credits roll, or they find a way to march into that final good night with grand aplomb. Those who have the benefit of living beyond their expectancy also have the advantage of reflecting on their lives and taking account of their actions, which makes for especially ripe drama in movies. American cinema, however, offers a curiously limited range of depictions of death for elder characters.

We have identified three filmic modes of depicting geriatric death, and they indicate the cultural resistance to and insecurities about the death and dying of the aged.[1] Curiously, there is not a similar level of resistance in other genres involving death: consider how much audiences have enjoyed films about war, monsters, and psychopathic killers over the years. Americans clearly have a fascination with characters being *murdered*, and even in melodramas, death is all but gleefully endured. Nonetheless, the otherwise noble accomplishment of a character reaching old age and facing a natural end of life is rarely celebrated and, again, is most often denied through various narrative traditions. Audiences are consequently encouraged to entertain one of three aspirations: that dying is glorious and fulfilling, that dying is peaceful and respectable, or that dying is continually postponed so that life may somehow go on forever.

The first of these modes is the dramatic death. In real life, the great majority of human deaths occur with little drama, and most Americans age sixty-five and over die in hospitals or other care facilities outside their homes.[2] Most of those people die in their sleep, quietly under sedation, or after life support machinery has been turned off. Relatively few people die in gun battles, on mountaintops, in plane crashes, or on sinking ships, even though, as Mark Gallagher has pointed out, "Hollywood films in particular have preferred spectacular, violent death to somber deathbed scenes or other avowedly realist depictions of the terminal stages of life."[3] Very few people die just after making an important proclamation, or saving a loved one, or solving a problem that has plagued them (or the world) for years. Nonetheless, movies persist with such examples whereby people of all ages go out in a blaze of glory, and if they are over the age of sixty, that glory carries an even greater gravity, since the older character usually has the opportunity to inform his or her children, or other successors, of vital life lessons. Further, the industry continually uses the tropes of dramatic death for aged characters to essentially displace tensions about the possibility of life after death. By giving us senescent characters who die in fascinating (or in any case aesthetically pleasing) ways, the movies give us the opportunity to view death as powerful and filled with potential for both the living and the dying, rather than as a depressing, painful, or, worst of all, absolutely final conclusion to life and existence.

The second mode, which is the most optimistic, is death with dignity. This is the vision most people have for their own expiration: no one wants to die suddenly with unfulfilled plans or while stuffed with tubes in a sterile hospital; everyone wants to die with calm resignation after a life full of satisfaction. Given Hollywood's penchant for happy endings, one might assume that this would be a common depiction of geriatric death, and yet it is the scarcest of the three approaches. A peaceful, honorable, or gracious death is bestowed on only the privileged few: often, pious idealists who are almost always cast as being somehow more deserving than common folk. A dignified death does not need to be anticipated or arranged by the elder, but it does require that the character pass away with a sense of control and completion, not in pain or with regret for deeds done and undone.

We borrow the term for the third mode of geriatric death from Ernest Becker's 1973 book, *The Denial of Death*, in which he argues that humans construct elaborate symbolic mechanisms, based on a heroic impulse, to convince themselves that their existence, or at least their significance, will extend beyond the longevity of their living bodies. Becker connects this belief to a utopian vision in which people can "live in an 'eternal now' of pure pleasure and peace," a fantasy that Hollywood often sells effectively.[4] Hollywood engages in this phenomenon by producing movies and endorsing awards that preserve the significance of movie stars and a few other artists in the cinematic field, and the dream factory takes this longing for meaning even further in most of its depictions of senescent characters nearing death. Elders facing their mortality regularly escape the grasp of the Grim Reaper by the film's end and persist with some hope that tomorrow will be a better day. This mode of presentation is most consistent with Hollywood's resistance to negativity, although given how often this approach to geriatric death has been followed in movies, we cannot merely blame the studios for their repression—that repression reveals just how deeply our cultural mythology is embedded with the longing for endless life. Hollywood accordingly displaces the tensions we all feel about the inevitability of death and exacerbates cultural delusions of immortality in many movies that depict dying elders who somehow escape or suspend the closure of their lives, a closure that might otherwise be confronted with sensitivity and admired with reverence.

Emphasizing a thematic examination of these modes in the last chapter of a book built on a relatively chronological structure may seem unnecessarily gloomy. Yet as the preceding chapter on penultimate journeys illustrates, Hollywood continues insistently to promote the denial (or at least deferment) of geriatric death in many films, and despite the industry's move toward a more honest depiction of elder love and sex in recent years, movies have nonetheless remained anxious, even downright delusional, about the ultimate fate of older characters. Evidence of this anxiety is most apparent in films of the past few decades, and thus our analysis leads to the contemporary cinema of the twenty-first century. But some history of the changing nature of death in America since the late nineteenth century is warranted, if only to understand the corresponding responses that cinema either incorporated into its narratives of elder death, or revised and resisted.

Most deaths of people at any age occurred in their homes until the twentieth century. In the late 1800s, the few hospitals that kept patients until death usually did so for those with long-term chronic diseases such as tuberculosis. Yet for most people, the act of dying was not prolonged. As more hospitals were constructed in America—particularly after the Hill-Burton Act of 1946—and as improvements in public health and medical care (sanitation, antibiotics, anesthesia) proliferated, life expectancy not only expanded rapidly, but people's deaths began occurring more often away from home, in hospitals or at another increasingly common locale, the eldercare facility.[5]

After World War II, the incidence of "sudden death" among Americans (from accidents or unexpected fatal health events) accounted for only 10 percent of deaths; the vast majority died from progressive diseases, which changed the cultural experience of dying in many ways. People began dying under medical care that often prolonged life, giving older patients naturally close to their life expectancy enough time to "put their affairs in order," thus allowing elders time for reflection or even travel, and providing families time to prepare for their relatives' deaths and their attendant rituals.

Yet in representations of death, the passing of a beloved or heroic protagonist in an anodyne facility could not be nearly as dramatic as death in random acts or more exposed settings, and so most movie characters who met their end on screen tended to perish on the battlefield, in the street, or under strange circumstances. The real and common occurrence of slowly degenerative death became all but exclusively the fate of older people, when it was shown at all. Curiously, the new medium of television better exploited the realities of death in soap operas, hospital procedurals, and "disease of the week" movies; such formats depicted death at unprecedented levels, and an implausibly high percentage of characters faced death and disease. For the cinema audience, such storylines were rarely appealing as escapist entertainment, and the studios only sporadically endorsed them.

The realities of death in America during the later twentieth century became ever scarcer in Hollywood movies, if only because the truth was less satisfying than fantasy. The prevailing social psychology supported this denial as younger people became more personally isolated from the death experience than previous generations, since their elders usually spent their final years away from their families, on their own (in their own homes or paid institutions) and dying in hospitals. Because the experience of natural death could not always be made dramatically rewarding nor denied altogether, Hollywood offered the exceptional and preferable yet reliably orchestrated option of death with dignity for the aged, in which the person facing death not only has some agency in the impending ending, but also manages to alleviate suffering for self and others.

To this day, death remains the *essential* confrontational topic for elder representation in American cinema, even though it is the most universally shared experience. The ways in which movies have depicted death and dying for elder characters thus reveal a matrix of cultural and industrial concerns that are often in conflict with actual geriatric existence, pointing to the ultimate contradiction between the aged on screen and in life.

EARLY ELDER DEATH

Examples of elder protagonists dying in American movies were relatively uncommon until the later twentieth century, when the postwar geriatric population gained more prominence. Many minor senescent characters died—especially sickly dotards and prudent martyrs—yet dying on screen was rarely the fate of the main characters on whom films focused, if only because the resolutions would have been unappealing. A rare example from the silent era was *The Glory of Youth* (1915), in which a spavined millionaire threatens to kill his young wife after discovering she loves an athlete, yet ultimately kills himself instead. More common were the natural deaths of elder figures after climactic moments, as in *According to the Code* (1916), when a Confederate veteran dies after a trial that reveals his long-lost son.

A small number of other Hollywood tales surveyed the subject of geriatric death during the silent era, and in these cases, the studios remained fond of exciting fatalities. *The World and His Wife* (1920) features a venerable Spanish swordfighter who is mortally wounded in a duel over the honor of his young beloved. In *Beyond the Rocks* (1922), an older man volunteers for an Arabian journey certain to result in his death, in order to ensure his young wife finds true love with a younger man. And the Western *Riders of the Sand Storm* (1925) begins in classic fashion with the death of a codger who sends a young cowboy in search of his hidden treasure.

Films that actually centered on the death of an elder, such as *If I Had a Million* (1932), in which a terminally ill tycoon doles out his fortune to a series of random strangers, often cheated their own contrivances by ending without the protagonist passing away. *East of Fifth Avenue* (1933) and *The Last Gentleman* (1934) were exceptions for the time. In the former, an aged couple dies in the course of the story and bequeaths their wealth to the tenants of their boardinghouse; in the latter, a wealthy patriarch achieves righteous deliverance after his family learns their financial fates from his will, which he has recorded on film. The value of elders *approaching* death, in these films and many others of the Depression era (*The Unholy Garden* [1931], *Prosperity* [1932], *You Can't Buy Everything* [1934], *The Young in Heart* [1938]), was directly equated to the inheritable assets they could leave behind. As the nation entered World War II, one film challenged the true worth of a senescent plutocrat's assets: *Citizen Kane* (1941) not only began with the ominous death of the lonely protagonist, but devoted the entire story to understanding his dying word, a mystery that goes unsolved in the end as his expensive effects are forgotten and his prized childhood toys vaporize in flames. Each of these instances represents one of the prevailing Hollywood approaches to depicting geriatric death: denial, dignity, and drama.

While numerous on-screen elder deaths continued to occur in the dramatic mode over the years, they were primarily limited to marginal characters, in films such as *Angels in White* (1936), *Keep Smiling* (1938), *Five Came Back* (1939), *The Black Cat* (1941), and *This Gun for Hire* (1942). Few films featured elder death in the manner of *Heaven Can Wait* (1943), which is not so much about dying as about living a buoyant life. A recently deceased septuagenarian details his willfully philandering ways, and his tempestuous marriage, at the gates of hell. He passes away in solitude after a delicious dream, a vision that must have indeed appeared heavenly to an audience at the height of World War II. A less popular film three years later, *The Cockeyed Miracle*, tells another story of an elder facing the afterlife: a sexagenarian meets his dead father in heaven, who guides him in helping his family cope with his death and avoid financial ruin.

Hollywood managed to maintain such optimistic perspectives on geriatric death in the decade after World War II, and in the few instances when an elder protagonist faced death, it tended to occur outside the story, as in the comedy *Breakfast in Hollywood* (1946), in which a delicate older lady (played by Beulah Bondi of *Make Way for Tomorrow*, still acting much older than her fifty-seven years) is hit by a car and hangs on to life until the film reaches its happy ending. Doom was likewise elided in two very different 1948 features: in *Miracle in Harlem*, a religious elder woman with premonitions of her death is compelled to abandon rehearsing her funeral after surviving a criminal plot, and in *Apartment for Peggy*, a retired professor rationalizes a decision to commit suicide but changes his mind after helping a young couple cope with the death of their child.

Over the next ten years or so, more ancillary elder characters perished on screen—in *Streets of Laredo* (1949), *No Man of Her Own* (1950), *Come Fill the Cup* (1951), and *The Eddie Cantor Story* (1954). Perhaps the most dignified death of this era occurs in *Kim* (1950), when a holy man perishes from a fight after experiencing a sacred revelation. The heightened realism of 1960s cinema then amplified emotions regarding the passing of elders. In *Wild River* (1960), Jo Van Fleet plays one of her many martyred matriarchs, forced off her river island to make way for a dam, and dying in a new house that will never be her home.[6] *Hud* (1963) also depicts the death of a bitter elder fighting for his property; Melvyn Douglas won an Oscar for his portrayal of a farmer who dies in the arms of his ingrate son after surveying his doomed ranch. Then *The Night of the Iguana* (1964) showcased one of the most dramatic of all elder deaths, although of a character relegated to the background: a nonagenarian poet must write and recite, with his last breaths, a final composition on a topic no less solemn than the circle of life and the acceptance of mortality.

As with elder romance, Hollywood began to explore the topic of death for the aged more thoroughly in the later twentieth century, although still sometimes with attempts at reassuring levity, as in *Where's Poppa?* (1970), which labored to find laughs in the story of a man who longs for his annoying anile mother to pass away because he can't place her in a nursing home.[7] The far more famous death of the mafia don Vito Corleone (Marlon Brando) in *The Godfather* (1972) was also darkly humorous: he theatrically topples over while playing with his grandson in a sunny garden, instead of being gunned down, as so many of his compatriots were. In an instance of further comfort with the delicate topic, the Walt Disney studio depicted elder death in the children's movie *Napoleon and Samantha* that same year, when a ten-year-old boy, who lives with a loving grandfather played by Will Geer, returns from school one day to find him dead, and even enlists the help of friends to bury the body. *Going in Style* (1979; discussed in chapter 4) reached for an all but absurd irony as a trio of senescent men carries out a harebrained scheme to rob a bank but soon thereafter start dying. The last man happily chooses prison before death arrives so that he can be cared for until he dies, a subtle denunciation of the not dissimilar nursing home system.

Drama also characterized more elder deaths on screen in the 1970s, as previously discussed concerning *Harold and Maude* (1971), and as seen later in John Wayne's valedictory film, *The Shootist* (1976), featuring his heroic character dying (for only the seventh time in Wayne's lengthy career) in a spectacular gun battle that brings righteousness to a wretchedly cancerous outlaw.[8] In the final scene of the 1977 Merchant-Ivory production *Roseland*, built around the famous ballroom in New York City, an elder woman profoundly attached to the hall suddenly collapses and dies while spinning, in poignant recognition of her eternal romance with dance.

By contrast, *Being There* (1979) earned Melvyn Douglas a second Best Supporting Actor Oscar as a terminally ill billionaire who befriends a simple-minded gardener. Because of his wealth, Douglas is able to effectively install an intensive care unit in his home. This arrangement affords him one of the most slowly dignified deaths in all of American cinema: he takes time to recognize that his long life has been rewarding, he frees himself from chronic pain, and he finds in the gardener a supposedly suitable new partner for his wife. Given the story's heavy reliance on hyperbole, it seems to suggest that death with dignity is all but superstition.

This handful of examples in the 1970s was barely expanded in the 1980s, even during the presidency of the geriatric Ronald Reagan and with the ongoing extensions of elder lives through medical advances. Dramatic deaths maintained some repute in movies such as *St. Helens* (1981), the true story of an obstinate landowner (played by Art Carney) who is doomed by the famed volcano, and in *Rocky III* (1982), with the inevitable end of the classically crusty boxing trainer Mickey (Burgess Meredith), in arguably the most exciting death of an older person on screen that decade. Mickey suffers a heart attack just before the eponymous champion is about to swiftly lose a

Eve (Shirley MacLaine) cares for her ailing husband, Benjamin (Melvyn Douglas), in Being There *(1979), leading to one of the few truly dignified deaths of an elder on screen.*

big bout, and then in his last gasps after the fight, he misunderstands that his indomitable disciple lost, dying with the delusion that Rocky remained the best.

Denials of geriatric death remained the dominant approach throughout the decade, even in films that purported to kill off their protagonists, as in *Max Dugan Returns* (1983) and *Grace Quigley* (1984). In the former, Jason Robards plays the title character, who returns to his daughter and grandson after many years away, loaded with stolen cash but having only six months to live. The belated emotions of a family brought together after decades of deception are nonetheless dismissed by the film's emphasis on their elevation in class status, and the supposedly impending death of the mysterious Max is discarded when he simply takes off to live out his final days in tropical decadence. Katherine Hepburn plays the title character in *Grace Quigley*—which is often erroneously identified as her last film—who hatches the unlikely plot of hiring a hit man to kill her and her aging, agonizing friends.[9] The even more unlikely comic aspirations of the story sank the film at the box office, and the fact that Grace and her prospective assassin escape mortal and moral consequences renders its oddly sardonic social commentary on euthanasia as murder-suicide rather vacuous.

Outright resistance to geriatric death peaked at the height of the Reagan

The largely aging cast of Cocoon *(1985) are astonished at the immortal vigor they mysteriously discover, including Gwen Verdon and Don Ameche, who are inspired to dance on the beach.*

era in *Cocoon* (1985) and its sequel *Cocoon: The Return* (1988).[10] Both were quite atypical in bringing together a substantial cast of aged actors, and in the science fiction genre, no less. The story focuses on four older couples, played by some of the most illustrious stage and screen performers of the century, including Don Ameche, Jessica Tandy, Hume Cronyn, and Gwen Verdon. They are living out their fading days at an assisted-care facility, which happens to be next to an empty large house with an impressive swimming pool, to which three of the men sneak off for surreptitious frolic. Without any of the characteristic fanfare, space aliens posing as humans rent the house; they need a large pool in which to incubate large cocoons containing their brethren who were left behind on a previous mission many centuries earlier. When the senescent men swim in the pool containing the cocoons, they are infused with an energetic life force, leading them to some confusion and certain reinvigoration of their sex lives. Yet as Janet Maslin pointed out, "Once restored, they choose to romp in very ordinary ways, and they bring very little ambivalence to the transformation."[11] Indeed, such a fable is founded on an oddly orthodox belief: elder men cannot, of their own volition, rediscover their youthful verve, and diagnoses of disease—and the cultural positioning of the geriatric as impaired and impotent—can be overcome only by supernatural powers.

The powers of the cocoons go far beyond their ability to provide vitality because the aliens are so advanced that they feel no pain and never die, and they offer the elder couples the opportunity to return with them to their planet and live out similar lives. One man in the group decides, after his wife dies, that he would rather stay on Earth, but the rest of the couples decide to leave this mortal coil and go on with the aliens. The story offers up an obvious contrivance for why the aliens can't take more humans with them—there is limited space on their ship—so the escaping elders depart together in an act that is, ironically, tantamount to group suicide. The prospect of eternal life is so appealing that they are willing to leave their loved ones behind, who will not be so fortunate.

Granted, the ending of the film is open-ended enough to suggest that the humans can return, and indeed all the major stars of the original film did just that in the inferior sequel, *Cocoon: The Return* (1988). To be fair, the sequel allows one of the older humans to die with dignity back on Earth so that he can save his wife, and further allows another couple to remain on Earth to aid their grandson. But the original film ends with the surviving (and mostly younger) family members of the elders gathering to grieve them, which further implicates the departed group in causing immense trauma for their relatives, and further draws attention to the fact that only those close to death, in this instance, were able to cheat it. These survivors must face the fact that they will eventually die, a fate that a film like this clearly does not want to confront, and that so many other, more realistic American movies have likewise avoided.

Another late-1980s film gathered aging titans of American cinema, in this case Lillian Gish (age ninety-three) and Bette Davis (age seventy-nine), as codependent octogenarian sisters in *The Whales of August* (1987). They spend a summer day bickering about their neighbors and their house, and much of the tension in the story is derived from the uncertainty about how long each still has to live. Following *On Golden Pond* (1981) and other films built on similar tensions, a predictable deception is at work here, because the anticipated threat is suspended, and once again relevant geriatric issues—such as whether one sister can keep caring for the other at home, and how either will cope once the other dies—are dodged for the sake of preserving a typical denial of elder death. In many ways, this result is in keeping with the classic Hollywood legends of the two esteemed actresses, whose beauty and confidence look all but eternal on screen. The mythology of immortality so broadly promoted by the industry is preserved as the two find a new energy in each other and make plans to install a patently metaphorical picture window at the end of the day, a day that is not the end.

A film from the following year, *Rocket Gibraltar*, was a radical exception to the tradition of denial. Burt Lancaster plays Levi, a well-off widower welcoming his four grown children and their eight kids to visit him for the weekend of his seventy-seventh birthday at his huge house on Long Island. His grandchildren have little reason for concern about the family patriarch until they ask him what he wants for his birthday, and in a nighttime chat on the beach, he tells the assembled tots that he wishes he could be buried as in a Viking ceremony: his body would be left on a boat in the ocean, a flaming arrow shot from shore would set it alight, and with his gathered family watching it burn, his ashes would dissolve into the sea. This portentous moment inspires the grandchildren to fix up an old sailboat they find on the beach, which they rechristen the *Rocket Gibraltar*, so that they can give it to grandpa as a birthday present. Little do they know that Levi is weakening from an aortic aneurysm, but after he has a mild heart attack and they overhear a conversation revealing this frightful twist, the stage is set for a marvelous departure.

To its unexpected credit, the film resists a dramatic death for the charismatically salty Levi, but does not deny it either. On the day of his birthday, his children give him some simple gifts like books and a movie, not knowing of their father's condition. As he is quietly reading and watching the movie in his room, Levi simply drifts away, happy with his surroundings, in a remarkably placid death scene. When his grandchildren find him soon thereafter, they are steeled for what has happened and become single-minded in moving his body out to the beach where the *Rocket Gibraltar* awaits. They do need to purloin a catering van for the mission, resulting in a morbidly comic fiasco as their parents give chase, but they succeed in bringing their grandfather's corpse to his ersatz Viking ship. Then, before their parents can stop them, the children push the dead Levi out to sea on the boat and shoot at it with flaming arrows until it ignites, whereupon the whole family becomes quickly resigned to watch this cremation on the water. Thus, Levi's *funeral* is one of the most dramatic of any elder character ever rendered on screen, but his painless passing and the precise fulfillment of his dying wish bring to his death a dignity that American cinema had rarely attempted to this point. Such dignity, not merely rare in a movie, is achieved only through a series of almost preposterous alignments, insinuating that Levi's already ancient and clandestine farewell would never be possible under contemporary conditions.

A more common scenario featuring an uncommonly strong family bond was presented the next year in *Dad* (1989), with Jack Lemmon as a somewhat senile seventy-eight-year-old whose self-absorbed corporate son returns to the family homestead to care for his father after his mother has a heart attack. The story clearly indicts the 1980s power-hungry businessmen who abandoned family for fortune, providing a corrective model through the dutiful attention that the son provides for his dad. His devotion grows more determined when the father is diagnosed with cancer, and even though he enjoys a briefly energetic remission, the senescent man begins to succumb to the disease and is afflicted with fanciful figments of a life he never lived (a subplot that is curious but cumbersome). *Dad* is special for its portrayal of a middle-aged child as the primary caregiver of an aged parent—a far more customary occurrence in real life than on screen—and for its celebration of the older man's physically active rediscovery of life before death. Further, while the father's actual passing is omitted at the end in standard Hollywood fashion, the story grants the character credit for his success as a parent, a theme that became increasingly important in later movies in which elders face the end of life.

DEATH GETS DARKER

Elder death in 1990s films took on striking thematic magnitude in most cases, but the number of films about death among the aged still remained rather consistent overall. The first half of the decade was lukewarm on the topic, and why the era later became more preoccupied with sadder stories is difficult to discern. The 1990s were a generally stable decade after the Cold War ended and the economy recovered from a recession during the first few years; perhaps this relative calm made movie studios more daring in tackling otherwise pessimistic topics about death among older Americans. The ongoing expansion of nursing home care and the increasing longevity of citizens were also likely factors in giving movies the confidence to address rather negative experiences among an aging population facing its end.

Some satirical sides of geriatric death had appeared by mid-decade, none with noteworthy success. A middle-aged couple find themselves amateur sleuths in the droll *Manhattan Murder Mystery* (1993) when an older neighbor dies of an apparent heart attack but they suspect her husband killed her, and then later uncover through many machinations that the dead woman was the female neighbor's sister; eventually, both the elder husband and wife end up murdered as well. Also that year, *The Cemetery Club* garnered minor attention as an uncommon film starring three women in their sixties who share friendship after the deaths of their husbands, a story understandably focused on the widows coping, using a lightly facetious touch palatable to audiences. *Roommates* (1995) offered a merry flair as well, with the improbable premise of Peter Falk as a grandfather raising his grandson for thirty-two years—to the age of *107*—playing up their differences until the centenarian quietly passes away, knowing that he has been properly paternal. And with a death left deliberately indifferent for the sake of the film's morbidly dark humor, *Getting Away with Murder* (1996) kills off a suspected Nazi commandant, played with suitable astonishment by Jack Lemmon, accentuating the grave turn that elder death had taken as a topic that decade.

That turn had begun emerging the year before in *Two Bits* (1995), whose principal concentration on imminent death was oddly enthusiastic. Gennaro (Jerry Barone) narrates the film as an adult, looking back on the summer day in 1933 when, as a twelve-year-old, he was enthralled with La Paloma, a new cinema opening in his neighborhood. His grandpa (Al Pacino), who spends his days lounging in a backyard chair, has promised Gennaro a quarter when he dies, which happens to be the price of a movie ticket. Honest in a way that only children can be, Gennaro tells Grandpa that he does not want him to die just so he can go to the movies, and he diligently spends all day in pursuit of the twenty-five cents he needs, leading him to some strange schemes. Gennaro and his grandpa are clearly comfortable talking about death in a way that his mother is not; the elder describes the house in heaven he envisions God is building for him, trying to reassure the boy that death is liberating. After Grandpa later suffers a fall, he tells Gennaro that when he was unconscious, he had a vision of heaven as La Paloma.

Two Bits joined *Cocoon* and *Rocket Gibraltar* in portraying grandchildren who have a greater acceptance of death than their parents, yet here the protagonist's respect for the dying becomes excessively calculated. Gennaro visits an aged woman whom Grandpa feels he shamed as a young man when he took her virginity; all these years since, he has carried that guilt and sought forgiveness, which Gennaro provides when he walks a few blocks to the woman's house and apologizes for Grandpa. At the end of the day, Gennaro has at last accumulated the twenty-five cents he needs for the movies, only to find that La Paloma charges fifty cents, setting up a deplorably predictable ending in which Grandpa fades away and dies that evening. Grandpa may have achieved some peace earlier through Gennaro's errand, but his death is less than dignified: he lies on the ground, whispering a final wish to his grandson that goes unheard, and dramatically allowing the coveted quarter to roll out of his lifeless hand. With barely a pause, Gennaro runs off to La Paloma and adds the two bits to his other change so he can at last go to the movies, hearing Grandpa's voice telling him the theater looks like heaven. The film closes on this superficial note of sacrifice, which reduces Gennaro's love for his grandfather to a cash value.

Marvin's Room (1996) was markedly somber, with a story that nonetheless employs typical terms of denial about the title character (Hume Cronyn), who has been rendered speechless by strokes late in life. The true protagonist is his oldest daughter, Bessie (Diane Keaton), who cares for his many needs even though the script keeps them largely limited to the psychological rather than the physical; we see her amuse him with the reflected light from a mirror many times, but she almost never handles his unwieldy body. Bessie calls on her estranged sister and nephews in hope that they can provide bone marrow to help her fight leukemia, but the effort is futile, and she faces her own looming deterioration. (Marvin, who had his first stroke twenty years earlier, has been in an elongated decline for some time.) The two sisters spar and cope until the film conveniently ends before Bessie or Marvin face the deaths that the entire story has been leading to, and thus its fantasies about the ease of elder caregiving *and* diseased degeneration can be mutually sustained.

In *Meet Joe Black* (1998), Anthony Hopkins plays William, a billionaire media mogul about to celebrate his sixty-fifth birthday while handling a massive merger with another company. Little does he expect that Death will show up in the form of Brad Pitt, who has "borrowed" the body of a young man who fatefully died moments after meeting William's daughter Susan (Claire Forlani), a physician. Like Ingmar Bergman's classic *The Seventh Seal* (1957) and other tales in which people bargain with the Grim Reaper to escape his scythe, here Death offers William an opportunity for a slight extension of existence if the rich—and morally upstanding—gentleman will be his "guide" on a tour of the human lives that Death continues to snuff out. Little does Death expect, however, that he will fall in love with Susan, and she with him, setting up a familial conflict alongside the business intrigue that William must manage in the space of a few days before he dies.

This plot seems to guarantee a dramatic demise for William, yet the film's handling of his promised death is ostentatious even for a fairy tale. William does not want the company that he built and ran for many years to be sold off to a competitor and then fade into corporate oblivion, which a rival board

Meet Joe Black *(1998) introduces Death (Brad Pitt) to the billionaire William (Anthony Hopkins), and the two agree on a morbid deal for living a little longer.*

member proposes to do by implementing William's devitalizing retirement on the day he turns sixty-five. The equation is clearly made between William's death and his forced firing, but Death, whom William has named Joe Black, steps in and becomes his adviser. The cinematic critique of capitalism—so prevalent in the 1980s—with its tacit threats to family unity and personal honor, is here transformed into redemption for the wealthy by the most fatal authority of all. In the process of saving the company that bears William's name, Death preserves a noble legacy for the dying man even as he selfishly beguiles Susan with his faux naïveté and extremely handsome charms.

The story requires many contrivances in order to resolve the romance between Susan and Joe, which predictably becomes a contest between whom Death will take: the young doctor, who saves lives, or the senescent man, who has accomplished his life's work. As the film builds to a protracted climax at William's retirement party, Death not only defeats the final threat to William's corporate integrity, but also leaves Susan behind and takes William across an awfully symbolic bridge to the great beyond. In this way, William's death fulfills its spectacular ambition—punctuated by fireworks—and is yet dignified in settling essentially every problem in his life. To reassure William that Susan will live a fruitful life, Death reincarnates the young man whom she found so alluring at the start of the film, leaving death as solely the domain of the aged and contented. This conclusion demands perhaps greater suspension of disbelief than the story itself, and thus unfortunately makes the Hollywood presentation of death with dignity for elders ever more despicably improbable.

The budget of *Gods and Monsters* (1998) was over 95 percent less than that of *Meet Joe Black*, which may account for its far lesser amount of pretension by comparison. It tells the story of the famed Hollywood director James Whale, played by the Oscar-nominated Ian McKellen, who by his late sixties was living in comfortable obscurity in 1950s Los Angeles. Notwithstanding the fact that Whale directed *Frankenstein* (1931) and other horror classics, this story of his life has relatively little to say about the macabre, even though it begins with Whale overcoming a stroke that leaves him somewhat mentally impaired. The narrative builds around Whale's relationship with a handsome gardener named Clay (Brendan Fraser), who befriends the director despite his unease with the older man's expressed homosexuality.

A clear parallel is made between Whale's stories of lonely monsters and the gay life that left him so often distraught. The friendship he finds in Clay leads to a physical confrontation in which Whale makes a sexual advance, only to ask Clay to kill him. The next morning, recalling other famous Hollywood deaths (*Sunset Blvd.* being the richest reference), Clay finds Whale floating dead in his pool, having left a suicide note. Such a scene is morbidly befitting a man who had enjoyed scaring audiences and yet felt so often misunderstood for his desires. And though suicide rates increase for Americans as they age beyond sixty-five (Whale killed himself at sixty-seven), this is one of the rare portrayals of geriatric suicide in movies.[12] Whale's note goes unread at the end, and we are left to surmise that his decision was based on a vague combination of physical pain and mental anguish, thereby compromising his reasoning for the desperate act.

This generally dour decade of elder death came to a decidedly lugubrious close with roles in three films that did not focus on older characters but made vivid impressions all the same. Denial was brought to an altogether new height in *The Green Mile* (1999), in which the protagonist recounts how he inherited a mystical spirit of enduring existence; now at the unlikely age of 108, he has been doomed to watch his loved ones die before him, yet we are spared seeing this saintly soul perish himself. *Magnolia* (1999) is an ensemble picture of tormented types facing personal traumas, one of whom is a rich dying man played by Jason Robards, who does little more than pass away slowly in home hospice care. (The nurse who looks after him in his final hours is notably attentive, in one of the only depictions of palliative care in American cinema.) His arrogant son and lecherous wife spend the duration of the story coping with their contempt for him, leading to a catharsis of criticism for his abuses and providing the kind of histrionic resolution that

In Magnolia *(1999), Frank T. J. Mackey (Tom Cruise) confronts his father (Jason Robards) on his deathbed with a dramatic admission.*

only Hollywood can deliver. The drama and denial of death are even more extreme in *Requiem for a Dream* (2000), an ensemble story about the depravities of drug abuse. Ellen Burstyn plays an elder mother who becomes hooked on speed pills and descends into madness, cracking up with hallucinations and psychosis on her way to a mental hospital, where she is left to expire in anonymity without the dignity of a merciful death.[13]

ELDER LEGACIES

Inexplicable as the darker aspects of 1990s elder death stories may have been, the more redemptive tone set by many movies about the topic in the new century was equally so. The emphasis on family legacies remained prominent in these films, and the children of elders provided a more crucial role in the process and in the aftermath of their parents' passing. Some evidence of this can be found in *Hanging Up* (2000), a rather insipid comedy about three affluent adult sisters coping with the impending death of their septuagenarian father, Lou, played by Walter Matthau. The middle daughter, Eve (Meg Ryan), is the most dutiful of the trio, arranging for her father to be given a series of tests at a hospital before deciding what kind of longer-term care he needs. That decision is conveniently postponed through a series of uninformed medical developments typical of a comedy—the closest attempt at a diagnosis for his condition is a "mini-stroke," and alcoholism is left as an implicit cause—so that the story can occupy itself with sororal bickering. Even that bickering is tame, given the years of repressed obligation that Eve has endured while her sisters have tended to their indulgent professional lives. Neither of them has seen their father get drunk and depressed, nor his embarrassing episodes of losing his memory and lucidity, the most odious of which occurs when Lou comes on to Eve, thinking she is an old flame.

Alas, the comic ambitions of the film derail the climactic death, which has been awaited throughout the story, with the three sisters gathered next to their father's hospital bed as he lies in a timely coma. A running joke building ceaselessly toward its punch line has been Eve's attempt to name an actress from the 1950s; Lou suddenly snaps out of his coma to provide the name and then just as suddenly lapses into immediate death. Any possible humor in the moment is immediately corrupted by his passing, and more distracting for any informed viewer is the implausible arrival of a lone nurse to take his pulse and declare him deceased within a matter of seconds, without any further treatment. Lou's death delivers typical Hollywood drama, yet its patent lack of realism is insulting to a film addressing family dynamics around the death of an elder, which are made somewhat intriguing by the tangential fact that the daughters' mother is still alive yet wants nothing to do with her ex-husband. More impertinent yet is the denouement, in which the three sisters happily prepare Thanksgiving dinner together with no other family present, their father's specter safely contained in happy memories from their childhood. There is little threat of their recent ordeal disrupting their upwardly mobile lives. Lisa Schwarzbaum articulated the fallacious elitism of *Hanging Up*, claiming, "It seemingly congratulates baby boomers for dealing maturely with their aging parents—as opposed to what, leaving them in dumpsters?"[14]

A much more nuanced handling of elder death can be found in *Big Fish* (2003), another story of an older parent slowly passing away while gathering his family to reflect on his past. Most of the film is occupied with stories told throughout the life of Edward (Albert Finney), who has been regaling his son Will (Billy Crudup) with wild tales of his many respectable endeavors since Will was born. As an adult, Will has become a journalist seeking the truth in stories, in deliberate contrast to the mythological accounts of his father's life that have left him exasperated, particularly now that he is about to become the father of a boy. Edward narrates at various turns his own legend as a town's savior, a circus carny, a war hero, a bank robber, and a most romantic suitor of Will's mother, stories that Will has all but dismissed until the end of the film, when Edward momentarily emerges from a stroke.

The conclusion then offers one of the most deliriously dignified endings for any movie character. On his deathbed, Edward asks Will to tell the final story of his life: Will envisions the two of them escaping from the hospital, whereupon he carries his father down to a sunlit river where *every* character from Edward's long life has gathered to say goodbye, celebrating his significance one last time as Will immerses him in the water. Edward then turns into a very large fish, which the apparent schmaltz connotes as the essence of what he has been all along, and with this closure to the make-believe vision, Edward dies. The fable that has been Edward's life, however, is revealed to be more true than Will ever expected when so many people from his father's past gather at his funeral, appearing more modestly believable than they had been described in Edward's stories. Will solemnly reflects in the end that his father's stories had indeed *become* him and thus offered Edward immortality, regardless of reality. The family legacy in this case is preserved in Will's own son, who imparts the excessive exploits of his grandfather to his young friends. This Hollywood fantasy of glory in death may be dramatic beyond belief, yet the human ambition to remain relevant after dying is upheld as a righteous cause that persists well past the limits of truth.

Themes of familial legacies continued to permeate elder death stories for most of the decade. *Illusion* (2004) features Kirk Douglas in his last big-screen role (in his late eighties) as a dying movie director forced to behold numinous visions of a son he never came to love; the film perceptively conveys his curative liberation from egotism as he achieves grace in his final hours.[15] *Checking Out* (2005) extends the curiously increasing use of theatricality as a topic in elder death films. Peter Falk plays a stage actor who gathers his three children on the eve of his ninetieth birthday, planning to kill himself the next day. The uncomfortably comical story glances at issues of unresolved family secrets and rationalized suicide—the elder here is healthy and reasonably sane—before settling on the selfsame denial of death that the protagonist proclaims he abhors. *Proof* (2005) deals more deeply with the mental health of an aging math professor, played by Anthony Hopkins, who lives on through the memories of his unstable daughter after his death from an aneurysm. The film bravely tackles the social disregard the woman feels as she cares for her deteriorating father in his final few years, and it builds intrigue regarding the hereditary influence she fears has doomed her to a life of psychic pain like his.

While films like *Proof* and *Little Miss Sunshine* (2006) continued to showcase families dealing with elder death and gained some recognition, most films dealing with the matter were unpopular. In *Little Miss Sunshine*, a family goes to absurd lengths to deny the sudden death of a grandfather during a trip to a beauty competition for his granddaughter; they even carry his corpse with them like excess baggage. The dysfunction within the family is

Lila (Meryl Streep) arrives just in time to see her dying sister Ann (Vanessa Redgrave) in Evening *(2007).*

only drawn out more by his death, which happens quietly in his sleep, and the resulting mania among the living characters makes the story perversely appealing. Alan Arkin earned wide acclaim and an Oscar for his supporting role as the grandfather, but in that same year he played the lead in *Raising Flagg* as an older man who calls his adult children together, believing he will soon die, a film that went virtually unseen. A similarly obscure 2006 film, *The Last Request*, features Danny Aiello as a patriarch who asks his seminarian son to produce a grandchild for him before he dies, leading to entertaining family hijinks.

Lower-budget films such as these may have understandably failed to find an audience without major studio support, but *Evening* (2007) had a large budget and stellar cast, so its lack of appeal was more confounding. Not unlike *The Notebook* from a few years earlier, the film features an older woman (played by Vanessa Redgrave) recollecting her first true love, but her two daughters, who attend to her deathbed delirium, are not privy to her memories. The film predominantly relies upon the youthful romance and resulting intrigue at its core, and largely dodges the lessons learned by the dying matriarch, whose own resolution about her lost love is ultimately uninformed and almost arbitrary. When she passes away at the end, the story moves immediately to a swift, silent coda without any reflective denouement.

By contrast, an unassuming film like *The Savages* (2007) was far more satisfying in its somewhat humorous approach to two siblings dealing with the senility of their father, and it became a sincerely realistic depiction of a family's ordeal in dealing with dementia and death, unlike any other in recent years. Lenny (Philip Bosco) has lived with his girlfriend for about twenty years after retiring to sunny Arizona, and though her family has paid for a caregiver, he has degenerated into untreated Alzheimer's. His adult children Wendy (Laura Linney) and Jon (Philip Seymour Hoffman) fly in from Buffalo after Lenny's girlfriend suddenly dies, and they are faced with the dire question of where and how their father should live. Lenny has already taken to extreme behavior—smearing his feces on walls—and he barely remembers his children when they visit. Ty Burr comments, "Their father's frailty isn't just a family crisis, it's the first thing in years to snap the siblings out of their self-absorbed wallow. We all deal with this shock to our systems eventually, *The Savages* implies, and the hard truth is that we need to."[16]

Wendy wrestles with enormous guilt over the hard truth that Jon finds so practically simple: they will take Lenny back to Buffalo and put him in a nursing home. Unlike many films that delve into their characters' backgrounds to detail their motivations, *The Savages* focuses on the process of care for elders as it subtly reveals the protagonists' lifelong "wallow," which has brought them to this point. Both Wendy and Jon have become professionally engaged in literal drama—she as an aspiring playwright, he as a theater professor—and yet they rarely recall any of the past with their abusive father and missing mother, or the internal struggles of a present with no stable romantic partners and many unfulfilled professional ambitions. They instead focus on the process of providing care to Lenny, which they know they can't do on their own.

The film covers contemporary eldercare routines that most Americans experience yet virtually never see portrayed in popular media. Jon secures a place at a sterile "rehabilitation center" in Buffalo for Lenny, which he coldly admits to Wendy is a nursing home under any other guise. The children speak with an administrator at the facility, and are dumbfounded when she quickly asks them how they plan to handle their father's funeral and burial. Having never spoken to their father about such matters, they endeavor to ask him, but his confused and brusque response—"Pull the plug!"—gives them little guidance. Wendy and Jon, whose mother disappeared long ago, are left to suddenly endure these alienating worries about their father and evade their personal concerns about money and employment. They have sought validation in theatricality because their parents never provided appreciation at home; Wendy repeatedly applies for fellowships beyond her reach, and Jon is interminably writing a book on a playwright who emphasized message over emotion. They are each unable to sustain a romance because they have no model for enduring affection, and even their affection for each other is operative, a performance for the sake of necessity.

All these tensions are discarded on the margins of their lives as they continue to deal with Lenny, who is inevitably unhappy in, and puzzled about, his new confines. Trying to work off some of her guilt, Wendy takes him for an interview at a higher-quality nursing home, where he proves unable to meet their competence criteria, leading Jon to blame her for denying the impending death of their father. As he eloquently points out, these homes exist not for the residents but for the relatives, to provide a mirage of luxury around their loved ones so they can ignore the ugly facts of death: "Right inside that beautiful building right now, it's a fucking horror show! And all this wellness propaganda and the landscaping, it's just there to obscure the miserable fact that people *die*! And death is gaseous and gruesome and it's filled with shit and piss and rotten stink!"

Wendy persists in denial and Jon embraces stark pessimism, confronting his sister about her failed career and relationships. She continues to divert her energies into providing trivial items for her father's blithe comfort, including a brand-name pillow and a lava lamp, while a male nurse provides her with some welcome yet evanescent reassurance that she is attractive. These tactics notwithstanding, Wendy calmly faces the quiet consequences of the situation and joins Jon in Lenny's room after his toes begin to curl, a sign portending his impending death. After spending the night, Wendy awakens to see her father motionless. She touches his hand and realizes he has died. Having overcome her denial, and without any drama, Wendy turns to Jon and says over her father's lifeless body, "That's it." This calm, clear acceptance of death is strikingly rare in movies.

And in a surprisingly positive result, after six months apart, Wendy and Jon reunite to mark the changes they have at last been able to make: she is mounting a play about their father's abuse, and he is going to Europe to reconsider his love for the girlfriend he has rebuffed. With none of the didacticism of Hollywood studio fare, a small independent film like *The Savages* is able to assess the germane dissensions within a family facing the death of an elder, an elder who does not achieve grace and is not reframed in heroic terms, but is as common as everyone else faced with debilitations at the end of life.

The humility inherent in *The Savages* is wrought with much more vivid conflict in *Gran Torino* (2008), which perhaps had no choice but to highlight the stifled heroic nature of Walt, a Korean War veteran played by the still-macho director Clint Eastwood at the age of seventy-eight.[17] Eastwood had announced the film as his swan song from acting, which perhaps was intended to justify his incredibly dramatic death at the climax when Walt tries to save a Hmong family from menacing thugs.[18] With his wife recently deceased and his two sons preoccupied with their own concerns, Walt finds unexpected and even unwanted redemption in his sacrificial act, preserving the unity of a family very much unlike his own.

A small cluster of films addressed assisted-living issues for declining elders after *The Savages*, opening up a particularly diverse array of anxieties about the topic, including *Choke*, *Diminished Capacity*, and *Schism* (all 2008), *Hannah Free* and *The Private Lives of Pippa Lee* (both 2009), and *Another Harvest Moon* and *Beginners* (both 2010). The cynical commentary of *Choke* is notable because it focuses on a man who painstakingly works to keep his maniacal mother in a private mental hospital, only to learn that the doctor he believes has been treating her is a patient herself. When his mother passes away immediately after a dramatic confession, the fake doctor is unable to revive her, and indeed the entire facility is revealed to have no effective staff: the senile and psychotic have been left to care for themselves. Such a critical assessment of clinical eldercare may have signaled a healthy introspection for American culture, but *Choke* and other films of the time that dealt with this socially sidelined topic were not commercially popular, suggesting the ongoing resistance of audiences to confront the increasingly relevant incidence of imminent death for the aged. The further disregard for films dealing at all with eldercare testifies to this lingering resistance.

One film at this time did endeavor to present a sincere illustration of dying in a clinical setting, bravely tackling the hospice environment. *Reach for Me* (2008) dismisses the medical details afflicting the patients at its deceptively sunny home of decay, and deviates from the stress placed on familial impact in other elder death stories, by presenting a protagonist who has no living family. The septuagenarian Alvin (Seymour Cassel) happily exaggerates his distant days of sexual frolic, disconnected from a wife who died many years before, leaving no children. He becomes enraged after his roommate dies and a much younger man with terminal cancer, Kevin (Johnny Whitworth), is brought in. Kevin is both clearly unable to relate to Alvin's resentment of a world that has left him behind, and resplendent in his remaining present through the devotion of a saintly girlfriend. Kevin's youthful romance, short though it will be, stirs in Alvin two changes, for he slowly recalls the failure he felt in his marriage, which led to his wife's suicide, and he pursues his own romance with a vivacious sexagenarian who, like Alvin, has filed DNR ("Do not resuscitate") orders with the clinic. Alvin also comes to care deeply for Kevin, even helping him with his catheters and ostomy bags, and is again enraged when this new friend also dies.

The predictability of Alvin's transformation aside, his pursuit of last love is all but unique in the history of American cinema, and worthy of more consideration than the low-budget constraints of the film could deliver. Played by the 1970s bombshell Adrienne Barbeau, Valerie easily sees through Alvin's gruff veneer to the insecure though libidinous coot he is at heart; she is also a proud cancer survivor who, in certainly the film's most powerful scene, courageously presents herself to him nearly nude, exposing her bare chest, which is absent one breast.[19] The moment is devastating, for Alvin had been sneaking peeks at her, anticipating a forbidden erotic thrill, and is met with her determined resolve to still be confidently sexual. She also makes the first move in their sensual contact, abruptly kissing him during a conversation before he can explain his own desires. The couple first share a bed after Alvin learns that Kevin has died, whereupon Valerie tenderly soothes him. In the final scene, they make a queen bed together, having given up their DNR orders so that they can hang on to whatever time they can still experience with each other. Granted, this ending plays to the Hollywood practice of denying death, holding out hope for the audience that these perishing patients may yet find renewed life, though their heartening resignation is entirely warranted. Alvin and Valerie recognize the fleeting pleasure that remains for them, and they intend to enjoy it with a private poise that disrupts the trappings of most cultural repressions around death.

In the 2010s, Hollywood has taken less interest than before in stories of elder debility. One example from the end of the previous decade is worth celebrating: *Get Low* (2009) features a poignant, underrated performance by Robert Duvall as Felix Bush, a character based on a true Tennessee hermit who decided to invite people to his "funeral party" while he was still alive. The movie takes liberties with the original story, which gained national attention in 1938, as Felix prepares for the big event while also confronting a secret in his past. A preacher friend has labored for forty years to convince Felix to confess his tortured sin, and a local woman, Mattie (Sissy Spacek), has also implored him to reveal it, since he was once in love with her deceased sister.

The suspense of Felix's secret overtakes the plot's interest in the strange ritual that he has proposed, a huge event that people from a wide area come to attend, especially after he announces a raffle to give away his land when he does die. Yet Felix is not yet fully dead; his illness of torment has simply rotted within him for decades. He finally releases it in a speech at the incongruously festive "funeral." As we learn, he once loved Mattie's sister Mary, but she was married, and the man beat her severely when he learned of the affair. In the process of trying to run away with Mary, Felix accidentally set her house on fire, and fled when he caught on fire himself, unable to save her. With his secret loosed upon the indifferent community, Felix is able to marvel at a life spent in emotional and literal isolation from the society around him. In that way, despite its generational remove, the story is another timeless example of the damage wrought by young trauma that festers through repression in elders. With no family to console, or to console him, Felix finds his redemption in a quiet moment when Mattie later visits him, at last able to understand how her sister died.

Felix's death occurs outside the narrative, preserving the apocryphal nature of his character. The contrast between his climactic celebration and his revelation is quite deliberate, pointing to many ironies in our cultural rituals around dying. Few people attend his interment, because only a few people actually knew him; the forgiveness he sought from the community where he felt so deeply ashamed was within him all along. Lessons like this are perhaps rarely celebrated in life, and would presumably be celebrated in movies about elder figures who have the time and wisdom to reflect on their past. Yet Hollywood generally continues to elide those depictions, and *Get Low* remains a rare example of an elder's sincere confrontation with life and catharsis before death. Other examples since 2000 have been few, tending toward the melodramatic, as in *Big Fish*, *The Notebook*, *Evening*, and *Gran Torino*.

Hollywood studios meanwhile evade the saddening topic of geriatric decline and death, further embracing the denial that forever fosters taboo about the topic and disavowing the possibility of handling end-of-life issues with maturity and dignity. Few films about death among the aged have gained any attention in recent years, even in the independent market. *Another Harvest Moon* (2010) went unreleased theatrically despite starring Ernest Borgnine, Piper Laurie, and Anne Meara in a sensitive story of nursing home patients resisting dementia diagnoses. The endearing *Beginners* (2010) garnered some attention after Christopher Plummer won the Best Supporting Actor Oscar for his role as a dying man coming out as gay (in scenes of a surprisingly dignified nature), but the film was generally inconspicuous. The little-noticed mock documentary *Bernie* (2011) managed to mine some humor in its true story of a mortician who becomes the caretaker and, later, killer of a crotchety rich lady played by Shirley MacLaine, whose role in this stylish gem is otherwise reduced to a handful of annoying elder stereotypes, including mean greed and excessive mastication.

In a somewhat more popular production, *St. Vincent* (2014), the protagonist's wife, who is an Alzheimer's patient in a nursing home, suffers a doubly undignified death: she passes away while her unknowing husband is recovering from a stroke, so weeks elapse before he learns this tragic news. When he returns to the facility for her body, he has forgotten that her will requested cremation, and the tactless home director nonchalantly hands the bereaved widower an office file box containing her ashes. The film is admittedly a dark comedy, yet this poignant scene is emblematic of how geriatric death is treated in contemporary American cinema, and often within the culture at large. Her death occurred without distinction or veneration, made all but invisible by industries—healthcare and Hollywood—that labor to erase elders' dying and grieving. The natural process of geriatric death, and its potential affirmation, remains, inappropriately, all but alien in American cinema, even as a European film such as *Amour* (2012) earned five Oscar nominations and universal critical acclaim for its sensitive story of a man slowly brought to the agonizing decision to euthanize his persistently vegetative wife.

Death is indeed inevitable for everyone, and those fortunate enough to live into their geriatric years—however defined—would be better off facing the pragmatic conditions and emotional responsibilities that most Hollywood films deny their elder characters. Those who live that long can accept the great likelihood that death will not contain the drama that so many movies bestow on elder characters allowed to die on screen, and can be assured that there is no shame in dying while sleeping, or in a nursing home, or on an operating table. Perhaps as the geriatric population continues to grow and gain more influence, Hollywood will be more confidently able to curtail the drama of geriatric death and allow elders to die with dignity and a sense of fulfillment. We can hope that as the children and grandchildren of elders learn to experience the death of older loved ones with more maturity and grace, they too will further resist the deceptive and delusional cinematic system in which geriatric death so often occurs.

Conclusion

We began this book from different agendas nearly a decade ago, and since then we have seen the film industry and the study of aging representation change considerably. In addition to the many films released during that time about elder characters, which have provided provocative issues to consider, the significant recent scholarly analyses detailed in the introduction, such as those by Amir Cohen-Shalev, Amelia DeFalco, Sally Chivers, and Pamela Gravagne, have further added to the dialogue about the roles of aged people in cinema, and also about how to best study them. Another indication of the growing interest in concerns about elder roles in fields beyond medical geriatrics and public health has been the emergence of an academic journal, *Age Culture Humanities*, which just began publishing in the spring of 2014.[1] *ACH* publishes traditional scholarly articles based on research in age studies and also promotes active dialogue through position papers and editorials on methodology and pedagogy in the field, as well as on specific topics, such as creativity, literature, and history.

While we have been intrigued (and often entertained) by the depictions of aging characters throughout American cinema history, there were also many occasions when we looked back at certain movies with critical contempt. After all, Hollywood films offer limited and often biased depictions of social reality and, like all media, are products of their times. This may explain the more negative attitudes toward elders we observed, from dismissive (at best) to derisive (at worst). More positive portrayals have represented elders respectfully or even reverently.

We have seen roles for aging characters since the early twentieth century become more nuanced and diverse, even if not always more mature. They have evolved from the "foxy" and crotchety coots who characterized Civil War veterans at the start of that century to often sophisticated and competent retirees who embrace a certain vibrancy in life after they have finished their careers, remaining active and energetic for a long time before infirmity sets in. At the same time, Hollywood has not always granted them the political relevance they carry in public life; a lingering assumption about elders still carried from the nineteenth century is that their social impact is proportional to their wealth and not to their wisdom. And on the personal level, many elders are still shown fostering close relationships only with younger characters, particularly children. Attachments *between* elders—from devoted friendships to intimate romance—remain relatively minimal, although we have seen some progress in this regard.

Hollywood movies continue to reflect other mistaken cultural assumptions about aging characters. The most glaring discrepancy is the disproportionate number of older male roles compared with those for women, when in fact the population of older women continues to be ever larger than that of older men.[2] Another bias is racial: extremely few roles for elders of color are offered in movies, even though 21 percent of the population age sixty-five and older in 2011 was composed of people from racial or ethnic minority groups.[3] Other misrepresentations include the role of religion in elders' lives, which increases in importance as Americans grow older, and which Hollywood all but ignores completely in aging depictions, most incompatibly for characters dealing with dying.[4] In addition to the repression of religion, participation in volunteer work and group associations (such as churches and social clubs) has been underrepresented. And again on a personal level, the sexual practices of elders remain, for the most part, sensationalist in the very few instances when they are shown.

In all of these cases, the movie industry has room to improve, assuming that the entertainment media want to provide the public with a better understanding of realistic elder life. As we discussed in the introduction, the very nature of Hollywood is to provide an often-preferred vision of life, to give us occasional escapes from reality, and to that end, the public may actually *not* want to see more realities of older age on screen. We question whether such blissful ignorance is healthy for aging people who cannot (and may not want to) escape from their real lives, and more so for the younger population, which is aging into their elder years with fanciful distortions about what they can expect. Are most of us able to critically divide the fantasies of senescence presented by Hollywood from the truth that we see in elders around us—or are movies promoting a more malignant division, between the economically, socially, and sexually active "young" and the unemployable, isolated, and lonely "old"?

We are encouraged by the promotion of longer careers for actors (again, more so for men than women), who enjoy more visibility on screen in vibrant

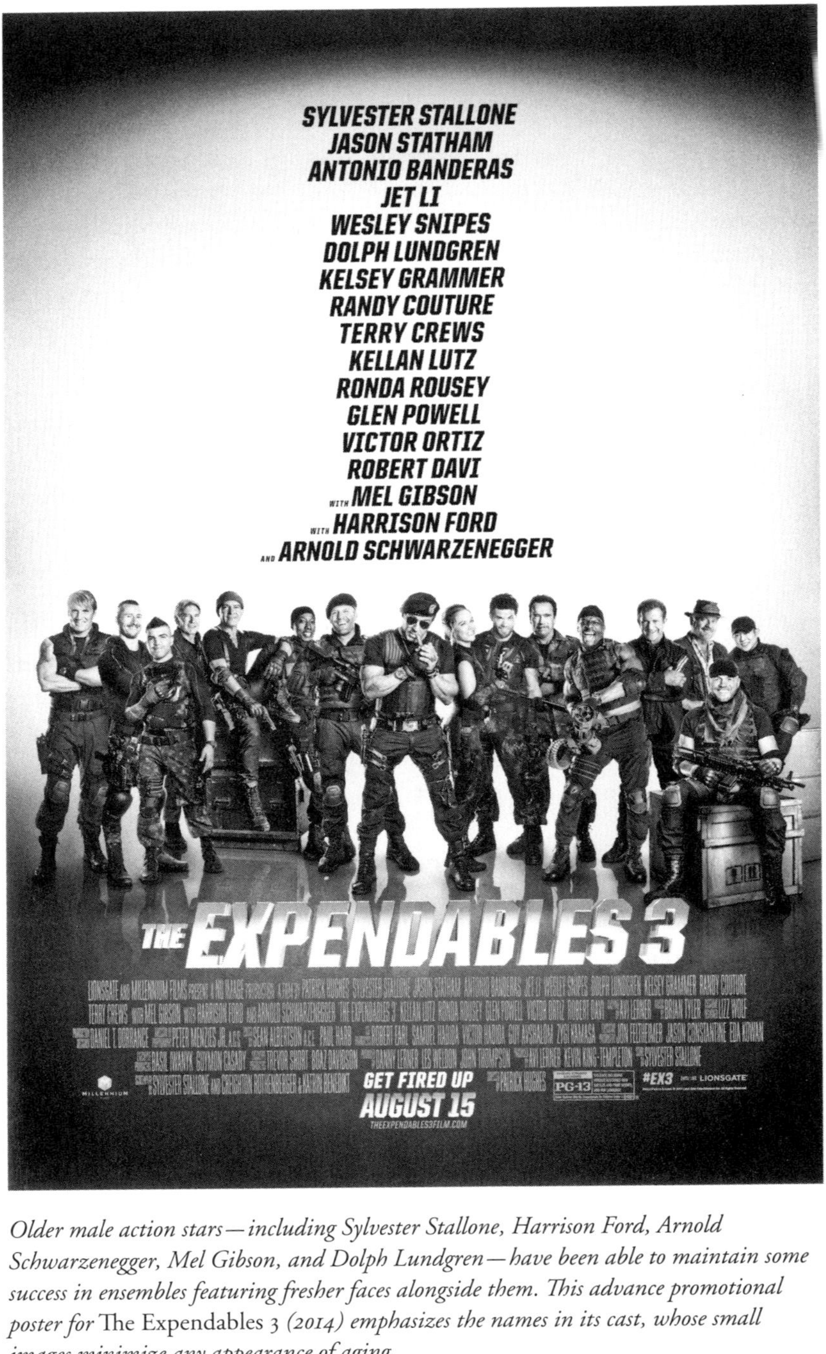

Older male action stars—including Sylvester Stallone, Harrison Ford, Arnold Schwarzenegger, Mel Gibson, and Dolph Lundgren—have been able to maintain some success in ensembles featuring fresher faces alongside them. This advance promotional poster for The Expendables 3 *(2014) emphasizes the names in its cast, whose small images minimize any appearance of aging.*

*In her mid-sixties, Meryl Streep has added to her record nineteen Oscar nominations by playing dying matriarchs (*August: Osage County*, 2013) and wicked witches (*Into the Woods*, 2014), yet also maintains youthful exuberance in roles such as the title character in* Ricki and the Flash *(2015).*

roles than their counterparts enjoyed in the past. We also welcome the tentative steps some movies are making toward confrontations with sensitive aging issues such as financial exploitation, sexual sustenance, familial reconciliation, and end-of-life care. At the same time, our chronology reveals scant attention paid to many topics of concern for elders—abuse by caregivers, dating and remarriage, proactive and palliative healthcare, psychological therapies—even as the aging population has expanded enormously in size, influence, and ability.

More critical studies of roles for older people in media are needed to augment what we and others have been able to examine. Despite locating over a thousand movies about elders in American cinema history, we were able to comment only on a few hundred of them, and the focus of our work prevented us from covering elder roles on television or in other entertainment media.[5] In addition, we were compelled to focus on only certain aspects of aging representation in relation to genres and themes, so further work is needed in areas we could not explore. Such studies could consider the intersections of race and class in elder depictions, the influence of specific elder "moguls" in the movie industry, or the impact of marketing to older demographic groups.

Overall, a greater appreciation for the aging population is needed at the most basic level to ensure that this ever-expanding group is not disenfranchised and misrepresented. The young need to be informed and compassionate in their roles with the aging. And much as it might still cater to escapism, American cinema can help the entire population by providing less extreme versions of elders—as decrepit, villainous, and kitschy—and giving the public a better sense of the real laughter and confusion, pleasure and pain, hope and doubt, and mysteries of *living* into older age.

APPENDIX A

Filmography of Significant Elder Roles in American Cinema

We provide the names of directors for titles we discuss in the text.

1890s

He and She (1897)
The Pretty Typewriter (1897)
An Interrupted Kiss (1898)
He Thought That He Had 'Em (1899)
Why He Resigned from the Lodge (1899)

1900–1914

How They Rob Men in Chicago (1900)
A Joke on Whom? (1901)
The Boys Take Grandpa's Cigars with Distressing Results (1902)
The Boys Think They Have One on Foxy Grandpa, But He Fools Them (1902, N/A)
The Boys Try to Put One Up on Foxy Grandpa (1902)
Foxy Grandpa and Polly in a Little Hilarity (1902)
Foxy Grandpa Shows the Boys a Trick or Two with the Tramp (1902)
Foxy Grandpa Shows the Boys He Is a Magician (1902)
Foxy Grandpa Tells the Boys a Funny Story (1902)
The Hair in the Soup (1902)
Mischievous Willie's Rocking Chair Motor (1902)
Naughty Grandpa and the Field Glass (1902, N/A)
The Burglar (1903)
How Tommy Got a Pull on His Grandpa (1903)
Poor Old Fido! (1903)
The Rock of Ages (1903)
Street Car Chivalry (1903)
Too Cautious (1903)
The Unappreciated Joke (1903)
Why Foxy Grandpa Escaped a Ducking (1903, N/A)
Boys' Trick on Grandpa (1904)
Grandfather as a Spook (1904)
The Seven Ages (1905)
Madam Flirt and Her Adopted Uncle (1908)
Through Darkness to Light (1908, N/A)
The Fugitive (1910, D. W. Griffith)
The House with Closed Shutters (1910, D. W. Griffith)

His Trust Fulfilled (1911, D. W. Griffith)
What Shall We Do with Our Old? (1911, D. W. Griffith)
The Rejuvenation of Aunt Mary (1914, Henry Cronjager)

1915

The Avalanche (Will S. Davis)
Don Quixote
The Glory of Youth (Robert Ellis)
The Iron Strain
Jewel
The Unwelcome Wife
The Waif
The Wild Goose Chase

1916

According to the Code (E. H. Calvert)
Ashes of Embers (Joseph Kaufman)
Discontent
God's Half Acre
The Kiss
The Man Who Stood Still
Nancy's Birthright
A Night Out
Pay Dirt (Henry King)
A Romance of Billy Goat Hill
The Salamander
The War Bride's Secret
The Wharf Rat

1917

Babbling Tongues
The Book Agent
Broadway Jones (Joseph Kaufman)
The Crab (Walter Edwards)
The Girl Glory
A Girl Like That (Dell Henderson)
God's Crucible (Lynn F. Reynolds)
The Hater of Men
The Heart of Ezra Greer (Emile Chautard)
Her Temptation (Richard Stanton)
A Jewel in Pawn
Madame Bo-Peep
The Man of Mystery (Frederick A. Thompson)
Miss Robinson Crusoe (William Christy Cabanne)
Money Magic (William Wolbert)
The Natural Law (Charles H. France)
Panthea (Allan Dwan)
Pots-and-Pans Peggy (Eugene Moore)
The Price She Paid (Charles Giblyn)
The Regenerates
A Soul for Sale (Allen J. Holubar)
Sunshine Alley
Sunshine and Gold
The Varmint
Wooden Shoes

1918

Arizona (Albert Parker)
The Flames of Chance
A Hoosier Romance (Colin Campbell)
How Could You, Jean?
The Love Net
The Power and the Glory
Rich Man, Poor Man (J. Searle Dawley)
The Rose of the World (Maurice Tourneur)
Winning Grandma (William Bertram)

1919

After His Own Heart
The Follies Girl
Hay Foot, Straw Foot
Home Wanted

In Honor's Web (Paul Scardon)
The Hoodlum
The Rebellious Bride
The Shepherd of the Hills (Harold Bell Wright)
Sue of the South
The Wishing Ring Man
You Never Saw Such a Girl

1920

Old Lady 31 (John E. Ince)
The Stolen Kiss
White Youth
The World and His Wife (Robert G. Vignola)

1921

Alias Ladyfingers
The Butterfly Girl
Brewster's Millions
The Charming Deceiver
The Price of Silence

1922

Beyond the Rocks (Sam Wood)
Borderland
A Dangerous Game
Gay and Devilish (William A. Seiter)
Grandma's Boy
Impulse
My Boy

1923

Crinoline and Romance
The Custard Cup
Daddy
Grumpy (William DeMille)
His Children's Children
Hollywood
Itching Palms
Lucretia Lombard (Jack Conway)
The Old Fool

1924

Greed
Hearts of Oak
Riders Up
Secrets
Wild Oranges

1925

The Danger Signal
Heir-Loons
Old Clothes
Range Buzzards
Riders of the Sand Storm (William Hughes Curran)
Siege
Three Wise Crooks
The Wall Street Whiz
Welcome Home (James Cruze)
The Wild Girl

1926

The Bonanza Buckaroo
Fools of Fashion
The Little Irish Girl
Men of the Night
The Truth About Men
Whom Shall I Marry?
The Yankee Señor

1927

The Callahans and the Murphys
The Jazz Singer (Alan Crosland)
Man Crazy
The Rejuvenation of Aunt Mary (Erle C. Kenton)
Spring Fever
Upstream

1928

Bringing Up Father
Lightnin' Shot
Love Me and the World Is Mine
Marry the Girl
The Patsy
Satan and the Woman
The Secret Hour
The Shepherd of the Hills (Albert Rogell)
The Shield of Honor
Speedy

1929

Disraeli
Linda
So Long Letty
The Vagabond Lover
The Younger Generation (Frank Capra)

1930

Anna Christie (Clarence Brown)
Cascarrabias
Caught Short
The Green Goddess
Grumpy
Hello Sister
Let Us Be Gay
Min and Bill (George Hill)
Old English
One Romantic Night
Playing Around
Romance

1931

Dude Ranch
The Millionaire
The Miracle Woman (Frank Capra)
Mother's Millions
Personal Maid
Politics
The Public Enemy (William A. Wellman)
Reducing
The Star Witness
The Unholy Garden (George Fitzmaurice)

1932

Border Devils
Emma (Clarence Brown)
The Expert (Archie Mayo)
If I Had a Million (Ernst Lubitsh et al.)
Little Orphan Annie
Men of America
Prosperity (Sam Wood)
Stranger in Town
A Successful Calamity

1933

Christopher Bean
Curtain at Eight
Dangerous Crossroads
Dangerously Yours
Dinner at Eight
East of Fifth Avenue (Albert Rogell)
Forgotten

In the Money
Lady for a Day
Night of Terror
One Man's Journey
The Stranger's Return
Tugboat Annie (Mervyn LeRoy)
The Working Man

1934

Among the Missing
City Park
The Count of Monte Cristo
Helldorado
The House of Rothschild
Lady by Choice
The Last Gentleman (Sidney Lanfield)
The Lemon Drop Kid
Mills of the Gods
Nana
Once to Every Woman
You Can't Buy Everything (Charles F. Riesner)

1935

Annapolis Farewell
Chasing Yesterday
A Dog of Flanders
The Eagle's Brood
Grand Old Girl
Hi, Gaucho!
I Live My Life
In Old Kentucky
Kind Lady
The Law of 45's
One Frightened Night
Pechmarie
Princess Charming
Rainbow Valley
She
Strangers All
Sunset of Power
Swifty
Three Kids and a Queen
Vanessa: Her Love Story

1936

Angels in White (Karl Brown)
The Captain's Kid
Chatterbox
Dancing Feet
Dodsworth (William Wyler)
Gentle Julia
Little Lord Fauntleroy
Mr. Deeds Goes to Town (Frank Capra)
My Man Godfrey (Gregory LaCava)
Rainbow on the River
Red Lights Ahead
The Return of Sophie Lang

1937

Conquest
Federal Bullets
Heidi
Make Way for Tomorrow (Leo McCarey)
Mama Steps Out (George B. Seitz)
Maytime (Robert Z. Leonard)
Night Must Fall
Paradise Express
Quality Street
Saratoga
She Asked for It
Smoke Tree Range
Wild and Woolly
Woman in Distress

1938

Danger on the Air
Forbidden Valley

Four's a Crowd
Ghost Town Riders
Keep Smiling (Herbert I. Leeds)
My Old Kentucky Home (Lambert Hillyer)
Nancy Drew: Detective
Saleslady
Stolen Heaven
You Can't Take It with You (Frank Capra)
Young Fugitives
The Young in Heart (Richard Wallace)

1939

Five Came Back (John Farrow)
Good Girls Go to Paris
Laugh It Off
Love Affair
Mickey the Kid
Nancy Drew and the Hidden Staircase
No Place to Go (Terry O. Morse)
On Borrowed Time
Reno
Sabotage
Those High Grey Walls

1940

Beyond Tomorrow
The Captain Is a Lady
Dreaming Out Loud
Eli Eli
Granny Get Your Gun
The Grapes of Wrath (John Ford)
The Last Alarm
Little Nellie Kelly
The Man with Nine Lives
My Love Came Back
The Old Swimmin' Hole
She Couldn't Say No
The Shop Around the Corner (Ernst Lubitsch)
The Texas Rangers Ride Again
Three Faces West
Young Buffalo Bill

1941

Among the Living
The Black Cat (Albert S. Rogell)
Cheers for Miss Bishop (Tay Garnett)
Citizen Kane (Orson Welles)
Dead Men Tell
The Devil and Daniel Webster
The Devil and Miss Jones
Highways by Night
Let's Make Music
The Lone Rider in Ghost Town
Lydia (Julien Duvivier)
Mr. Celebrity
The Penalty
Playmates
Prairie Stranger
Remember the Day (Henry King)
Romance of the Rio Grande
Saddle Mountain Roundup
The Shepherd of the Hills
Sunset in Wyoming
Thieves Fall Out
Unexpected Uncle

1942

The Bashful Bachelor
Bullets for Bandits
The Corpse Vanishes
The Great Gildersleeve
The Great Man's Lady
Lady in a Jam
The Mystery of Marie Roget
Scattergood Survives a Murder

So's Your Aunt Emma!
The Spoilers
That Other Woman
This Gun for Hire (Frank Tuttle)

1943

Gildersleeve's Bad Day
Happy Land
Heaven Can Wait (Ernst Lubitsch)
Lassie Come Home
Marching On!
The Meanest Man in the World
The More the Merrier
My Kingdom for a Cook
Sarong Girl
Someone to Remember
So This Is Washington
Two Weeks to Live

1944

Arsenic and Old Lace (Frank Capra)
The Climax
Going My Way
Goin' to Town
The Great Moment
Guns of the Law
The Impatient Years
Knickerbocker Holiday
Mrs. Parkington (Tay Garnett)
Murder, My Sweet
My Best Gal
None but the Lonely Heart
Reckless Age
San Fernando Valley
Strangers in the Night
Sunday Dinner for a Soldier
Wilson

1945

And Then There Were None
The Body Snatcher
China's Little Devils
The Enchanted Forest
Murder, He Says
Over 21
Pardon My Past
A Royal Scandal
Shady Lady
The Southerner
The Spiral Staircase

1946

Breakfast in Hollywood (Harold Schuster)
Cloak and Dagger
The Cockeyed Miracle (S. Sylvan Simon)
Colonel Effingham's Raid
Dragonwyck
Duel in the Sun
The Green Years
It's a Wonderful Life (Frank Capra)
Lady Luck
Margie
Partners in Time
Rolling Home
Song of the South
Three Wise Fools
Wake Up and Dream

1947

Angel and the Badman
Christmas Eve
Dick Tracy Meets Gruesome
The Ghost and Mrs. Muir (Joseph L. Mankiewicz)
Miracle on 34th Street

Moss Rose
Night Song
Philo Vance Returns
Sport of Kings

1948

Apartment for Peggy (George Seaton)
B. F.'s Daughter
Bodyguard
The Enchanted Valley
Enchantment (Irving Reis)
Hills of Home
Key Largo
Miracle in Harlem (Jack Kemp)
Portrait of Jennie
Red River
So Dear to My Heart
The Strange Mrs. Crane
The Treasure of the Sierra Madre
West of Sonora
Yellow Sky

1949

Abbott and Costello Meet the Killer, Boris Karloff
Challenge to Lassie
The Doctor and the Girl
Down to the Sea in Ships (Henry Hathaway)
The Fan
The Gal Who Took the West
The Great Sinner
In the Good Old Summertime
Intruder in the Dust
Lust for Gold
Mr. Belvedere Goes to College
Pinky
The Red Danube
The Red Pony
Sitting Pretty
Song of Surrender (Mitchell Leisen)
Streets of Laredo (Leslie Fenton)

1950

All About Eve (Joseph L. Mankiewicz)
Comanche Territory
The Furies
Gunmen of Abilene
Kim (Victor Saville)
Louisa (Alexander Hall)
The Magnificent Yankee
Mister 880
No Man of Her Own (Mitchell Leisen)
Sunset Blvd. (Billy Wilder)
West of Wyoming

1951

According to Mrs. Hoyle
Arizona Manhunt
As Young as You Feel
Bannerline
The Blue Veil (Curtis Bernhardt)
Buckaroo Sheriff of Texas
Come Fill the Cup (Gordon Douglas)
Deadline—U.S.A.
Death of a Salesman
The First Legion
Gold Raiders
Kind Lady
Lemon Drop Kid (Sidney Lanfield)
Love Nest (Joseph Newman)
The Man from Planet X
The Man with a Cloak
The Mating Season (Mitchell Leisen)
Mr. Belvedere Rings the Bell
Pardon My French
The Raging Tide
Raton Pass
Rough Riders of Durango
The Strange Door

When I Grow Up
The Whip Hand

1952

The Black Castle
Bonzo Goes to College
Captive of Billy the Kid
Castle in the Air
Dreamboat
Has Anybody Seen My Gal?
The Jazz Singer
Limelight (Charles Chaplin)
Monkey Business
My Son John (Leo McCarey)
No Room for the Groom
Park Row
Paula
Return of the Texan
Sally and Saint Anne
Something for the Birds
Wait Till the Sun Shines, Nellie

1953

Abbott and Costello Meet Dr. Jekyll and Mr. Hyde
El Paso Stampede
Forever Female (Irving Rapper)
The Homesteaders
Loose in London
Mister Scoutmaster
The Sun Shines Bright
Trouble Along the Way
Wonder Valley

1954

The Boy from Oklahoma
The Eddie Cantor Story (Alfred E. Green)
Four Guns to the Border
Hell and High Water
Magnificent Obsession (Douglas Sirk)
The Outlaw's Daughter
The Rocket Man
Sabaka
Sabrina (Billy Wilder)
Them!
Three Coins in the Fountain (Jean Negulesco)
Tobor the Great
Untamed Heiress
Woman's World

1955

All That Heaven Allows (Douglas Sirk)
The Ladykillers
Las Vegas Shakedown
A Man Called Peter
Night of the Hunter
Teen-Age Crime Wave
The Trouble with Harry

1956

Anastasia
Autumn Leaves (Robert Aldrich)
Blonde Bait
Dark Venture
Giant (George Stevens)
Glory
Good-bye, My Lady
Lisbon
Lum and Abner Abroad
The Naked Hills
Our Miss Brooks
Over-Exposed
The Searchers (John Ford)
World Without End

1957

An Affair to Remember
Boy on a Dolphin
Break in the Circle
God Is My Partner
How to Murder a Rich Uncle
Johnny Gunman
Johnny Trouble
Tammy and the Bachelor
Voodoo Island
The Way to the Gold
Zombies of Mora-Tau

1958

Dragstrip Riot
Frankenstein—1970
Gigi
I Bury the Living
The Last Hurrah
Macabre
The Old Man and the Sea (John Sturges)
The Sad Horse
Sing, Boy, Sing
Wink of an Eye

1959

The Best of Everything (Jean Negulesco)
Holiday for Lovers
The Last Angry Man
Look Back in Anger
Middle of the Night (Delbert Mann)
The Nun's Story
The Remarkable Mr. Pennypacker (Henry Levin)
Rio Bravo
Solomon and Sheba

1960

Beyond the Time Barrier
Bobbikins
A Dog of Flanders
For the Love of Mike
The Half Pint
The House of Usher (Roger Corman)
Inherit the Wind
The Leech Woman
Seven Thieves
Take a Giant Step
Weddings and Babies
Wild River (Elia Kazan)

1961

The Children's Hour
The Devil at 4 O'Clock
The Devil's Partner
Fanny (Joshua Logan)
Judgment at Nuremberg
Kipling's Women (Fred Hudson, Larry Smith)
A Majority of One (Mervyn LeRoy)
The Misfits
Pocketful of Miracles
The Roman Spring of Mrs. Stone (José Quintero)
Tammy Tell Me True
The Young Doctors

1962

Long Day's Journey into Night
My Geisha
Rome Adventure
Satan Never Sleeps
Shoot Out at Big Sag
Tales of Terror (Roger Corman)
Two Weeks in Another Town

What Ever Happened to Baby Jane? (Robert Aldrich)
The World's Greatest Sinner

1963

Beach Party (William Asher)
The Comedy of Terrors (Jacques Tourneur)
Hud (Martin Ritt)
Monstrosity
The Prize
The Raven (Roger Corman)
Tammy and the Doctor
The Terror
Twice-Told Tales

1964

The Chalk Garden
Dead Ringer (Paul Henreid)
Hush . . . Hush, Sweet Charlotte (Robert Aldrich)
I'd Rather Be Rich
Lady in a Cage (Walter Grauman)
The Masque of the Red Death (Roger Corman)
The Night of the Iguana (John Huston)
Open the Door and See All the People
Pajama Party (Don Weis)
7 Faces of Dr. Lau
The Shepherd of the Hills
Straight-Jacket (William Castle)
Where Love Has Gone
Witchcraft

1965

Beach Blanket Bingo (William Asher)
The Cincinnati Kid
Die! Die! My Darling! (Silvio Narizzano)
How To Stuff a Wild Bikini (William Asher)
I Saw What You Did (William Castle)
The Nanny (Seth Holt)
Never Too Late (Bud Yorkin)
The Night Walker (William Castle)

1966

A Funny Thing Happened on the Way to the Forum (Richard Lester)
The Ghost in the Invisible Bikini
7 Women
The Year of the Horse

1967

Fitzwilly
The Gnome-Mobile
Guess Who's Coming to Dinner (Stanley Kramer)
Rosie!
Tammy and the Millionaire

1968

Bandolero!
Berserk! (Jim O'Connolly)
Fever Heat
Finian's Rainbow
Never a Dull Moment
The One and Only, Genuine, Original Family Band
Rosemary's Baby (Roman Polanski)
Savage Intruder (Donald Wolfe)
The Subject Was Roses
Targets

1969

Goodbye, Mr. Chips
The Madwoman of Chaillot
Midas Run
The Reivers
Support Your Local Sheriff
True Grit (Henry Hathaway)
What Ever Happened to Aunt Alice? (Lee H. Katzin)

1970

The Cheyenne Social Club (Gene Kelly)
The Gang That Couldn't Shoot Straight
I Never Sang for My Father
Little Big Man (Arthur Penn)
A Man Called Horse
The McMasters
Myra Breckinridge (Michael Sarne)
Trog
A Walk in the Spring Rain (Guy Green)
Where's Poppa? (Carl Reiner)

1971

Alien Terror
The Brotherhood of Satan
Brother John
Bunny O'Hare (Gerd Oswald)
Harold and Maude (Hal Ashby)
Kotch (Jack Lemmon)
One More Train to Rob
Sudden Terror

1972

Black Girl (Ossie Davis)
Dear Dead Delilah
The Godfather (Frances Ford Coppola)
Jeremiah Johnson
Legend of Horror
Napoleon and Samantha (Bernard McEveety)
One Is a Lonely Number
The Other
Pickup on 101 (John Florea)
Scandalous John
Sleuth
Travels with My Aunt (George Cukor)

1973

Ash Wednesday (Larry Peerce)
A Delicate Balance
Executive Action
From the Mixed-Up Files of Mrs. Basil E. Frankweiler
Guns of a Stranger
Harry in Your Pocket
The Iceman Cometh
Running Wild
Soylent Green
Summer Wishes, Winter Dreams
Who Fears the Devil

1974

Amazing Grace
Black Eye
Bootleggers
Chinatown (Roman Polanski)
Don't Open the Door!
The Gambler
Harry and Tonto (Paul Mazursky)
Herbie Rides Again
Homebodies
Murder on the Orient Express
Silence

1975

Farewell, My Lovely
The Hiding Place
Legacy
Rooster Cogburn (Stuart Millar)
The Sunshine Boys (Herbert Ross)

1976

The Amazing Dobermans
Baker's Hawk
Burnt Offerings
Marathon Man (John Schlesinger)
No Deposit, No Return
The Return of a Man Called Horse
Rocky (John G. Avildsen)
The Shootist (Don Siegel)
St. Ives

1977

Axe
Black Oak Conspiracy
Evil Town
The Great Smokey Roadblock (John Leone)
The Hills Have Eyes
The Late Show
Martin
Oh, God! (Carl Reiner)
Roseland (James Ivory)

1978

The Betsy
The Children of Sanchez
Foul Play
House Calls
The Mafu Cage
Olly, Olly, Oxen Free
Return from Witch Mountain
Sextette (Ken Hughes)

1979

Being There (Hal Ashby)
Boardwalk
Going in Style (Martin Brest)
Just You and Me, Kid
A Little Romance
Rocky II
Scavenger Hunt
The Seduction of Joe Tynan
The Watcher in the Woods

1980

Atlantic City (Louis Malle)
Foolin' Around
The Jazz Singer
Melvin and Howard (Jonathan Demme)
Oh, God! Book II (Gilbert Cates)
Rough Cut
Tell Me a Riddle (Lee Grant)

1981

Clash of the Titans
Dead & Buried
Death Hunt
First Monday in October
Ghost Story
Harry's War
On Golden Pond (Mark Rydell)
St. Helens (Ernest Pintoff)

1982

Death Wish II
Rocky III (Sylvester Stallone)
That Championship Season

1983

Max Dugan Returns (Herbert Ross)
Something Wicked This Way Comes
Trading Places

1984

The Ambassador
Crackers
Delta Pi
The Evil That Men Do
Grace Quigley (Anthony Harvey)
Oh, God! You Devil (Paul Bogart)

1985

Cocoon (Ron Howard)
Death Wish 3
The Passing
The Trip to Bountiful (Peter Masterson)

1986

Crossroads (Walter Hill)
That's Life
Tough Guys

1987

**batteries not included*
Death Wish 4: The Crackdown
Evil Spawn
Flowers in the Attic
The Lost Boys
Mannequin (Michael Gottlieb)
September
Square Dance
The Whales of August (Lindsay Anderson)

1988

Appointment with Death
Cocoon: The Return (Daniel Petrie)
Da
18 Again! (Paul Flaherty)
Full Moon in Blue Water
Messenger of Death
Mr. North
Purple People Eater
Rocket Gibraltar (Daniel Petrie)
Things Change (David Mamet)

1989

Dad (Gary David Goldberg)
Do the Right Thing (Spike Lee)
Dream a Little Dream
Driving Miss Daisy (Bruce Beresford)
Field of Dreams (Phil Alden Robinson)
Grandmother's House
An Unremarkable Life (Amin Q. Chaudhri)
Wicked Stepmother

1990

An Empty Bed (Mark Gasper)
The Freshman
Mr. & Mrs. Bridge (James Ivory)
Oddball Hall
Rocky V

1991

The Arrival
Convicts
Daughters of the Dust
Fried Green Tomatoes
Jungle Fever

1992

Folks!
Glengarry Glen Ross
Passed Away
Prelude to a Kiss (Norman René)
Sister Act
Stop! Or My Mom Will Shoot (Roger Spottiswoode)
Storyville
Unforgiven (Clint Eastwood)
Used People

1993

The Cemetery Club (Bill Duke)
Dennis the Menace
Grumpy Old Men (Donald Petrie)
In the Line of Fire
Lost in Yonkers
Manhattan Murder Mystery (Woody Allen)
Mrs. Doubtfire (Chris Columbus)
Wrestling Ernest Hemingway

1994

The Color of Evening
Death Wish V: The Face of Death
Don Juan DeMarco (Jeremy Leven)
Greedy
Guarding Tess
The Last Good Time (Bob Balaban)
Love Affair
Maverick
Nobody's Fool (Robert Benton)
The Shawshank Redemption (Frank Darabont)

1995

Backfire!
Captiva Island
Dolores Claiborne
The Grass Harp
Grumpier Old Men (Howard Deutch)
Heavy
How to Make an American Quilt
Roommates (Peter Yates)
Something to Talk About
Two Bits (James Foley)

1996

The Evening Star
A Family Thing (Richard Pearce)
Get on the Bus (Spike Lee)
Getting Away with Murder (Harvey Miller)
I'm Not Rappaport
The Island of Dr. Moreau
Marvin's Room (Jerry Zaks)
Merlin's Shop of Mystical Wonders
The Mirror Has Two Faces
Mrs. Winterbourne
My Fellow Americans (Peter Segal)
The Nutty Professor (Tom Shadyac)
The Rock
The Spitfire Grill
The Substance of Fire
Unhook the Stars

1997

Absolute Power
Amistad (Steven Spielberg)
The Apostle
As Good as It Gets (James L. Brooks)
Farmer and Chase
Out to Sea (Martha Coolidge)
A Thousand Acres
Titanic (James Cameron)
Ulee's Gold
Washington Square

1998

Animals with the Tollkeeper
Apt Pupil
The Avengers
Better Living
Blackheart
Down in the Delta
Gideon
Gods and Monsters (Bill Condon)
Hope Floats
Mafia!
Meet Joe Black (Martin Brest)
Mel
The Mighty
The Odd Couple II (Howard Deutch)
Phantoms
Playing By Heart
Safe House
Twilight

1999

The Annihilation of Fish (Charles Burnett)
Diamonds (John Asher)
A Dog of Flanders
Entrapment
The Green Mile (Frank Darabont)
Instinct
The Last Great Ride (Ralph Portillo)
The Lost Treasure of Sawtooth Island
Magnolia (Paul Thomas Anderson)
On the Q.T.
Paradise Cove
Saturn
Shadows of the Past (Joe Camp III)
Spring Forward
The Straight Story (David Lynch)
True Crime
Walking Across Egypt
The Weekend

2000

Big Momma's House (Raja Gosnell)
Blue Moon
Castle Rock
Finding Forrester
Hanging Up (Diane Keaton)
Hoover
Meeting Daddy
Nutty Professor II: The Klumps (Peter Segal)
Requiem for a Dream (Darren Aronofsky)
Return to Me
Space Cowboys (Clint Eastwood)
Stanley's Gig
Very Mean Men
Where the Money Is (Marek Kanievska)

2001

Corky Romano
Hearts in Atlantis (Scott Hicks)
L.I.E.
Monster's Ball
The Pledge (Sean Penn)

The Royal Tenenbaums
The Score
Spy Game (Tony Scott)

2002

About Schmidt (Alexander Payne)
Assassination Tango (Robert Duvall)
Blood Work (Clint Eastwood)
Bubba Ho-tep (Don Coscarelli)
Divine Secrets of the Ya-Ya Sisterhood
The Little Unicorn
Road to Perdition
Undisputed

2003

Anger Management (Peter Segal)
Assisted Living
Big Fish (Tim Burton)
Carolina
Charlie's War
The Human Stain (Robert Benton)
It Runs in the Family
The League of Extraordinary Gentlemen
The Long Ride Home
Runaway Jury (Gary Fleder)
Secondhand Lions
Something's Gotta Give (Nancy Meyers)

2004

Alexander
Barn Red
The Clearing
The Dust Factory
Illusion (Michael A. Goorjian)
The Ladykillers
Meet the Fockers (Jay Roach)
Million Dollar Baby
The Notebook (Nick Cassavetes)
Proud
Welcome to Mooseport

2005

An American Haunting
Aurora Borealis
Bewitched
Boynton Beach Club (Susan Seidelman)
Checking Out (Jeff Hare)
Come Away Home
Diary of a Mad Black Woman (Darren Grant)
The Final Patient
In Her Shoes
Kicking & Screaming
Must Love Dogs (Gary David Goldberg)
The New World (Terence Malick)
Proof (John Madden)
Rumor Has It . . . (Rob Reiner)
The Skeleton Key
Sweet Land
The Thing About My Folks (Raymond De Felitta)
The Three Burials of Melquiades Estrada (Tommy Lee Jones)
An Unfinished Life

2006

All the King's Men
Big Momma's House 2 (John Whitesell)
The Departed (Martin Scorsese)
Grandma's Boy
Inside Man
The Last Request (John DeBellis)
Little Miss Sunshine (Jonathan Dayton, Valerie Faris)
Local Color (George Gallo)
Lucky Number Slevin

Madea's Family Reunion (Tyler Perry)
Mothers and Daughters
The Novice
Raising Flagg (Neal Miller)
Rocky Balboa (Sylvester Stallone)
10 Items or Less (Brad Silberling)
The Ultimate Gift
A Very Serious Person
The Wicker Man

2007

The Bucket List (Rob Reiner)
Evening (Lajos Koltai)
Feast of Love (Robert Benton)
Fracture (Gregory Hoblit)
In the Land of Women
In the Valley of Elah (Paul Haggis)
Into the Wild
Lions for Lambs
Man in the Chair (Michael Schroeder)
Oliviero Rising
The Savages (Tamara Jenkins)
Slipstream
Starting Out in the Evening (Andrew Wagner)
Steam (Kyle Schnicker)
Three Days to Vegas
The Walker (Paul Schrader)
You Kill Me (John Dahl)

2008

The American Standards
Choke (Clark Gregg)
The Curious Case of Benjamin Button (David Fincher)
Diminished Capacity (Terry Kinney)
Elegy (Isabel Coixet)
Frost/Nixon (Ron Howard)
Frozen Stupid
The Golden Boys
Gran Torino (Clint Eastwood)
Last Chance Harvey (Joel Hopkins)
Looking for Palladin
Lovely, Still (Nik Fackler)
Meet the Browns (Tyler Perry)
Reach for Me (LeVar Burton)
Righteous Kill
Schism (John C. Lyons)
Welcome Home, Roscoe Jenkins

2009

According to Greta
American Cowslip
Everybody's Fine (Kirk Jones)
Get Low (Aaron Schneider)
Hannah Free (Wendy Jo Carlton)
I Can Do Bad All by Myself (Tyler Perry)
In the Electric Mist
It's Complicated (Nancy Meyers)
The Lightkeepers
Madea Goes to Jail (Tyler Perry)
Play the Game (Marc Fienberg)
The Private Lives of Pippa Lee (Rebecca Miller)
Solitary Man (Brian Koppelman, David Levien)
Thick as Thieves (Mimi Leder)
Trash Humpers

2010

Another Harvest Moon (Greg Swartz)
Barney's Version
Beginners (Mike Mills)
Eager to Die
Esther's Diary
The Expendables (Sylvester Stallone)
The Extra Man (Shari Springer Berman, Robert Pulcini)
The Good Heart
Hello Lonesome

How Do You Know
Little Fockers (Paul Weitz)
Main Street
Please Give
RED (Robert Schwentke)
Shutter Island
Stone
True Grit (Ethan Coen, Joel Coen)
Wall Street: Money Never Sleeps
The Wolfman
You Will Meet a Tall Dark Stranger (Woody Allen)

2011

Another Happy Day
Bernie (Richard Linklater)
Big Mommas: Like Father, Like Son (John Whitesell)
Friends with Benefits
The Girl with the Dragon Tattoo (David Fincher)
Hugo
J. Edgar (Clint Eastwood)
Jeff, Who Lives at Home
Madea's Big Happy Family (Tyler Perry)
Montana Amazon (D.G. Brock)
Night Club
The Rite
Seven Days in Utopia
Someday This Pain Will Be Useful to You
Thin Ice
Thor (Kenneth Branagh)

2012

Assisted Fishing
Being Flynn
Cloud Atlas
Come Morning (Derrick Sims)
The Company You Keep (Robert Redford)
The Expendables 2 (Simon West)
The Forger
Hitchcock (Sacha Gervasi)
Hope Springs (David Frankel)
Jayne Mansfield's Car
Madea's Witness Protection (Tyler Perry)
The Magic of Belle Isle (Rob Reiner)
The Man Who Shook the Hand of Vincente Fernandez
Robot & Frank (Jack Schreier)
Silver Linings Playbook (David O. Russell)
Stand Up Guys (Fisher Stevens)
Starlet
Trouble with the Curve

2013

All Is Lost (J. C. Chandor)
Angel's Perch
August: Osage County
The Big Wedding (Justin Zackham)
A Birder's Guide to Everything
Coffin Baby
The Family
Fighting for Freedom
Grudge Match (Peter Segal)
Jackass Presents: Bad Grandpa (Jeff Tremaine)
Killing Season
Last Vegas (Jon Turteltaub)
Muhammad Ali's Greatest Fight
Nebraska (Alexander Payne)
A Night in Old Mexico
Northern Borders
RED 2 (Dean Parisot)
Redwood Highway (Gary Lundgren)
Thor: The Dark World (Alan Taylor)
Tyler Perry's A Madea Christmas (Tyler Perry)
The Ultimate Life
Walking with the Enemy
Wish You Well

2014

And So It Goes (Rob Reiner)
Beyond the Reach
Elsa & Fred (Michael Radford)
The Expendables 3 (Patrick Hughes)
The Forger
The Giver
The Homesman
The Humbling (Barry Levinson)
Into the Woods
The Judge
Land Ho! (Aaron Katz, Martha Stevens)
Love Is Strange (Ira Sachs)
Match
Noah (Darren Aronofsky)
St. Vincent (Theodore Melfi)
The Taking of Deborah Lohman
Tammy (Ben Falcone)
This Is Where I Leave You
X-Men: Days of Future Past

2015

Boulevard
Danny Collins
Don Quixote
5 Flights Up
Grandma (Paul Weitz)
Hands of Stone
I'll See You in My Dreams (Brett Haley)
The Intern
Krampus
Love the Coopers
Manglehorn
Needlestick
Old Soldiers
Ricki and the Flash (Jonathan Demme)
Rock the Kasbah
Self/Less
A Walk in the Woods (Ken Kwapis)
Wild Horses
Woman in Gold (Simon Curtis)

APPENDIX B

Subject Lists of Elder Films

These are subjects drawn from films specifically discussed in the text. We know that other topics are worthy of categorization and study (for example, class, criminality, grandparenting, inheritance, race), which we hope further research will explore.

ASSISTED CARE AND FACILITIES

What Shall We Do With Our Old? (1911)
God's Half Acre (1916)
Old Lady 31 (1920)
Welcome Home (1925)
The Expert (1932)
Forgotten (1933)
The Lemon Drop Kid (1934, 1951)
No Place to Go (1939)
The Captain Is a Lady (1940)
Eli Eli (1940)
Miracle on 34th Street (1947)
Marvin's Room (1996)
The Green Mile (1999)
Bubba Ho-tep (2002)
Assisted Living (2003)
The Notebook (2004)
The Savages (2007)
Choke (2008)
The Curious Case of Benjamin Button (2008)
Diminished Capacity (2008)
Reach For Me (2008)
Schism (2008)
Hannah Free (2009)
The Private Lives of Pippa Lee (2009)
Another Harvest Moon (2010)

DEATH AND DYING

The Glory of Youth (1915)
According to the Code (1916)
Money Magic (1917)
The World and His Wife (1920)
Beyond the Rocks (1922)
Riders of the Sand Storm (1925)
The Unholy Garden (1931)
If I Had a Million (1932)
Prosperity (1932)
East of Fifth Avenue (1933)
The Last Gentleman (1934)
You Can't Buy Everything (1934)
Angels in White (1936)
Keep Smiling (1938)
The Young in Heart (1938)
Five Came Back (1939)

The Black Cat (1941)
Citizen Kane (1941)
This Gun for Hire (1942)
Heaven Can Wait (1943)
Breakfast in Hollywood (1946)
The Cockeyed Miracle (1946)
Apartment for Peggy (1948)
Miracle in Harlem (1948)
Streets of Laredo (1949)
Kim (1950)
No Man of Her Own (1950)
Come Fill the Cup (1951)
The Eddie Cantor Story (1954)
Wild River (1960)
Hud (1963)
The Night of the Iguana (1964)
Little Big Man (1970)
The Godfather (1972)
Napoleon and Samantha (1972)
The Shootist (1976)
Roseland (1977)
Being There (1979)
Going in Style (1979)
St. Helens (1981)
Rocky III (1982)
Grace Quigley (1984)
Cocoon (1985)
The Whales of August (1987)
Cocoon: The Return (1988)
Rocket Gibraltar (1988)
Dad (1989)
The Cemetery Club (1993)
Manhattan Murder Mystery (1993)
Roommates (1995)
Two Bits (1995)
Getting Away With Murder (1996)
Gods and Monsters (1998)
Meet Joe Black (1998)
Magnolia (1999)
Hanging Up (2000)
Requiem for a Dream (2000)
Big Fish (2003)
Illusion (2004)
Checking Out (2005)
Proof (2005)
The Last Request (2006)
Little Miss Sunshine (2006)
Raising Flagg (2006)
The Bucket List (2007)
Evening (2007)
The Savages (2007)
The Curious Case of Benjamin Button (2008)
Gran Torino (2008)
Reach For Me (2008)
Get Low (2009)
Hannah Free (2009)
Beginners (2010)
Bernie (2011)
St. Vincent (2014)

ELDER KITSCH

The House of Usher (1960)
Tales of Terror (1962)
Beach Party (1963)
The Comedy of Terrors (1963)
The Raven (1963)
The Masque of the Red Death (1964)
Pajama Party (1964)
Beach Blanket Bingo (1965)
How To Stuff a Wild Bikini (1965)
A Funny Thing Happened on the Way to the Forum (1966)
Myra Breckinridge (1970)
Harold and Maude (1971)
The Sunshine Boys (1975)
Oh, God! (1977)
Sextette (1978)
Going in Style (1979)
Melvin and Howard (1980)
Oh, God! Book II (1980)
Oh, God! You Devil (1984)
Cocoon (1985)
Mannequin (1987)
Cocoon: The Return (1988)
18 Again! (1988)

Stop! Or My Mom Will Shoot (1992)
Mrs. Doubtfire (1993)
The Nutty Professor (1996)
Big Momma's House (2000)
Meet the Fockers (2004)
Diary of a Mad Black Woman (2005)
Madea's Family Reunion (2006)
Little Fockers (2010)
RED (2010)
Bernie (2011)
Madea's Big Happy Family (2011)
Jackass Presents: Bad Grandpa (2013)
RED 2 (2013)
Roommates (1995)
A Family Thing (1996)
Marvin's Room (1996)
Meet Joe Black (1998)
The Straight Story (1999)
Hanging Up (2000)
Meet the Fockers (2004)
Checking Out (2005)
The Savages (2007)
Everybody's Fine (2009)
Little Fockers (2010)
Silver Linings Playbook (2012)
Nebraska (2013)
Tammy (2014)

FAMILY

The Fugitive (1910)
The House with Closed Shutters (1910)
The Crab (1917)
The Heart of Ezra Greer (1917)
Winning Grandma (1918)
The Shepherd of the Hills (1919, 1928, 1941, 1964)
Welcome Home (1925)
The Younger Generation (1929)
Anna Christie (1930)
Min and Bill (1930)
Emma (1932)
Tugboat Annie (1933)
Make Way for Tomorrow (1937)
You Can't Take It with You (1938)
The Grapes of Wrath (1940)
The Mating Season (1951)
My Son John (1952)
Never Too Late (1965)
Guess Who's Coming to Dinner (1967)
Chinatown (1974)
Harry and Tonto (1974)
On Golden Pond (1981)
Max Dugan Returns (1983)
Rocket Gibraltar (1988)
Mr. & Mrs. Bridge (1990)
Nobody's Fool (1994)

FEMININITY AND MATRIARCHY (SEE ALSO PSYCHO BIDDIES)

The Rejuvenation of Aunt Mary (1914, 1927)
Pay Dirt (1916)
Old Lady 31 (1920)
Lucretia Lombard (1923)
Anna Christie (1930)
Min and Bill (1930)
The Miracle Woman (1931)
The Public Enemy (1931)
Emma (1932)
Tugboat Annie (1933)
My Man Godfrey (1936)
Mama Steps Out (1937)
Maytime (1937)
The Grapes of Wrath (1940)
Cheers for Miss Bishop (1941)
Lydia (1941)
Remember the Day (1941)
Arsenic and Old Lace (1944)
Mrs. Parkington (1944)
All About Eve (1950)
Louisa (1950)
No Man of Her Own (1950)
The Blue Veil (1951)
The Mating Season (1951)

Forever Female (1953)
All That Heaven Allows (1955)
The Best of Everything (1959)
Wild River (1960)
The Roman Spring of Mrs. Stone (1961)
Bunny O'Hare (1971)
Travels with My Aunt (1972)
Tell Me a Riddle (1980)
Grace Quigley (1984)
The Trip to Bountiful (1985)
The Whales of August (1987)
Driving Miss Daisy (1989)
The Cemetery Club (1993)
Something's Gotta Give (2003)
Boynton Beach Club (2005)
Hannah Free (2009)
RED (2010)
RED 2 (2013)
Tammy (2014)
Grandma (2015)
I'll See You in My Dreams (2015)
Ricki and the Flash (2015)
Woman in Gold (2015)

JOURNEYS

The Grapes of Wrath (1940)
Down to the Sea in Ships (1949)
The Searchers (1956)
The Old Man and the Sea (1958)
True Grit (1969, 2010)
The Cheyenne Social Club (1970)
Bunny O'Hare (1971)
Kotch (1971)
Pickup on 101 (1972)
Travels with My Aunt (1972)
Harry and Tonto (1974)
Rooster Cogburn (1975)
The Great Smokey Roadblock (1977)
Tell Me a Riddle (1980)
The Trip to Bountiful (1985)
Crossroads (1986)
Things Change (1988)
Driving Miss Daisy (1989)
Field of Dreams (1989)
Unforgiven (1992)
The Shawshank Redemption (1994)
A Family Thing (1996)
Get on the Bus (1996)
My Fellow Americans (1996)
Titanic (1997)
The Odd Couple II (1998)
Diamonds (1999)
The Last Great Ride (1999)
Shadows of the Past (1999)
The Straight Story (1999)
Space Cowboys (2000)
Where the Money Is (2000)
The Pledge (2001)
Spy Game (2001)
About Schmidt (2002)
Blood Work (2002)
The Thing About My Folks (2005)
The Three Burials of Melquiades Estrada (2005)
Little Miss Sunshine (2006)
10 Items or Less (2006)
The Bucket List (2007)
In the Valley of Elah (2007)
Everybody's Fine (2009)
Thick as Thieves (2009)
The Expendables (2010)
RED (2010)
Montana Amazon (2011)
Come Morning (2012)
The Company You Keep (2012)
The Expendables 2 (2012)
Robot & Frank (2012)
Stand Up Guys (2012)
All Is Lost (2013)
Last Vegas (2013)
Nebraska (2013)
RED 2 (2013)
Redwood Highway (2013)
The Expendables 3 (2014)

Land Ho! (2014)
Tammy (2014)
Grandma (2015)
A Walk in the Woods (2015)
Woman in Gold (2015)

MASCULINITY AND PATRIARCHY

The *Foxy Grandpa* films (1902–1903)
His Trust Fulfilled (1911)
A Girl Like That (1917)
God's Crucible (1917)
The Man of Mystery (1917)
Miss Robinson Crusoe (1917)
Rich Man, Poor Man (1918)
Grumpy (1923)
The Last Gentleman (1934)
Dodsworth (1936)
Mr. Deeds Goes to Town (1936)
The Shop Around the Corner (1940)
It's a Wonderful Life (1946)
Enchantment (1948)
Giant (1956)
The Searchers (1956)
Hud (1963)
True Grit (1969, 2010)
Rooster Cogburn (1975)
The Sunshine Boys (1975)
Rocky (1976)
The Shootist (1976)
Cocoon (1985)
Dad (1989)
An Empty Bed (1990)
Prelude to a Kiss (1992)
Grumpy Old Men (1993)
Nobody's Fool (1994)
Grumpier Old Men (1995)
Amistad (1997)
Gods and Monsters (1998)
Magnolia (1999)
Space Cowboys (2000)
Big Fish (2003)
The Three Burials of Melquiades Estrada (2005)
The Departed (2006)
Local Color (2006)
Rocky Balboa (2006)
Frost/Nixon (2008)
Gran Torino (2008)
Solitary Man (2009)
Beginners (2010)
The Expendables (2010)
J. Edgar (2011)
Thor (2011)
The Expendables 2 (2012)
Stand Up Guys (2012)
Grudge Match (2013)
Last Vegas (2013)
Thor: The Dark World (2013)
The Expendables 3 (2014)
Land Ho! (2014)
Noah (2014)
A Walk in the Woods (2015)

MAY-DECEMBER ROMANCE

Through Darkness to Light (1908)
The Avalanche (1915)
Ashes of Embers (1916)
Broadway Jones (1917)
Her Temptation (1917)
The Natural Law (1917)
Panthea (1917)
Pots-and-Pans Peggy (1917)
The Price She Paid (1917)
A Soul for Sale (1917)
Arizona (1918)
A Hoosier Romance (1918)
The Rose of the World (1918)
In Honor's Web (1919)
Gay and Devilish (1922)
Lucretia Lombard (1923)
The Ghost and Mrs. Muir (1947)
Song of Surrender (1949)

Sunset Blvd. (1950)
Limelight (1952)
Magnificent Obsession (1954)
Sabrina (1954)
All That Heaven Allows (1955)
Autumn Leaves (1956)
Middle of the Night (1959)
Fanny (1961)
The Roman Spring of Mrs. Stone (1961)
Harold and Maude (1971)
Atlantic City (1980)
The Last Good Time (1994)
As Good as It Gets (1997)
Assassination Tango (2002)
The Human Stain (2003)
Rumor Has It . . . (2005)
Starting Out in the Evening (2007)
Elegy (2008)
Beginners (2010)
You Will Meet a Tall Dark Stranger (2010)
The Magic of Belle Isle (2012)
The Humbling (2014)

PSYCHO BIDDIES

What Ever Happened to Baby Jane? (1962)
Dead Ringer (1964)
Hush . . . Hush, Sweet Charlotte (1964)
Lady in a Cage (1964)
Straight-Jacket (1964)
Die! Die! My Darling! (1965)
I Saw What You Did (1965)
The Nanny (1965)
The Night Walker (1965)
Berserk! (1968)
Rosemary's Baby (1968)
Savage Intruder (1968)
What Ever Happened to Aunt Alice? (1969)

ROMANCE AMONG ELDERS

Dodsworth (1936)
Make Way for Tomorrow (1937)
My Old Kentucky Home (1938)
Louisa (1950)
Love Nest (1951)
The Remarkable Mr. Pennypacker (1959)
A Majority of One (1961)
A Walk in the Spring Rain (1970)
Black Girl (1972)
Ash Wednesday (1973)
On Golden Pond (1981)
Cocoon (1985)
An Unremarkable Life (1989)
Mr. & Mrs. Bridge (1990)
Grumpy Old Men (1993)
Don Juan DeMarco (1994)
Grumpier Old Men (1995)
Out to Sea (1997)
The Annihilation of Fish (1999)
Something's Gotta Give (2003)
Boynton Beach Club (2005)
Must Love Dogs (2005)
Feast of Love (2007)
Steam (2007)
Last Chance Harvey (2008)
Lovely, Still (2008)
It's Complicated (2009)
Play The Game (2009)
You Will Meet a Tall Dark Stranger (2010)
Hitchcock (2012)
Hope Springs (2012)
The Big Wedding (2013)
And So It Goes (2014)
Elsa & Fred (2014)
Love is Strange (2014)
I'll See You in My Dreams (2015)

SENILITY AND ALZHEIMER'S DISEASE

Where's Poppa? (1970)
On Golden Pond (1981)
Driving Miss Daisy (1989)
Hearts in Atlantis (2001)
The Notebook (2004)
Proof (2005)
Fracture (2007)
Man in the Chair (2007)
The Savages (2007)
Choke (2008)
Diminished Capacity (2008)
Lovely, Still (2008)
Another Harvest Moon (2010)
Nebraska (2013)

SEX

Harold and Maude (1971)
Grumpy Old Men (1993)
The Human Stain (2003)
Something's Gotta Give (2003)
The Walker (2007)
Play The Game (2009)
Solitary Man (2009)
The Extra Man (2010)
The Big Wedding (2013)
And So It Goes (2014)
The Humbling (2014)

Notes

PREFACE

1. The oldest person for whom there is confirmed documentation was Jeanne Calment of Arles, France, who died in 1997 at the age of 122 years, 164 days. For life expectancy at birth, see National Center for Health Statistics, *Health, United States, 2013*, 82.

2. W. A. Achenbaum, "A History of Aging in America," in *Older Americans Almanac: A Reference Work on Seniors in the United States*, 15.

3. Rebecca Riffkin, "Average U.S. Retirement Age Rises to 62," *Gallup Economy*, Apr. 28, 2014.

4. Braedyn Kromer and David Howard, "Labor Force Participation and Work Status of People 65 Years and Older," *American Community Survey Briefs*, U.S. Census Bureau, Jan. 2013. If 16.2 percent workforce participation for those 65 and older does not seem significant, consider that the 2012 employment rate for Americans age 55–64 was 64.5 percent, and for age 25–54, 81.4 percent. The so-called unemployment rate in the United States (usually under 10 percent) is deceptive, since it refers only to those who apply for unemployment benefits in any given week; see Bureau of Labor Statistics, *Civilian Labor Force Participation*, Dec. 2013.

5. Laura L. Carstensen, "The New Age of Much Older Age," *Time*, Feb. 23, 2015, 69.

6. Felicitie C. Bell and Michael L. Miller, "Life Tables for the United States, Social Security Area 1900–2100," Actuarial Study no. 120, SSA Pub. no. 11-11536 (Aug. 2005).

7. For a chronology of median age in the United States in the twentieth century, see Frank Hobbs and Nicole Stoops, *Demographic Trends in the 20th Century*, US Census Bureau, Nov. 2002. The 2014 median age is estimated in Central Intelligence Agency, *The World Fact Book* (2014).

8. While most grandparents in American movies appear much older, in 2012

AARP found that the average age for first-time grandparents in the United States was forty-seven, much younger than the traditional retirement age (AARP, "New AARP Survey Finds Grandparents Play Essential Role").

INTRODUCTION

1. Motion Picture Association of America, *Theatrical Market Statistics, 2013*, 16.

2. US Department of Health and Human Services, Administration on Aging, *A Profile of Older Americans, 2012*, 2.

3. Ibid., 12.

4. Andrew Blaikie, *Aging and Popular Culture* (1999), 20.

5. See Michel Foucault, *Madness and Civilization: A History of Insanity in the Age of Reason* (1988); *The History of Sexuality, vol. 1: An Introduction* (1990); *The Birth of the Clinic: An Archaeology of Medical Perception* (1994); *Discipline and Punish: The Birth of the Prison* (1995).

6. Richard Maltby, "How Can Cinema History Matter More?" (2007).

7. Even teenage representation was not taken seriously in film studies until the 1980s, and most studies of childhood in the movies before that time had focused on popular actors rather than representations of youth. Timothy Shary describes the history of youth film studies, offering an explanation for the identification of "youth" that parallels our efforts at identifying "older" characters, in *Generation Multiplex: The Image of Youth in American Cinema since 1980* (2014), 20–28.

8. See Molly Haskell, *From Reverence to Rape: The Treatment of Women in the Movies* (1974); Marjorie Rosen, *Popcorn Venus: Women, Movies, and the American Dream* (1973).

9. Tom Robinson, Mark Callister, and Dawn Magoffin, "Older Characters in Teen Movies from 1980–2006."

10. The authors argue: "Despite changing gender roles in later life since the 1930s and despite social and economic changes for older Americans (earlier retirement age and better health are but two examples), their film roles have remained remarkably static in age and gender stereotyping" (137).

11. Gender continues to be the most common topic connected to aging studies in movies, even though concerns about sexuality *per se* are all but elided for elders in Hollywood movies; see Doris Bazzini and William D. McIntosh, "The Aging Woman in Popular Film: Underrepresented, Unattractive, Unfriendly, and Unintelligent" (1997); F. M. Hodges, "The Penalties of Passion and Desire: Love and the Aging Male in Early 20th-century Film" (2003); Elaine Roth, "Momophobia: Incapacitated Mothers and Their Adult Children in 1990's Films" (2005); Rose Weitz, "Changing the Scripts: Midlife Women's Sexuality in Contemporary U.S. Film" (2010).

12. While not entirely about movies, the 2010 collection *Staging Age: The Performance of Age in Theater, Dance, and Film*, edited by Valerie Barnes Lipscomb and Leni Marshall, features three essays on movies by eminent film studies scholars, indicating the developing interest in age studies across humanities disciplines.

13. Amir Cohen-Shalev, *Visions of Aging*, 132.

14. We list American films featuring elders in our filmography, appendix A. We provide the names of directors there for titles that we mention in the text.

15. Pamela H. Gravagne, *The Becoming of Age*, 36.

16. Ibid., 158.

17. Because we are unable to view many films released before World War II, and some thereafter, we rely on plot descriptions from catalogues to refer to films about aging that are unavailable. We are also limited in our access to descriptions of many early films, as the online *American Film Institute Catalog of Feature Films* reveals. Many early titles in the catalogue have little or no summary information, and in such cases we were unable to identify them as relevant to elder subjects. For example, the catalogue lists 1,267 titles for 1907, but none of them have descriptions with relevant elder terms—even likely titles such as *The Miser's Hoard*—and thus we list no films for that year, compared to the twenty-five we found in 1917.

18. Another conundrum for our labeling of elder characters would be George "Gabby" Hayes (1885–1969), who *played* old in many of his 193 film appearances going back to 1929, almost all of them Westerns, yet he only made twenty-two films after age sixty, and not one after age sixty-five. Determining in which of his films he did *not* portray an elder character would be contentious, because few films with Hayes featured his characters within the context of a story related to their aging condition.

CHAPTER 1: GENERATIONAL CONFLICT IN PREWAR HOLLYWOOD FILM

1. For a detailed analysis of the moviegoing public's response to Capra's character representations as told through fans' correspondence with Capra, see the dissertation that initiated Nancy McVittie's work on this book, "Elder Kitsch: The Development of a Comedic and Cultural Trope in Postwar America" (PhD diss., University of Michigan, 2013), specifically "I Love the Old Folks at Home: Elder Representation in Hollywood from 1936–1946," 41–85.

2. Richard Abel, *Americanizing the Movies and Movie-Mad Audiences, 1910–1914*, 145.

3. US Department of Health and Human Services, *Profile of Older Americans*, 3.

4. "Case 395," *New York Times*, Jan. 1, 1933, 2.

5. The Social Security Act (HR 7260, Public Law No. 271, 74th Congress), enacted Aug. 14, 1935.

6. See the Social Security Administration's historical document chronology: www.ssa.gov/history/1930.html.

7. Tino Balio, *Grand Design: Hollywood as a Modern Business Enterprise, 1930–1939*, 2.

8. Stoddard, *Saints and Shrews*, 37.

9. *The Younger Generation* appears very much to have been inspired by, or at least

to be quite similar to, *The Jazz Singer* (1927), with Al Jolson, a prominent picture at the time with a celebrated partial synch-sound "talkie" soundtrack. *The Jazz Singer* similarly tells the story of a first-generation Jewish American struggling to integrate into American society, in this case, as a jazz performer, while not angering his jazz-hating, Orthodox father. Unlike the Capra film, however, the sympathy appears to lie much more with Jolson and his supportive, saintly mother than with his traditional, immigrant father, though Jolson's father relents by the end of the film.

10. For an example of this type of advertisement for *Mr. Smith Goes to Washington*, see the *Motion Picture Herald*, Sept. 23, 1939, 34.

11. For an example of this type of advertisement for *You Can't Take It With You*, see the *Los Angeles Times*, Sept. 29, 1938, 14.

12. For an example of this type of advertisement for *You Can't Take It With You*, see the *Motion Picture Herald*, Sept. 6, 1938, 46.

13. Abraham Epstein, *Facing Old Age: A Study of Old Age Dependency in the United States and Old Age Pensions*, 6–7.

14. Lois Gordon and Alan Gordon, *The Columbia Chronicles of American Life, 1910–1992*, 221.

15. Robert Sklar, "The Imagination of Stability: The Depression Films of Frank Capra," 122.

16. Peter Filene, *Him/Her/Self: Sex Roles in Modern America*, 161–162.

17. Achenbaum, *Shades of Grey*, 46.

18. Ibid., 49. "Title II" refers to the 1939 expansions of Title I of the Social Security Act of 1935.

19. Ibid., 50.

20. May, *Homeward Bound*, 58.

21. Quoted in ibid., 51.

22. Ibid., 150.

23. Ibid., 152.

24. Achenbaum, *Shades of Grey*, 40.

25. Belle Boone Beard, "Are the Aged Ex-Family? An Inquiry into the Place of the Aged in Family Life with Special Reference to the Treatment of the Aged in Sociology Textbooks on the Family" (275).

26. Some sources attribute the popularization of the term "nuclear family" to the sociologists Talcott Parsons and Neil Smelser in their *Economy and Society: A Study In the Integration of Economic and Social Theory* (1956), though we have not been able to confirm this.

27. Beard, "Are the Aged Ex-Family?," 275.

CHAPTER 2: THE SENSATIONAL SPECTER OF AGING

1. Norma H. Goodhue, "Film Officer of P.T.A. Tells Opportunity: New Audience of 35,000,000 Seen for Adult Pictures," *Los Angeles Times*, May 2, 1947, A5.

2. Ibid.

3. Barbara Klinger, *Melodrama and Meaning: History, Culture, and the Films of Douglas Sirk*, 37.

4. Douglas Gomery, *Shared Pleasures: A History of Movie Presentation in the United States*, 84.

5. See Robert Coughlan, "Now It Is Trouble That Is Supercolossal in Hollywood," *Life*, Aug. 13, 1951, 112–114, 120–124; see also Samuel Goldwyn, "Is Hollywood Through?" *Colliers*, Sept. 29, 1951, 18–19; Geoffrey Wagner, "The Lost Audience," *Quarterly of Film, Radio, and Television* 6, no. 4 (Summer 1952), 328–350.

6. Gomery, *Shared Pleasures*, 84.

7. Wagner, "Lost Audience," 340.

8. Leo Handel, *Hollywood Looks at Its Audience*, 104. Gilbert Seldes quotes similar numbers, attributing them to studies completed by the Audience Research Institute, to which Seldes was privy: "Checks made by different researchers at different times and places turn up minor variations in percentages, but it works out that between the ages of thirty and fifty, more than half of the men and women in the United States, steady patrons of the movies in their earlier years, do not bother to see more than one picture a month; after fifty, more than half see virtually no pictures at all" (Gilbert Seldes, *The Great Audience*, 12).

9. Handel, *Hollywood Looks at Its Audience*, 107.

10. J. A. Rogers, "Made-in-America Movies Have to Take Back Seat to Most Foreign Films," *Pittsburgh Courier*, Feb. 8, 1947, 6.

11. Seldes, *Great Audience*, 14.

12. Ibid., 22.

13. Ibid., 245.

14. "Mae Tinee" was the pseudonym given to a variety of film critics for the *Chicago Tribune* from 1915 to 1966. Given the feminine nature of the name and the anonymity of the authors who wrote under it, we here refer to "her" in conjunction with the surname "Tinee." Some explanation of the tradition is provided in the obituary for the *Tribune*'s famous critic of the later twentieth century, Gene Siskel: Mark Caro, "A Man of Influence," *Chicago Tribune*, Feb. 22, 1999; http://articles.chicagotribune.com/1999-02-22/features/9902220139.

15. Mae Tinee, "20th Produces a Tense Film of Stark Realism," *Chicago Daily Tribune*, Aug. 20, 1951, B4.

16. "TV and Radio Seen on Juvenile Level: Times Writers Tell Teachers of the Need for Improving Industries' Standard," *New York Times*, May 2, 1951, 36.

17. Philip K. Scheuer, "Daisy Kenyon Adult Loves Story with Three Stars," *Los Angeles Times*, Nov. 28, 1947, A13.

18. Richard L. Coe, "All My Sons Is a Powerful Film," *Washington Post*, June 25, 1948, C7.

19. Seldes, *Great Audience*, 37.

20. Bosley Crowther, "For the 'Over 30s': Adults in Films Do Not Mean Adult Pictures," *New York Times*, Feb. 4, 1951, 81.

21. Tinee, "Film Rating: Adults, Dull, Teens, Fine!" *Chicago Daily Tribune*, Nov. 3, 1954, A8.

22. Ibid.

23. Crowther, "For the 'Over 30s,'" 81.

24. "Audience Research Book is Published," *Hollywood Reporter*, Aug. 8, 1950, 8.

25. Gomery, *Shared Pleasures*, 248.

26. An example of this type of ad for *All About Eve* can be viewed in the *Washington Post*, Nov. 2, 1950, 17.

27. *Hollywood Reporter*, Oct. 18, 1950, 8–18.

28. An example of this type of ad for *Sunset Blvd.* can be viewed in the *Portland Press Herald*, Sept. 7, 1950, 21.

29. For an example of this type of ad for *Sunset Blvd.*, see the *Washington Post*, Sept. 7, 1950, 15.

30. An example of this type of ad for *Sunset Blvd.* can be viewed in the *Trenton Evening Times*, Sept. 27, 1950, 30.

31. For an example of this type of ad for *Sunset Blvd.*, see the *Motion Picture Herald*, Aug. 1, 1950, 412.

32. Handel, *Hollywood Looks*, 103.

33. "Seven-Month Campaign Builds High Interest in 'Sunset Blvd,'" *Hollywood Reporter*, Aug. 8, 1950, 8.

34. "Swanson to Canada," *Hollywood Reporter*, Aug. 7, 1950, 5.

35. "15 Key City Dates Set for 'Sunset Blvd.,'" ibid.

36. "Fox President Announces Plan to Bar Patrons after Start of Film," *Hollywood Reporter*, Aug. 12, 1950, 21.

37. Ibid.

38. William R. Weaver, "Hollywood Roots for 'Scheduled Showings'," *Motion Picture Herald*, Sept. 16, 1950, 33.

39. *Motion Picture Herald*, Sept. 30, 1950, 5.

40. "'Eve' Is Going on Continuous Basis; Roxy Switches Fri," *Hollywood Reporter*, Oct. 18, 1950, 1.

41. Christine Gledhill, "Rethinking Genre," 228.

42. Klinger, *Melodrama and Meaning*, 56.

43. Thomas Schatz, *Hollywood Genres: Formulas, Filmmaking, and the Studio System*, 233.

44. Ibid., 223.

45. Judith Hess Wright, "Genre Films and the Status Quo."

46. We examine this topic of movie juvenilization, made popular by Thomas Doherty's work, in chapter 3. Doherty first published *Teenagers and Teenpics: The Juvenilization of American Movies in the 1950s* in 1988, and then a new edition in 2002.

CHAPTER 3: THE HORRIFIC AND THE HILARIOUS

1. Doherty, *Teenagers and Teenpics* (2002), 42–43.

2. Wright, "Genre Films," 60.

3. Robin Wood, "An Introduction to the American Horror Film," 201.

4. Peter Shelley, *Grande Dame Guignol Cinema*, 8.
5. Chivers, *Silvering Screen*, 51–56.
6. See ibid., 40–41; see also Mary Russo, "Aging and the Scandal of Anachronism."
7. Linda Williams, "Film Bodies: Gender, Genre, and Excess."
8. Chivers, *Silvering Screen*, 43.
9. Ibid., 57.
10. Doherty, *Teenagers and Teenpics* (1988), 153–154.
11. Timothy Shary covers these developments in *Teen Movies: American Youth on Screen*, 17–36.
12. Vincent Canby, "Screen: Mae West, 87, Does an Encore, Trying for Sixth Marriage," *New York Times*, June 8, 1979, C1.
13. A one-year spin-off of the show, *The Golden Palace*, ran for the 1992–1993 TV season; three of the four original characters were played by the same actors.
14. The popularity of Tyler Perry's Madea was arguably foreshadowed by the success of two other portrayals of large older women by African American comics: Eddie Murphy in his remake of *The Nutty Professor* (1996) and its 2000 sequel, and more so, Martin Lawrence in *Big Momma's House* (2000) and its two sequels (in 2006 and 2011). These films' caricatures, like Perry's, often disturbed critics, yet audiences were apparently enamored. *Mrs. Doubtfire* (1993), with Robin Williams in the title role as a man impersonating an older nanny, predated these films and was likewise a box-office hit, although it received comparatively little critical condemnation for its caricature—which raises the question of the extent to which race had a dominant influence in the reception of the later roles.
15. Roger Ebert, review of *Diary of a Mad Black Woman*, Feb. 24, 2005, www.rogerebert.com/reviews/diary-of-a-mad-black-woman-2005.
16. Wesley Morris, review of *Madea's Big Happy Family*, *Boston Globe*, Apr. 25, 2011, www.boston.com/ae/movies/articles/2011/04/25/theres_a_lot_of_meanness_in_madeas_big_happy_family.
17. *Jackass Presents: Bad Grandpa* was nominated for the Best Makeup and Hairstyling Oscar in 2014.

CHAPTER 4: THE EMERGENCE OF THE ELDER ODYSSEY

1. Richard F. Weingroff, "June 29, 1956: A Day in History."
2. Raymond Fielding, "Hale's Tours: Ultra-Realism in the Pre-1910 Motion Picture."
3. Joseph Campbell's foundational work on heroism was *The Hero with a Thousand Faces* (1949), in which he advanced his famous theory of the "monomyth," which permeates so many heroic tales across cultures and time: the hero travels away from life as it has been and encounters forces over which he or she must prevail in order to return with knowledge that will help others. A notable distinction in films about elder odysseys is that the stories often end before their elder heroes return to the place from whence they started.

4. Robert Yahnke credits Charles Nicholas with coining the term "elderquest," which he applied more broadly than our subgenre of the "elder odyssey." In Yahnke's terms, an elderquest is a "movie or story [that] follows the senior through a quest for resolution to a conflict or completion of a significant task as part of his or her life's journey" (Yahnke, "The Golden Years on the Silver Screen").

5. See producer Samuel Arkoff's commentary on the film in his autobiography, *Flying Through Hollywood by the Seat of My Pants.*

6. Mazursky discusses his original casting ideas for the film on the commentary track of the DVD (Twentieth Century Fox Home Video, 2005), starting with his selection of James Cagney at 00:02:35.

7. Roger Ebert, review of *Harry and Tonto*, Jan. 1, 1974, www.rogerebert.com/reviews/harry-and-tonto-1974.

8. Another 1980 film, *Melvin and Howard*, offered a somewhat short but certainly intriguing elder odyssey for the aging Howard Hughes (Jason Robards), who is rescued by Melvin (Paul Le Mat), a well-meaning truck driver, after crashing his motorcycle in the Nevada desert. In a single extended sequence during which they drive overnight to Las Vegas, Howard finds a certain poignant connection with the uncouth yet sincere Melvin, who does not believe the eccentric billionaire when he reveals his identity. Yet with the exception of a flashback that closes the film, Howard is abandoned as a character, and even though his brief journey inspires him to bequeath Melvin many millions in his will (the story is supposedly true), the elder odyssey here is explored for its effects on others rather than on the elder himself.

9. Vincent Canby, review of *The Trip to Bountiful*, *New York Times*, Dec. 20, 1985, sec. 3, 1.

10. Other than May-December romances (discussed in chapter 5), which are of course motivated by romantic or sexual desire, nonfamilial teen-elder pairings were scarce until recent years; *Just You and Me, Kid* (1979), in which George Burns aids and abets the runaway Brooke Shields, was one of the rare exceptions before *Crossroads*. But lately, other costarring combos have multiplied: *Apt Pupil* (1998), *Finding Forrester* (2000), *Local Color* (2006), *Man in the Chair* (2007), *Gran Torino* (2008), *A Birder's Guide to Everything* (2013), and the 2010 remake of *True Grit.*

11. Eastwood's career since 1990—when he turned sixty—has arguably been the most extraordinary of any elder star in Hollywood history. He made *Unforgiven* (1992) as director, producer, and actor (winning Oscars for two of those roles), continued acting in (and in some cases directing) successful features (*In the Line of Fire* [1993], *The Bridges of Madison County* [1995], *Absolute Power* [1997], *Space Cowboys* [2000]), again won two Oscars from three nominations for *Million Dollar Baby* (2004), and has directed over a dozen other features since turning seventy, including *Mystic River* (2003), *Flags of Our Fathers* and *Letters From Iwo Jima* (both 2006), *Changeling* and *Gran Torino* (both 2008), *Invictus* (2009), and *American Sniper* and *Jersey Boys* (both 2014). The $350 million domestic box office for *American Sniper* makes it easily the highest-grossing film ever made by an octogenarian director. See Christine Holmlund's analysis, "The Aging Clint," in *Impossible Bodies: Femininity and Masculinity*

at the Movies. Other perspectives include "The Old Man and the C Masculinity and Age in the Films of Clint Eastwood," by Walter Metz, "A Good Vintage or Damaged Goods? Clint Eastwood and Aging in Hollywood Film," by Philippa Gates, and "A Finish Worthy of the Start: The Poetics of Age and Masculinity in Clint Eastwood's *Gran Torino*," by Art Redding. For commentary specific to the journey film, see Al Collins, "Outside the Walls: Men's Quest in the Films of Clint Eastwood."

12. Officially a Canadian film, *Camilla* was set in and shot primarily in Georgia. Tandy died on September 11, 1994, and *Camilla* appeared on November 25 of that year; her last movie appearance was in *Nobody's Fool* (1994), which had a limited release a month after *Camilla* and was dedicated to Tandy in the credits.

13. Edvins Beitiks, review of *The Odd Couple II*, *San Francisco Examiner*, Apr. 10, 1998, D3.

14. Martha Nochimson, "*The Straight Story*: Sunlight Will Out of Darkness Come."

15. Some readings of the film place enormous emphasis on the seizure of Rose's children, blaming either Alvin or Lyle for letting a fire break out that caused one of her children to be burned, and thus led the state to take them away. In fact, a lengthy review by Tim Kreider and Rob Content (*Film Quarterly* 54, no. 1: 26–33) argues that Alvin did not travel to see Lyle to seek forgiveness for their schism, but to atone for his abusive alcoholism, which caused Rose's children—and perhaps his other six children—to leave his life. If one accepts such a backstory to explain Alvin's motivations, especially after his family has been broken like so many sticks, then his effort to reach Lyle is more astonishing, a penance he endures in hope of connecting with the one family member who may still welcome his return.

16. Chivers, *Silvering Screen*, 144.

17. Gravagne, *Becoming of Age*, 172.

18. Chivers (*Silvering Screen*, 140–145) considers Farnsworth's suicide in the context of cultural concerns about geriatric death, specifically in contrast to the death of the younger Italian actor Massimo Troisi after *Il Postino* (1995).

19. Evidence of the increasing placement of older characters in genre films, and certainly one of the most bizarre films about *any* elder in the twenty-first century, was *Bubba Ho-Tep* (2002), a comedy-horror hybrid, the oddity of which even the campiest 1960s films may not have achieved. Bruce Campbell stars as Elvis Presley, still alive and living out his ailing last days in a rest home, who becomes embroiled in an ancient Egyptian mummy curse along with a fellow patient who thinks he is John F. Kennedy (Ossie Davis). Together the two save the old souls of the home from the clutches of evil.

20. Lisa Schwarzbaum, review of *About Schmidt*, *Entertainment Weekly*, Dec. 13, 2002, 43.

21. "Kicking the bucket" as a euphemism for death has an unclear etymology. According to one theory, people who hung themselves may have kicked a bucket out from under them in the process; a more likely derivation comes from the archaic word for a beam on which animals were slaughtered.

22. Todd McCarthy, review of *The Bucket List*, *Variety*, Dec. 11, 2007, 77.

23. See Philippa Gates, "Acting His Age? The Resurrection of the '80s Action Heroes and Their Aging Stars."

24. Sylvester Stallone had already made another notable comeback in 2006 at the age of sixty, playing his original Rocky character thirty years later in *Rocky Balboa*, in which the aging boxer comes out of retirement to fight a much younger reigning champion, for reasons so uninspired that his eventual valiant bout—which he loses by one point on the scorecards—feels entirely inconsequential; see the recent collection reflecting on his career, *The Ultimate Stallone Reader*, edited by Chris Holmlund.

25. A. O. Scott, review of *Nebraska*, *New York Times*, Nov. 15, 2013, C1.

26. David Edelstein, review of *Nebraska*, *New York*, Nov. 10, 2013, 57.

27. *Jackass Presents: Bad Grandpa* (2013)—discussed in chapter 3—is a film that explicitly exploits aspects of the elder odyssey subgenre: an "old man" (portrayed in heavy makeup by a younger actor) takes his grandson on a road trip with the corpse of his wife in tow, leading to petty crimes and social outrages and culminating in a children's beauty pageant that is unabashedly copied from *Little Miss Sunshine*.

CHAPTER 5: THE REPRESSION AND RELEASE OF OLD ROMANCE

The full citation for the chapter epigraph is A. M. Broadley and Walter Jerrold, eds., *The Romance of an Elderly Poet: A Hitherto Unknown Chapter in the Life of George Crabbe Revealed by His Ten Years' Correspondence with Elizabeth Charter, 1815–1825* (London: Paul, 1913).

1. Alfred C. Kinsey, Wardell B. Pomeroy, and Clyde E. Martin, *Sexual Behavior in the Human Male* and *Sexual Behavior in the Human Female*; William H. Masters and Virginia E. Johnson, *Human Sexual Response*; Edward M. Breecher, *Love, Sex, and Aging.*

2. William H. Masters, Virginia E. Johnson, and Robert C. Kolodny, *Human Sexuality*, 260.

3. See the pointed argument of Merryn Gott in "Why are Sexuality and Old Age Incompatible? Unpicking the Myth of the 'Asexual Old Age.'" Many concepts of child sexuality were codified by the time of Sigmund Freud's essay "Infantile Sexuality" (1905). With G. Stanley Hall's contemporaneous study *Adolescence* (1904), psychology in the early twentieth century had ample evidence of youthful sexuality. The fact that geriatric sexuality was given scant attention until the 1960s, and remains shrouded in repression to this day, suggests that sexual practice may be more taboo on the later end of the age scale than in the early years of life.

4. We noticed in our research that the online AFI *Catalog of Feature Films* contains 953 titles for 1917, which is the most of any year in that decade, although only 5 percent more than 1916, and 12 percent more than 1918. The apparent increase in films about elders in that particular year may be the result of idiosyncrasies in the catalog's classification terms rather than symptomatic of any industry trends.

5. A study of Dressler that particularly considers her age and body representation is Victoria Sturtevant's *A Great Big Girl Like Me: The Films of Marie Dressler.*

6. *Enchantment* (1948), a distinctive film of the era, employs the wistful-memory device with a male protagonist, a retired World War II general who urges his grand-niece to not deny herself love as he did. Times had certainly changed a little over a decade later: the mildly pornographic (and covert) *Kipling's Women* (1961) features an older man remembering his varied sexual exploits, which supposedly inspired the title author. In the early 1950s, the Supreme Court's "Miracle Decision" (in *Joseph Burstyn, Inc. v. Wilson*) had restored certain First Amendment rights to movies, and nudity was one of the off-limits areas to be breached as a result; stories featuring sexually active elders, however, were generally limited to the underground pornography market until the 1990s.

7. Many sources trace the use of "senior citizen" to the 1930s; the *Oxford English Dictionary* lists a 1938 origin.

8. Extremely few cases of pregnancy in women over fifty have been recorded; see Hamisu M. Salihu et al, "Childbearing Beyond Maternal Age 50 and Fetal Outcomes in the United States."

9. As mentioned in chapter 4, *The Golden Palace* ran as a spin-off show during the 1992–1993 TV season.

10. The grosses for *On Golden Pond* are available at www.boxofficemojo.com/movies/?id=ongoldenpond.htm.

11. US Census Bureau, "A Century of Population Change in the Age and Sex Composition of the Nation"; Jonathan Vespa, Jamie M. Lewis, and Rose M. Kreider, *America's Families and Living Arrangements, 2012.*

12. Peter Travers, review of *Prelude to a Kiss*, *Rolling Stone*, July 10, 1992, www.rollingstone.com/movies/reviews/a-prelude-to-a-kiss-19920710.

13. Mick LaSalle, review of *The Last Good Time*, *San Francisco Chronicle*, Apr. 28, 1995, www.sfgate.com/movies/article/Last-Good-Time-A-Waste-of-Time-3036264.php.

14. Stephen Holden, review of *The Notebook*, *New York Times*, June 25, 2004, www.nytimes.com/2004/06/25/movies/25NOTE.html.

15. Erectile-dysfunction and enhancement medications like Viagra (sildenafil) became popular at the end of the 1990s, and were soon the source of much humor in the culture at large, as well as concern for doctors who treated many older (and younger) men for overexertion due to sexual excess. *Something's Gotta Give* offered one of the first examples of such a stimulant being used by a elder male, although curiously, only when he intends to engage his much younger partner and not the woman closer to his age. The same scenario was used in another film that year, *The Human Stain*, in which Anthony Hopkins plays a professor having an affair with Nicole Kidman, a few decades younger. Viagra is put to elder use also in *Play the Game* (2009), *Little Fockers* (2010), *You Will Meet a Tall Dark Stranger* (2010), and *Stand Up Guys* (2012). An argument could be made that the medical endorsement of male sexual vigor has provided an opportunity to further exaggerate salacious masculine prowess in depictions of elder males.

16. The same double standard that Hollywood has applied to nudity in younger characters persists for elders: women can be shown completely naked, and men cannot. The "balance" of nudity in *Something's Gotta Give* is achieved through humorous shots of Nicholson's bare buttocks seen through a hospital gown. For a more complete appreciation of Keaton in terms of her later career, see "'Glorious, Glamorous, and That Old Standby, Amorous': The Late Blossoming of Diane Keaton's Romantic Comedy Career" by Deborah Jermyn, in *Female Celebrity and Ageing: Back in the Spotlight* (2014).

17. Earlier scenes clearly establish that Harry never consummated his relationship with Marin, alleviating the potentially incestuous mother-daughter sharing of the same partner.

18. Pamela Gravagne has mixed feelings about the film: "Despite the many ways in which *Something's Gotta Give* conforms to the perspective of growing older contained in the narrative of decline and keeps youthful gendered differences largely intact, it does present the viewer with older characters who are creative and successful and who, in spite of their initial resistance to stepping away from the attempt to maintain hegemonic masculinity and the belief that older women should insulate themselves from the vagaries of love, do allow unexpected love and romance to alter the trajectory of their lives" (*Becoming of Age*, 104).

19. Ben Kingsley made *You Kill Me* in 2007, in which his alcoholic hit man falls in love with a woman around thirty years younger, although their romance is a minor aspect of the film's focus on his character's attempt to recover his killing skills.

20. Jacqui Jackson has since become Jax Jackson, living openly as a transgender man.

21. When Christopher Plummer won the Best Supporting Actor Academy Award for this role at the age of eighty-two, he became the oldest actor to ever win an Oscar in competition. The oldest actor nominated for an Oscar was Gloria Stuart, who was eighty-seven when she was nominated for *Titanic* (1997). Seven actors have won Honorary Oscars after the age of eighty-two: Groucho Marx, eighty-three (1974); Lauren Bacall, eighty-five (2009); Gena Rowlands, eighty-five (2015); Myrna Loy, eighty-five (1991); Angela Lansbury, eighty-eight (2013); Maureen O'Hara, ninety-four (2014); and Eli Wallach, ninety-four (2010).

22. Gravagne, *Becoming of Age*, 119.

23. The 2011 biopic *J. Edgar* is worth mentioning, even though most of its story focuses on the titular FBI director in his pre-elder years. The framing story has Hoover (Leonardo DiCaprio) reflecting on his life and career as an older man, including his relationship with his longtime companion, which, the film suggests, was never allowed to flourish as a romance.

24. Joe Morgenstern, review of *Hope Springs*, *Wall Street Journal*, Aug. 9, 2012, http://online.wsj.com/news/articles/SB10000872396390443537404577577243030504690?mod=WSJ_ArtsEnt_LifestyleArtEnt_2.

25. US Department of Health and Human Services, *Profile of Older Americans*.

CHAPTER 6: DECEPTIONS AND DELUSIONS OF ELDER DEATH

1. While we often use the term "geriatric" throughout the text as an adjective describing an older person afflicted with aging-related conditions, we here use the phrase "geriatric death" to refer to the concept of actual aged people dying, and "elder death" to refer to aged characters in movies who die on screen.

2. Nearly 60 percent of all American deaths among people age sixty-five and older in 2009 occurred in hospitals, nursing homes, or long-term-care facilities. An increasing number of geriatric deaths in recent years have been at home, from 15 percent in 1989 to 24 percent in 2009, although many deaths classified as "other" occurred in hospitals' outpatient or emergency rooms and inpatient hospice facilities (Federal Interagency Forum on Aging-Related Statistics, "Special Feature: End of Life").

3. Mark Gallagher, "'Be Patient, Dear Mother . . . Wait for Me': The Neo-Infirmity Film, Female Illness and Contemporary Cinema," 213.

4. Ernest Becker, *The Denial of Death*, 266.

5. The Hill-Burton Act, as it came to be known, was originally the Hospital Survey and Construction Act, signed into law by President Truman in 1946. The law, which provided federal money to help expand the number of municipal hospitals across the country, was aimed particularly at impoverished rural areas.

6. Like Beulah Bondi, Jo Van Fleet was one of the few stars to gain a reputation for often playing older characters, starting in 1953 at the age of thirty-nine when she played the contentious grandmother in *The Trip to Bountiful*, on both television and the Broadway stage. In *I'll Cry Tomorrow* (1955), she played the mother of Susan Hayward, who was only three years younger. In *Wild River*, she played, at the age of forty-six, a hardened grandmother suspected of senility. Thereafter, she began taking on roles more closely aligned with her age in films such as *Cool Hand Luke* (1967) and *The Gang That Couldn't Shoot Straight* (1971).

7. Another 1970 production, the Western comedy *Little Big Man*, offered subtler evidence of Hollywood's ongoing resistance to elder death depictions. Dustin Hoffman plays a survivor of the Battle of Little Big Horn whose tales are made even more stupendous by the fact that he reflects on them from the age of 121. The opening and closing scenes feature Hoffman in absurdly heavy makeup that indicates a lack of realistic reference for someone so old. The character, like Western mythology, is an enigma that simply will not die.

8. John Wayne appeared in 167 movies, playing leading roles in at least 150 of them. Yet in only 7 movies did his character die (only 3 times after the age of fifty), always by being murdered.

9. *Grace Quigley* was reedited many years later to its original title, *The Ultimate Solution of Grace Quigley*, which had a minimal release. The film can only be called Hepburn's last *starring* role in a theatrical feature: she had a small role in the feature *Love Affair* in 1994, and she starred in five television movies from 1984 to 1994, when she was eighty-seven. She died in 2003 at the age of ninety-six.

10. Another denial of death that spoke to the Reagan era's conflicted ethos appears in *Nothing in Common* (1986), in which the upwardly mobile Tom Hanks slowly suspends his successful advertising career to care for his declining salesman father, Jackie Gleason, who all but succumbs to seriously neglected diabetes. To save his life, the elder reluctantly agrees to an amputation, represented as a worthy exchange for the retirement of his enduring resentments. He thereby forgoes death, thanks to having a son who is wealthy enough to support him.

11. Janet Maslin, review of *Cocoon*, *New York Times*, June 21, 1985, C3.

12. Suicide Prevention Resource Center, *Elderly Suicide Fact Sheet*, 2006.

13. Mark Gallagher presents a compelling argument for the "neo-infirmity" trend in movies made since the turn of the millennium, in which supporting elder female characters are depicted as close to death or dying. While his diverse examples—such as *Spider-Man* (2002), *Collateral* (2004), and *Superman Returns* (2006)—are not focused on their elder characters, he makes the case that "women's deathbed and hospital-bed scenes in contemporary cinema validate anew the maternal role and the figure of the mother, transporting the woman-centered discursive space of melodrama into narrative terrain often hostile to women's presence" ("'Be Patient, Dear Mother,'" 210). Such research again reminds us of the further work to be done at the intersection of aging studies with fields such as gender and genre studies.

14. Lisa Schwarzbaum, review of *Hanging Up*, *Entertainment Weekly*, Feb. 25, 2000, www.ew.com/ew/article/0,,275501,00.html.

15. See Adam Balz's thoughtful review of *Illusion*—one of the few published—on the website *Not Coming to a Theater Near You*, www.notcoming.com/reviews/illusion/.

16. Ty Burr, review of *The Savages*, *Boston Globe*, Dec. 21, 2007, www.boston.com/ae/movies/articles/2007/12/21/a_lucid_look_at_family_and_limitations/.

17. Sally Chivers addresses the older persona of Clint Eastwood, specifically with regard to the racism in *Gran Torino* (*Silvering Screen*, 114–119).

18. Eastwood returned to acting on screen in *Trouble with the Curve* four years later.

19. Adrienne Barbeau, who was sixty-three at the time of *Reach for Me*, is something of an older-age marvel. She gave birth to twin boys at the age of fifty-one, and reportedly joked that she was "the only woman on the maternity ward who was a member of AARP" (www.abarbeau.com). The fact that she played buxom damsels throughout her 1970s and 1980s heyday and in this film was willing to expose her elder body almost naked, and with one breast missing, testifies to a level of endearing self-possession on her part.

CONCLUSION

1. See http://ageculturehumanities.org/WP/. Arguably the leading journal in the field, the *Gerontologist*, is a publication of the Gerontological Society of America, which published the *Journal of Aging, Humanities, and the Arts* until 2010. In 2011, the

Gerontologist began to publish a "Humanities and Arts" section, and has frequently provided media reviews.

2. Within the population of Americans age sixty-five and older in 2011, there were 131 women for every 100 men. For those age eighty-five and older, the ratio rose to an extraordinary 203 women for every 100 men. See US Department of Health and Human Services, *Profile of Older Americans: 2012*, 2.

3. Ibid., 6.

4. See Frank Newport, "Seven in 10 Americans Are Very or Moderately Religious."

5. Nancy McVittie devotes a chapter of her dissertation to elder characters in American television of the 1950s, "Blue Hair and the Blue Glow: The Older Star and Early Television" ("Elder Kitsch," 132–160).

Bibliography

AARP, "New AARP Survey Finds Grandparents Play Essential Role." March 29, 2012. http://www.aarp.org/about-aarp/press-center/info-03-2012/New-AARP-Survey-Finds-Grandparents-Play-Essential-Role.html.

Abel, Richard. *Americanizing the Movies and Movie-Mad Audiences, 1910–1914*. Berkeley: University of California Press, 2006.

Achenbaum, Andrew. "A History of Aging in America." In *Older Americans Almanac: A Reference Work on Seniors in the United States*, edited by Ronald J. Manheimer, 3–22. Detroit: Gale, 1994.

———. *Shades of Grey: Old Age, American Values, and Federal Policy since 1920*. Boston: Little, Brown, 1983.

Arkoff, Samuel. *Flying through Hollywood by the Seat of My Pants*. Baltimore: Midnight Marquee, 2000.

Balio, Tino. *Grand Design: Hollywood as a Modern Business Enterprise, 1930–1939*. Berkeley: University of California Press, 1993.

Bazzini, Doris, and William D. McIntosh. "The Aging Woman in Popular Film: Underrepresented, Unattractive, Unfriendly, and Unintelligent." *Sex Roles* 36, nos. 7–8 (1997): 531–543.

Beard, Belle Boone. "Are the Aged Ex-Family? An Inquiry into the Place of the Aged in Family Life, with Special Reference to the Treatment of the Aged in Sociology Textbooks on the Family." *Social Forces* 27, no. 3 (Mar. 1949): 274–279.

Becker, Christine. *It's the Pictures That Got Small: Hollywood Film Stars on 1950s Television*. Middletown, Conn.: Wesleyan University Press, 2008.

Becker, Ernest. *The Denial of Death*. New York: Free Press, 1973.

Bell, Felicitie C., and Michael L. Miller. "Life Tables for the United States, Social Security Area 1900–2100." Actuarial Study no. 120. SSA Pub. no. 11-11536 (Aug. 2005). www.ssa.gov/oact/NOTES/as120/images/LD_fig2b.html.

Blaikie, Andrew. *Aging and Popular Culture*. Cambridge: Cambridge University Press, 1999.

Breecher, Edward M. *Love, Sex, and Aging*. Boston: Little, Brown, 1984.

Bureau of Labor Statistics. "Employment Projections: Civilian Labor Force Participation Rates by Age, Race, and Ethnicity." Dec. 2013. www.bls.gov/emp/ep_table_303.htm.

Campbell, Joseph. *The Hero with a Thousand Faces*. 3rd ed. Novato, Calif.: New World Library, 2008. First published 1949.

Carstensen, Laura L. "The New Age of Much Older Age." *Time*, Feb. 23, 2015: 68–72

Central Intelligence Agency. *The World Fact Book* (2014). https://www.cia.gov/library/publications/the-world-factbook/fields/2177.html.

Chivers, Sally. *The Silvering Screen: Old Age and Disability in Cinema*. Toronto: University of Toronto Press, 2011.

Cohen-Shalev, Amir. *Visions of Aging: Images of the Elderly in Film*. Portland, Ore.: Sussex Academic Press, 2009.

Collins, Al. "Outside the Walls: Men's Quest in the Films of Clint Eastwood." *San Francisco Jung Institute Library Journal* 23, no. 4 (2004): 62–73.

Coughlan, Robert. "Now It Is Trouble That Is Supercolossal in Hollywood." *Life*, Aug. 13, 1951, 112–114, 120–124.

DeFalco, Amelia. *Uncanny Subjects: Aging in Contemporary Narrative*. Columbus: Ohio State University Press, 2010.

Doherty, Thomas. *Teenagers and Teenpics: The Juvenilization of American Movies in the 1950s*. Boston: Unwin Hyman, 1998. Rev. ed., Philadelphia: Temple University Press, 2002.

Ello, Linda M. "Older Adult Issues and Experiences through the Stories and Images of Film." *Journal of Teaching in Social Work* 27, nos. 1–2 (2007): 271–282.

Elsaesser, Thomas. "Tales of Sound and Fury: Observations on the Family Melodrama." *Monogram* 3 (1972): 2–15.

Engel, Leonard. *Clint Eastwood: Actor and Director*. Salt Lake City: University of Utah Press, 2007.

———. *New Essays on Clint Eastwood*. Salt Lake City: University of Utah Press, 2012.

Epstein, Abraham. *Facing Old Age: A Study of Old Age Dependency in the United States and Old Age Pensions*. New York: Knopf, 1922.

Federal Interagency Forum on Aging-Related Statistics. "Special Feature: End of Life." www.agingstats.gov/Main_Site/Data/2012_Documents/SpecialFeatures.aspx.

Ferguson, Susan J. "The Old Maid Stereotype in American Film, 1938 to 1965." *Film and History* 21, no. 4 (Dec. 1991): 130–144.

Fielding, Raymond. "Hale's Tours: Ultra-Realism in the Pre-1910 Motion Picture." In *Film before Griffith*, edited by John Fell, 116–130. Berkeley: University of California Press, 1983.

Filene, Peter. *Him/Her/Self: Sex Roles in Modern America*. 2nd ed. Baltimore: Johns Hopkins University Press, 1986.

Fisher, Bradley J. "Exploring Ageist Stereotypes through Commercial Motion Pictures." *Teaching Sociology* 20, no. 4 (1992): 280–284.

Foucault, Michel. *The Birth of the Clinic: An Archaeology of Medical Perception*. New York: Vintage, 1994.

———. *Discipline and Punish: The Birth of the Prison*. New York: Vintage, 1995.

———. *The History of Sexuality*. Vol. 1: *An Introduction*. New York Vintage, 1990.

———. *Madness and Civilization: A History of Insanity in the Age of Reason*. New York: Vintage, 1988.

Freud, Sigmund. "Infantile Sexuality." In *Three Essays on the Theory of Sexuality*, translated and edited by James Strachey. London: Imago, 1949.

Gallagher, Mark. "'Be Patient, Dear Mother . . . Wait for Me': The Neo-Infirmity Film, Female Illness, and Contemporary Cinema." *Feminist Media Studies* 9, no. 2 (2009): 209–225.

Gates, Philippa. "Acting His Age? The Resurrection of the '80s Action Heroes and Their Aging Stars." *Quarterly Review of Film and Video* 27, no. 4 (2010): 276–289.

———. "A Good Vintage or Damaged Goods? Clint Eastwood and Aging in Hollywood Film." In *New Essays on Clint Eastwood*, edited by Leonard Engel, 168–189. Salt Lake City: University of Utah Press, 2012.

Gledhill, Christine. "Rethinking Genre." In *Reinventing Film Studies*, edited by Christine Gledhill and Linda Williams, 221–243. London: Oxford University Press, 2000.

Goldwyn, Samuel. "Is Hollywood Through?" *Colliers*, Sept. 29, 1951, 18–19.

Gomery, Douglas. *Shared Pleasures: A History of Movie Presentation in the United States*. Madison: University of Wisconsin Press, 1992.

Gordon, Lois, and Alan Gordon. *The Columbia Chronicles of American Life, 1910–1992*. New York: Columbia University Press, 1995.

Gott, Merryn. "Why are Sexuality and Old Age Incompatible? Unpicking the Myth of the 'Asexual Old Age.'" In *Sexuality, Sexual Health, and Ageing*. London: Open University Press, 2004.

Gravagne, Pamela H. *The Becoming of Age: Cinematic Visions of Mind, Body, and Identity in Later Life*. Jefferson, N.C.: McFarland, 2013.

Hall, G. Stanley. *Adolescence*. New York: Appleton, 1904.

Handel, Leo. *Hollywood Looks at Its Audience*. Urbana: University of Illinois Press, 1950.

Haskell, Molly. *From Reverence to Rape: The Treatment of Women in the Movies*. Baltimore: Penguin, 1974.

Hobbs, Frank, and Nicole Stoops. *Demographic Trends in the 20th Century*. US Census Bureau, Nov. 2002. www.census.gov/prod/2002pubs/censr-4.pdf.

Hodges, F. M. "The Penalties of Passion and Desire: Love and the Aging Male in Early 20th-Century Film." *Aging Male* 6, no. 1 (2003): 18–23.

Holmlund, Christine. *Impossible Bodies: Femininity and Masculinity at the Movies*. London: Routledge, 2002.

———, ed. *The Ultimate Stallone Reader*. New York: Columbia University Press and Wallflower, 2014.

Jermyn, Deborah. "'Glorious, Glamorous, and That Old Standby, Amorous': The Late Blossoming of Diane Keaton's Romantic Comedy Career." In *Female Celebrity and Ageing: Back in the Spotlight*, edited by Deborah Jermyn. London: Routledge, 2014.

Kinsey, Alfred C., Wardell B. Pomeroy, and Clyde E. Martin. *Sexual Behavior in the Human Female*. Philadelphia: Saunders, 1953.

———. *Sexual Behavior in the Human Male*. Philadelphia: Saunders, 1948.

Klinger, Barbara. *Melodrama and Meaning: History, Culture, and the Films of Douglas Sirk*. Bloomington: Indiana University Press, 1994.

Kromer, Braedyn, and David Howard. "Labor Force Participation and Work Status of People 65 Years and Older." American Community Survey Briefs. US Census Bureau, Jan. 2013. www.census.gov/prod/2013pubs/acsbr11-09.pdf.

Lipscomb, Valerie Barnes, and Leni Marshall. *Staging Age: The Performance of Age in Theater, Dance, and Film*. New York: Palgrave Macmillan, 2010.

Maltby, Richard. "How Can Cinema History Matter More?" *Screening the Past*, no. 22 (Dec. 2007). http://tlweb.latrobe.edu.au/humanities/screeningthepast/22/board-richard-maltby.html.

Markson, Elizabeth, and Carol Taylor. "The Mirror Has Two Faces." *Ageing and Society* 20, no. 2 (2000): 137–160.

Masters, William H., and Virginia E. Johnson. *Human Sexual Response*. Boston: Little, Brown, 1966.

Masters, William H., Virginia E. Johnson, and Robert C. Kolodny. *Human Sexuality*. 2nd ed. Boston: Little, Brown, 1985.

May, Elaine Tyler. *Homeward Bound: American Families in the Cold War Era*. New York: Basic Books, 2008.

McVittie, Nancy. "Elder Kitsch: The Development of a Comedic and Cultural Trope in Postwar America." PhD diss., University of Michigan, 2013.

Metz, Walter. "The Old Man and the C: Masculinity and Age in the Films of Clint Eastwood." In *Clint Eastwood: Actor and Director*, edited by Leonard Engel, 207–221. Salt Lake City: University of Utah Press, 2007.

Motion Picture Association of America. *Theatrical Market Statistics, 2013*. www.mpaa.org/wp-content/uploads/2014/03/MPAA-Theatrical-Market-Statistics-2013_032514-v2.pdf.

National Center for Health Statistics. *Health, United States, 2013*. Washington, DC: Government Printing Office, 2014.

Newport, Frank. "Seven in 10 Americans Are Very or Moderately Religious." *Gallup Politics*, Dec. 4, 2012. www.gallup.com/poll/159050/seven-americans-moderately-religious.aspx.

Nochimson, Martha. "*The Straight Story*: Sunlight Will Out of Darkness Come." *Senses of Cinema*, issue 7 (June 2000). http://sensesofcinema.com/2000/7/straight.

Ohmer, Susan. *George Gallup in Hollywood*. New York: Columbia University Press, 2006.

Parsons, Talcott, and Neil Smelser. *Economy and Society: A Study in the Integration of Economic and Social Theory*. Glenview, Ill.: Free Press, 1956.

Perry, Merry G. "Animated Gerontophobia: Ageism, Sexism, and the Disney Villainess." In *Aging and Identity: A Humanities Perspective*, edited by Sara M. Deats and Lagretta Lenker, 201–212. Westport, Conn.: Greenwood, 1999.

Redding, Art. "A Finish Worthy of the Start: The Poetics of Age and Masculinity in Clint Eastwood's *Gran Torino*." *Film Criticism* 38, no. 3 (2014): 2–23.

Riffkin, Rebecca. "Average U.S. Retirement Age Rises to 62." *Gallup Economy*, Apr. 28, 2014. www.gallup.com/poll/168707/average-retirement-age-rises.aspx.

Robinson, Tom, Mark Callister, and Dawn Magoffin. "Older Characters in Teen Movies from 1980–2006." *Educational Gerontology* 35, no. 8 (2009): 687–711.

Rosen, Marjorie. *Popcorn Venus: Women, Movies, and the American Dream*. New York: Coward, McCann, and Geoghegan, 1973.

Roth, Elaine. "Momophobia: Incapacitated Mothers and Their Adult Children in 1990's Films." *Quarterly Review of Film and Video* 22, no. 2 (2005): 189–202.

Russo, Mary. "Aging and the Scandal of Anachronism." In *Figuring Age: Women, Bodies, Generations*, edited by Kathleen Woodward, 20–33. Bloomington: Indiana University Press, 1999.

Salihu, Hamisu M., M. Nicole Shumpert, Martha Slay, Russell S. Kirby, and Greg R. Alexander. "Childbearing beyond Maternal Age 50 and Fetal Outcomes in the United States." *Obstetrics and Gynecology* 102, no. 5 (2003): 1006–1014.

Schatz, Thomas. *Hollywood Genres: Formulas, Filmmaking, and the Studio System*. New York: Random House, 1981.

Seldes, Gilbert. *The Great Audience*. Westport, Conn.: Greenwood, 1951.

Shary, Timothy. *Generation Multiplex: The Image of Youth in American Cinema since 1980*. Austin: University of Texas Press, 2014.

———. *Teen Movies: American Youth on Screen*. London: Wallflower, 2005.

Shelley, Peter. *Grande Dame Guignol Cinema*. Jefferson, N.C.: McFarland, 2009.

Sklar, Robert. "The Imagination of Stability: The Depression Films of Frank Capra." In *Frank Capra: The Man and His Films*, edited by Richard Glatzer and John Raeburn, 121–138. Ann Arbor: University of Michigan Press, 1975.

Spigel, Lynn. *Make Room for TV: Television and the Family Ideal in Postwar America*. Chicago: University of Chicago Press, 1992.

Stoddard, Karen M. *Saints and Shrews: Women and Aging in American Popular Film*. Westport, Conn.: Greenwood, 1983.

Sturtevant, Victoria. *A Great Big Girl like Me: The Films of Marie Dressler*. Urbana: University of Illinois Press, 2009.

Suicide Prevention Resource Center. "*Elderly Suicide Fact Sheet*." 2006. www.sprc.org/library_resources/items/elderly-suicide-fact-sheet.

US Census Bureau. "A Century of Population Change in the Age and Sex Composition of the Nation." Sept. 12, 2013. www.census.gov/dataviz/visualizations/055.

US Department of Health and Human Services. Administration on Aging. *A Profile of Older Americans: 2012*. www.aoa.gov/Aging_Statistics/Profile/2012/docs/2012profile.pdf.

Vespa, Jonathan, Jamie M. Lewis, and Rose M. Kreider. *America's Families and Living Arrangements, 2012: Population Characteristics*. United States Census Bureau, Aug. 2013. www.census.gov/prod/2013pubs/p20-570.pdf.

Wagner, Geoffrey. "The Lost Audience." *Quarterly of Film, Radio, and Television* 6, no. 4 (Summer 1952): 338–350.

Walsh, Andrea. "'Life Isn't Yet Over': Older Heroines in American Popular Cinema of the 1930s and 1970s/80s." *Qualitative Sociology* 12, no. 1 (1989): 72–96.

Weingroff, Richard F. "June 29, 1956: A Day in History." 2015. Federal Highway Administration. www.fhwa.dot.gov/interstate/thisday.cfm.

Weitz, Rose. "Changing the Scripts: Midlife Women's Sexuality in Contemporary U.S. Film." *Sexuality and Culture* 14, no. 1 (2010): 17–32.

Williams, Linda. "Film Bodies: Gender, Genre, and Excess." *Film Quarterly* 44, no. 4 (1991): 2–13.

Wood, Robin. "An Introduction to the American Horror Film." In *Movies and Methods, Volume 2*, edited by Bill Nichols, 195–219. Berkeley: University of California Press, 1976.

Wright, Judith Hess. "Genre Films and the Status Quo." In *Film Genre Reader 3*, edited by Barry Keith Grant, 60–68. Austin: University of Texas Press, 2003.

Yahnke, Robert. "The Golden Years on the Silver Screen." Feb. 2007. Vital Aging Network, www.vital-aging-network.org/Resources_for_Vital_Living/Finding_Your_Way/22/The_Golden_Years_on_the_Silver_Screen.html.

———. *The Great Circle of Life: A Resource Guide to Films on Aging*. Owings Mills, Md.: National Health Publications, 1988.

Index

Note: *Italic* page numbers refer to illustrations.